The Passion and Reason of True Worship

WORSHIP THAT PLEASES GOD

Loving God with Heart, Soul, Mind, and Strength

Stephen R. Phifer

Order this book online at www.trafford.com
or email orders@trafford.com

Most Trafford titles are also available at major online book retailers.

Printed in the United States of America.

ISBN: 978-1-4120-6237-4 (sc)
ISBN: 978-1-4122-3747-5 (e)

Trafford rev. 11/13/2014

www.trafford.com
North America & international
toll-free: 1 888 232 4444 (USA & Canada)
fax: 812 355 4082

Dedication

To worshipers and their leaders who turn to the Scriptures for instruction in worship. May we all ascend the hill of the Lord and stand in the Holy Place together.

Acknowledgements

I wish to acknowledge the contribution of those who have believed in me as a writer: my parents J. D. and Ruth Phifer, my brother Dr. James D. Phifer, my wife Freeda, our children and their husbands Matt and Nicole Huett and Manny and Jennifer Foret, and my three best friends: Rev Larry Hartley, Rev. Steve Swain, and Dr. Tom McDonald. The consistent faith and encouragement of family and friends have been essential to this book.

Cover design: Emmanuel Foret. Cover icon: *Mary of Bethany at Jesus' Feet*. Courtesy of Atelier Saint-Andre, a Community of Traditional Byzantine Iconographers (<u>www.ateliersaintandre.net</u>).

The Flame

May the candle of my passion burn for You, Lord.
Let the stuff of my existence fuel its flame.
May the darkness of this world flee before it,
And may all who turn to see it,
see the glory of Your name.

May the truth of who You are consume my reason.
May the fire of holy justice burn in me.
Till the darkness of this world is defeated,
And the brightness of Your mercy
sets the human spirit free.

—Stephen R. Phifer

Contents

Other Works by Steve Phifer

*Loose Him and Let Him Go—Releasing the Ministry of the
    Christian Artist*
Worship—A Pentecostal Perspective
Ancient Future Pentecost—A Study in 21st Century Possibilities
*Experiment In Prayer—The Convergence of Fixed and Extempo-
    raneous Prayers in the Daily Private Worship of Congregants
    at Word of Life International Church, Springfield, Virginia*
    (Doctoral Thesis for the Institute of Worship Studies)
Seasons of Praise Vol. I
    A collection of columns encouraging worship through
    the year.
Short Dramatic Works for the Worship Service
Prevailing Winds
    A Collection of Poems
Worship Columns
    Sprit and Truth ("Communicator" Magazine)
    Fire and Form—Spirit-led Worship with Dr. Steve Phifer
    (211 Network)

Foreword

Mark 12:28-31 — Jesus to a Teacher of the Law

He asked him, "Of all the commandments, which is the most important?"

"The most important one," answered Jesus, "is this: 'Hear, O Israel, the Lord our God, the Lord is one. Love the Lord your God with all your heart and with all your soul and with all your mind and with all your strength.'

"The second is this: 'Love your neighbor as yourself.' There is no commandment greater than these."

John 4:24 — Jesus to the Woman at the Well

God is spirit, and his worshipers must worship in spirit and in truth.

Passion and Reason. These two great statements of Jesus form the foundation stones of this book:

"Love the Lord your God with all your heart and with all your soul and with all your mind and with all your strength." Both passion and reason are essential to worship. It is not possible to love God with your "heart and soul" without passion. Likewise, it is impossible to love Him with your "mind and strength" without reason.

"Worshipers must worship in spirit and in truth." Worshiping God with spirit implies passion. Worshiping Him in truth demands reason.

Discovering the passion and reason of True Worship is the goal of this biblical study. Too many people and too many traditions have emphasized one over the other. But in the twenty-first century it is time to put the two together. We must wholeheartedly thank the Lord and proclaim His excellence with the full force of our spirit, employing our capacity for passion. And, we must wholeheartedly seek out His truth using our ability to reason. We must then adjust our preferences to His preferences as they are revealed in God's Word. That is, we must let reason inform and focus our passion, and we must let passion set fire to the truth we have discovered.

Because of this sweeping statement Jesus made to the Woman at the Well, "spirit and truth" will be the scriptural lenses through which we will view all the passages from the Holy Bible. Just as with a pair of eyeglasses or contact lenses, we must use both lenses to see clearly. Readers who have primarily used one or the other—they have looked at worship as either a "spiritual experience" or an "intellectual exercise"—will be stretched beyond their comfort zones. Actually, this is a necessary part of True Worship. As we look to the Scriptures, it becomes obvious that when a person has an encounter with the Living God, many times the first casualty of that encounter is his or her comfort zone:

- Abraham was told to leave his home and go to a land God would show him.
- Jacob's name was changed, and he walked with a limp the rest of his life.
- Moses' experience at the Burning Bush sent the desert-dwelling stutterer to Pharoah's palace in Egypt as spokesman and prophet.
- David's worship life with God turned a psalm-singing shepherd into a stone-slinging soldier.
- Twelve men of various occupations were transformed into disciples when Jesus looked at them and invited them to follow Him. Fishing nets and tax rolls were abandoned.
- Eleven of them became apostles when the Holy Spirit came upon them. All previous plans were canceled and

a new and unforeseeable adventure stretched before them.

Obviously, this list could go on and on. The point is, passionate and well-reasoned worship will change us. Through it God will clean us up and then send us out to do His will. We will be different people, no longer tied to the past like Abraham but called by a new name like Jacob (deceiver), turned Israel (Prince with God). Like Moses, our halting speech will sing with prophesy. Like David our worship will turn to warfare, and we will see giants fall. Like the disciples, we will abandon our old nets for new ones—those which catch men—glistening with the promise of an unpredictable road reaching to horizons we never have imagined.

The Presence of God. When we worship in spirit and truth, with passion and reason, we enter the manifest presence of God. In the pages of this book you will find an analysis of the differing aspects of the presence of God. This analysis leads to an understanding of how we may come before the presence of a God who is omnipresent. When we worship God in spirit and truth, He responds with His presence and His sovereign-ty. The King James Version of Psalm 22:3 tells us of His pre-sence—"But thou art holy, O thou that inhabitest the praises of Israel." The New American Standard version of this same verse tells of His sovereignty—"Yet You are holy, O Thou who art enthroned upon the praises of Israel." Both translations are valid. Think of it! When we worship God, He responds with His all-pervading presence and His all-encompassing sover-eignty. When we worship Him, He visits us and begins to rule in us. His kingdom begins to come in us and His will begins to be done in us. He dwells and rules in the heart that truly wor-ships Him, for that heart is centered on Him.

The kingdom of God. The primary effect of True Worship is to establish the kingdom of God in our hearts, our homes, our work places, and our houses of worship. The kingdom of God is defined in Scripture as "righteousness, peace and joy in the Holy Spirit" — "For the kingdom of God is not a matter of eating and drinking, but of righteousness, peace and joy in the Holy Spirit, because anyone who serves Christ in this way is pleasing to God and approved by men." (Romans 14:17-18)

These qualities of the kingdom become the three major divisions of the book.

PART ONE: RIGHTEOUSNESS. Under this heading a theology of True Worship is presented, for it is only by the righteousness of Christ applied to our lives that we worship the Lord. This theology involves definitions based on original word meanings, on seven biblical models of worship, and on the purity of heart demanded by True Worship.

PART TWO: PEACE. The second section develops the philosophical aspects of the priority of worship in the life of the congregation. A church full of peace, not strife, will result from passionate and reasoned worship. Ethnic and generational conflicts can be solved when the priority of worship is taught and practiced at every level by the local church.

PART THREE: JOY IN THE HOLY SPIRIT. The life of the believer who is a True Worshiper should be a life of joyful victory. This section explores the topics of *Craftsmanship*— God's people do good work offered as praise and worship to the Lord; *Creativity*—God's people do original work offered as praise and worship to the Lord; and *Spiritual Warfare*—God's people are victorious in their living, and the forces of darkness flee before them. The result is "joy in the Holy Spirit".

The Expression of a Relationship. True Worship is an interactive experience based on a relationship that people may have with God through Jesus Christ. God wants a close relationship with us, but our sins stand in the way. Sin in our life means that we are centered on ourselves and not on God. Our passions are not those of heaven, and our reason is flawed by disobedience and error. God the Father sent His Son, Jesus, into the world to pay the price for our sins. Only when the sin problem is solved for each of us at Calvary are we qualified to enter into the relationship God desires with us. The blood of Jesus makes it possible for us to worship God. It is the only qualifier we can find.

Worshiping God expresses the dynamics of our relationship with God. As we worship Him with the meditation of the heart, the words of the mouth, and the works of the hands, we are loving Him with all our heart, soul, mind, and strength. Worshiping God empowers us to love our neighbor as our self. This is the ministry of every believer, not just of the people on the church platform. It is not something best left to the professionals for *it is from each believer's worship relationship with God that all other ministry flows.*

For all the above reasons and more, we see that passionate and reasoned worship is of necessity the highest priority in life. True Worship centers life on God. Worship with passion and reason is the interaction of God with His people. As we interact with the Almighty, an exchange of spiritual but very real properties takes place. God has given us His Word. We give Him our attention and time when we read, study, and obey it. He has given us His Son. When we accept and follow Jesus as our Savior, we give our lives back to Him. He opens for us the awesome access of prayer.

As we enter the Holy of Holies to worship and bring our petitions, we give Him our love. He gives us a Sabbath day, and we give Him our service of worship. In that worship service, the initiative becomes ours. We give Him our praise, and He responds with His manifest presence. We give Him our worship and He imparts to us the majesty of His kingdom. When we worshipfully sing and pray, God responds with his presence and His sovereignty.

As we sit, stand, and move about in stately procession, and as we proclaim, honor, and respond to the Word of God, we are interacting with our Heavenly Father. This is worship. When we present ourselves to Him for personal or family prayer and Bible study we experience a personal interaction with God. This is worship. When we fill our days with the craftsmanship of our lives and present the work of hands to Him, this, too, is worship.

The Scriptures. The goal of this study is to examine the Scriptures in search of God's eternal plan and purpose for our worship. The Scriptures will be our chief source of light, not because man's teaching on worship is necessarily flawed but because we must judge all of man's thinking on worship by God's thoughts. I do not attempt to pass judgment on man's traditions or to justify any particular style of worship. I seek to discover God's truth and elevate it to a higher plane than man's concepts. We need truth that transcends culture. The expression or passion of worship is culture (music, ceremony, etc.). The substance or reason of worship is the same in every culture (truth). I have taught these things in North America, Asia, and Northern and Eastern Europe with full confidence that biblical truth applies equally everywhere and with full knowledge that worshipers in each culture will express them-selves in different ways.

This book is not about current trends. It is certainly not about styles of music. It is about worshiping God passionately from an informed viewpoint, as a reasonable response to the revelation in Scripture of His desires. My dream is to see an informed priesthood in each culture of the earth entering into True Worship with passion and reason.

Twenty-first Century Worship. The following passage from the Psalms predicts a time of unprecedented visitation. God will hear from heaven and respond to the needs of a broken humanity. True Worship, as the church fully centers herself on God himself, will be the triggering force. I believe this is a prophesy of the twenty-first century church. The last line of the passage is actually the triggering mechanism for the fulfillment of the prophecy.

Let this be written for a future generation,
that a people not yet created may praise the LORD:

"The LORD looked down from his sanctuary on high,
from heaven he viewed the earth,
to hear the groans of the prisoners
and release those condemned to death."

So the name of the LORD will be declared in Zion
and his praise in Jerusalem
when the peoples and the kingdoms
assemble to worship the LORD.

—Psalm 102:18-22

I believe this century will bring a visitation from the Lord that has never been seen in history. When the "peoples", that is, the ethnic divisions of mankind, and the "kingdoms", that is, the political divisions of humanity meet for the express purpose of worshiping the Lord, God's love will flow to a hurting humanity as never before. Lord, hasten the day when "peoples and the kingdoms assemble to worship the Lord." Let it begin in me!

Structure: Narrative, Exposition, Application and Illustration. Each chapter will begin with a short narrative based on a character from the Scriptures. These very short stories are products of my imagination and are not intended as a presentation of the way these biblical events happened. With these I wish to illustrate from the Scriptures important points about worshiping or failing to worship God with passion and reason. Each truth is presented first with exposition, followed by application or illustration. Frequently these are short homilies suitable for use in sermons.

Here is an example from Chapter One:

With a poor and contrite spirit we must worship the Jesus revealed to us in the pages of the Bible. He is not the Jesus of imagination, created in our own image by the design of our flawed personality. He is not the Jesus of society, marred by the clumsy minds of men. He is the Jesus slain before the foundation of all creation. He is the image of the invisible God by whom all the worlds were made and the virgin-born Servant emptied of all but love, who became the Lamb of God, the sacrifice for all sin. He is the preacher to souls in captivity and their avenging hero. He is the conqueror of death, hell, and the grave who rose by the power of the Spirit to new and eternal life. Jesus is the One whose coronation heaven witnessed. He is now seated at the Father's right hand, and His name is above every other name. He is the One before whom every knee will bow and to whom every tongue will confess that He indeed is Lord, Master, and Sovereign. Only this Jesus, the Jesus of the Bible, prompts our worship for no other Jesus could.

The Cycle of True Worship. This cycle will precede each of the three sections of the book. This book is about much more than what happens on Sunday morning. It is a picture of the all-encompassing nature of True Worship. Follow the flow of God's life as the power of spirit-and-truth worship extends around the circle to personal worship, public worship, and the worship lifestyle. As the personal worship experience of the believer is infused with spirit and truth, it becomes more and more powerful. That power then flows to the public service.

When this believer gathers with others to worship God, the public worship service is empowered by his worship. Likewise the daily life of this worshiper becomes a more joyful and victorious experience as the power of the public service goes with him into his work week. His work becomes praise and worship to God and thus is worthy for God's habitation and sovereignty. This daily walk in the Spirit enriches the personal worship life, and the cycle begins anew. When each station of life, from personal worship to public worship to daily crafts-manship, is infused with spirit and truth, it sends the power of God along to the next station. It is a cycle of power, an upward spiral to which every believer is called.

Worship Paradigms. These illustrations serve as sum-maries of the Big Picture of worship. This diagram will help us avoid losing sight of the whole vision as we delve into the particulars. "Heart to God" represents our righteousness before the Lord. "Hands to God" represents our faithfulness to biblical methodology. "Hands to Man" represents the impact of our worship as the Lord reaches through our lives to touch and heal a hurting humanity.

Your Study of Worship. No book other than the Bible has the whole truth on worship. If you are a worship leader (musician or preacher) you are also a student of worship. My prayer is that my study will aid your personal study. Many of the biblical truths discussed in this study are themselves worthy subjects for books. The Scriptures are a treasure field and my job is to mark the places for all of us to dig. Scripture quotations will be from the New International Version unless otherwise noted. May the Lord bless you as you study His Word on this subject so close to His heart. Let us set our hearts to be the end of His centuries-old search for True Worshipers.

—Stephen R. Phifer

Worship That Pleases God
The Passion and Reason of True Worship

PART ONE

THE KINGDOM OF GOD IS RIGHTEOUSNESS

Jesus' righteousness makes it possible for us to have a relationship with God.

The Holy Bible provides a system of thought, a theology for understanding and entering into this relationship.

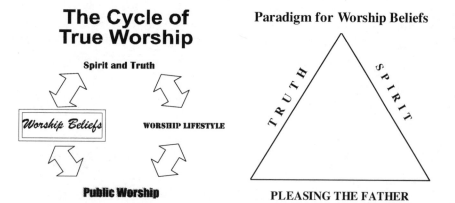

Chapter One

PLEASING GOD

Mary of Bethany

T he aroma of the contents of a broken alabaster jar filled the room in the little house in Bethany where Jesus enjoyed a meal with close friends. Few of the men noticed as Mary produced this jar of ointment, a concoction ripe with pungent scent. The men were busy talking, eating. Only Jesus saw her steal away to her hiding place, find her most precious possession, break the container, and lovingly anoint his feet with the spice. But the aroma gave her away, pulling back her curtain of privacy and thrusting her to the public stage.

The men were not pleased. They rebuked her. This simply was not the best way to use this valuable commodity. It was worth a year's wages to the common man. Once committed to this line of reasoning, an alternative use had to be proposed. Let's see, ah yes, the poor, always a handy cause to plead to gain the Master's favor. The air was heavy with the smell of the ointment and with anticipation of how Jesus would handle this foolish woman.

Around that table were men whose names would become known throughout the world for centuries to come. At this moment they were obscure little men with glimmers of greatness that only Jesus could see. Among them was John, so filled with fun and free with emotion; Peter, his opposite, so rough and full of pride; Thomas whose knife-like mind always sliced away the nonessentials in an issue; James, John's mischievous brother, a "Son of Thunder" he was called; Matthew the former tax collector; the other Gallileans; and . . . Judas, who kept the money. A diverse group, hand-selected, not for what they were but for what they could become if they centered their lives on God. All were silent now, waiting for Jesus to answer their question. Mary had wasted a valuable resource, hadn't she?

"Leave her alone," Jesus said. "Why are you bothering her? She has done a beautiful thing to me." He went on to say that she had done what she could, that she had anointed His body for burial, and that wherever the gospel is preached, her story would be told.

The men were shamed. He had taken the woman's side over theirs. But as they listened, something began to stir within them. It always did when He spoke. Soon, their embarrassment was forgotten, and before long all but one was wishing that he had something valuable to pour over Jesus' feet.

True Worship

Mary's story is that of a passionate and truthful worshiper, one who pleased the heart of Jesus her King. Of all the accounts in Scripture of people worshiping God, this one speaks to me on the deepest level. When I worship the Lord, this story serves as a model. I try to think of worship in terms of sitting at His feet. When I lift my voice to sing or take my instrument to play, I think of my expression as my "alabaster jar," my very best. As I worship, I break it and pour its contents on my Savior. In my spirit, I can even sense His approval as He says to me, "Steve, you have done a beautiful thing to me."

What did this simple woman of Bethany know that we have forgotten? Although men witnessed her worship, it was not for them. *She ministered to Jesus, centering her life on Him.* Her passion was to please Him with little regard for the opinions of His followers. Her actions were reasonable in that light, and they meant far more than she could know. Still, the meaning of it all was not her concern. Two realities dominated her heart, a jar of costly ointment and a priceless Savior. Her love for Jesus compelled her to lavish one on the other. She held nothing back. Her devotion was complete. Reason demanded no less passion than this. The analytical, practical disciples earned a rebuke but Mary won a commendation; she pleased the Lord. Like Mary of Bethany, you and I have the capacity to touch the heart of Jesus with our offerings of gratitude and adoration. He is faithful to respond to us just as He did to Mary.

As congregations, too, we can please the Lord. We can set our passion on Him. When led by the Holy Spirit, entire congregations can sit at Jesus' feet in worship. It is intensely personal and yet it is meant to be done by all, before all. This kind of worship heals the worshiper's heart and the aroma of it rises to heal a hurting humanity. Just as fragrance filled that room in Bethany, so the presence of the Lord rises with our adoration of Him to fill our hearts, our homes, our houses of worship, and even all creation.

Jesus connected Mary's heart-level worship with the preaching of the gospel to all the nations. God intends a partnership of pew and pulpit. The worshiper's tears soften the soil for the seed the preacher sows. Worship is the plow of the Holy Spirit that breaks up the fallow ground of the heart, preparing it for the seed of the Written Word. In this promise the Great Commandment (loving God) and the Great Commission (preaching the gospel) are vitally connected. Like passion and reason, each empowers the other.

But, how can we, the children of a fallen humanity, please a Holy God?—only by God's grace. Only the righteousness of Christ can fully please the Father. This book is not about obtaining salvation. Our concern is with worshiping God, the interaction of a saved people with their Savior. The danger of displeasing God with our worship is not that we would lose our salvation, but rather that we would fail to know Him and live for Him as we should. Just as salvation is only possible through grace, so True Worship is only possible through grace. First Peter 2:5 makes this clear—"You also, like living stones, are being built into a spiritual house to be a holy priesthood, offering spiritual sacrifices acceptable to God through Jesus Christ." When we fall short of perfection as we endeavor with all our hearts to worship God, Jesus makes each offering perfect before the Father.

By God's astounding grace we are counted worthy of a relationship with God. But grace is not license. We are commanded to present our bodies as living sacrifices of worship and to set about actively proving the good and perfect will of God in our lives (Romans 12:1,2). In other words, we are commanded to learn what pleases God. Mary pleased Him. The disciples didn't. This book is about learning how to please God with a lifestyle of passionate and reasonable praise and worship.

Pleasing God is the most important thing in life; other pursuits pale in comparison. If we thrill our parents, win the admiration of peers, and are loved by many friends but have not pleased God, those we have pleased will stand silent and unable to defend us when we stand before God to give an account of our Christian living. If our life's work has pleased the Lord, we will experience the double joy of seeing it withstand the fires of His judgment (I Corinthians 3:10-15) and hearing Him say, "Well done, good and faithful servant. Enter into the joy of the Lord" (Matthew 25:14-30). In the light of that moment, pleasing God is what really matters in life.

As we mature in Christ, we learn how to please God rather than ourselves or others. We learn how to center our lives on Him. The Bible speaks to this issue often.

- Pleasing God rather than men is the path of victory (Proverbs 16:7).
- It is the pathway to his presence and joy (Isaiah 56:4-8) and is an essentially spiritual approach to life (Romans 8:8).
- It is not to be confused with pleasing others (Galatians 1:10) and leads to abundant living (I Thessalonians 4:1).

- Through True Worship, we engage in a victorious spiritual warfare (II Timothy 2:4).
- Faith is an essential element to worship and carries an assurance that God will reward those who please him (Hebrews 11:6).

Many people long for a simpler life. Living is too fast, and decisions are too difficult. Relationships are too demanding. The future is too frightening. But a worship relationship with God changes all of that. Setting one's heart to please God greatly simplifies life: Time is in the hands of the timeless one, decisions are based upon His Word, relationships can be built that will last forever, and the future is the brightest prospect of all. Life can achieve a manageable order if we set our hearts to please Him first, above all others. God is worthy of no less a place in our hearts than the absolute center. The overriding message of Scripture to the believer is this: Love God first, above all others, and delight in Him. Let His ways become your heart's passion. Let His truth be the basis of all your reasoning. Please Him today. Tomorrow and eternity will take care of themselves, for they are in His hands. Only He knows how to lead us through this day in the manner that will prepare us for tomorrow.

The Way that Seems Right

The question then becomes, "How do I know what pleases God in worship?" How can we know that God is pleased with the cycle of our personal devotion, our public worship, and our daily lives? We must prayerfully sort His ways from our ways. This is not easy. His ways and ours have been so thoroughly blended we have great difficulty discerning what pleases God from what pleases us. Two ways face us: the way that seems right and the way that is right.

Think of this analogy. When looking for an address in a strange city, we do not turn down streets because they *feel* right to us. Consulting with people we meet along the way may or may not get us where we want to go. The only sure way is to consult a map, a dependable source of truth. *As we seek the right way in our journey toward True Worship, we cannot depend on our feelings or the directions of others.* The One we seek has drawn us a map to His house. He will even assist us in reading the map and prompt us at every turn.

As we seek God's heart, we must face two important possibilities. First, well-intentioned people who love us may send us on a route that takes us far from our goal of True Worship. Second, our own feelings may be conditioned responses birthed in us by our culture. The Bible puts it this way: "There is a way that seems right to a man, but in the end it leads to death" (Proverbs 14:12). "For my thoughts are not your thoughts, neither are your ways my ways," declares the LORD" (Isaiah 55:8).

Let's explore these possibilities with these questions:

- Could our worship be pleasing to men and displeasing to the Lord?
- Or could it be that our worship could displease men and please the Lord?
- Could what pleases or displeases us in worship activity, really affect the Lord Jesus in the opposite way?
- How can we know if God is pleased? Is our pleasure a dependable gauge of His pleasure?

Some who would never accept a "seems right" attitude toward morality or ethics will worship God according to their own feelings without questioning whether He is pleased. Others may worship to the point of their own satisfaction with little thought of whether God is satisfied. If believers fail to seek out God's ways and deliberately stop short of pleasing God, they have elevated their ways to an equal footing with God's ways. There are frightful consequences. They erect boundaries around their organizations and are cutoff from the current move of the Holy Spirit. Like walled cities, they are locked in by their lack of vision and cut off from those who are following God. Not only is the extent of ministry limited, but the engine that powers the ministry will be fueled by the power of man not the power of God. The power politics of man will replace the kingdom authority of God.

Worship in our own strength is as powerless to please Him as our works are to save us from our sins. The utter failure of man to find his own way is illustrated by the story of Israel's first king. Saul could have been a great king. God did not choose him for failure but gave him a new heart and a new set of friends, the prophets. The ministry of these men could have kept the presence of the Lord as near to the king as his very breath. They could have helped Saul focus his passion on God and helped him keep his reasoning clear.

But Saul only engaged in worship activities when it was politically expedient. He demonstrated no interest in the Ark of God's presence. He tried to use forms of worship to build his own kingdom. His kingly anointing could have been the source of a vibrant, life-long relationship with Almighty God. Instead, his refusal to nurture his new heart became a cancer, draining life from him until sanity left him, the crown departed from his house, and his own sword became his undoing. Saul's slow demise is a warning to all who would forsake the ways of the Lord in their lives. By trying to do what God had called him to do in his own way, without the touch of God, this bashful young man became a tortured, embittered, spear-throwing monster. His passion turned inward, and reason deserted him.

It still happens today. No magical evolution over the centuries has enabled us to do God's will without God's power and wisdom. We still must walk, work, and worship *His* way, not ours.

Through this study we will attempt to discover His thoughts and ways. As we begin to adjust our passion and reason to His, He will arise in our hearts as never before. As His thoughts and ways are presented to you, keep these questions in mind:

- Will I worship to please myself?
- Will I worship to please others?
- Will I worship to please God?

These questions will help us sort things out.

Will I worship to please myself? Have *my* goals for worshiping God become paramount? Do I come to Him just for the benefits? Do I refuse to sing songs in public worship because they displease me? Am I offended by the praise and worship of others even when I know there is Scripture encouraging that very type of worship? We must see that our personal preferences have been formed by the action of different forces upon us: personality, culture, and the Word of God. Our personal preferences will call upon us to worship God in the way that *seems* right to us. But the metal of our preferences was forged in the fires of heredity and hammered on the anvil of experience.

Will I worship to please others? The "others" might be the people of another generation or a power block in the church. Whoever they might be, they form a cultural influence. Traditions of men can be powerful influences for good in a society, but only if the tradition is in keeping with truth. Our traditions must constantly be measured by biblical truth. A vital Christianity is one that is in a continual state of renewal. We must not blindly hold to our traditions as if they were the teachings of God. The pathway to apostasy leads to the equalization of church tradition and biblical revelation. This brought public anger in the earthly ministry of Jesus. "You have let go of the commands of God and are holding on to the traditions of men." And he said to them: "You have a fine way of setting aside the commands of God in order to observe your own traditions!" (Mark 7:8,9). We must constantly seek the unfolding truth of God in the Bible and adjust our traditions to what the Holy Spirit is saying to the churches. If we do not, culture will invade our traditions and what in one generation was a fresh move of God becomes the methodology of the next generation and the tradition of the third. Only by constant renewal can we see the difference between methodology (cultural techniques) and truth (eternal, trans-cultural revelation from Scripture) and keep the influence of culture at bay. Culture will cry out to us to worship God in the way that seems most fitting to the collective image of Him in society. But modern culture is beset by profound darkness with only an occasional sliver of light from a forgotten time when God's truth was the true enlightenment.

Will I worship to please God? The Holy Spirit calls us through the Word of God to worship God in the way that pleases *Him* most because the Holy Spirit is the revealer of God's heart. By seeking out the things that please God as He has revealed them in the Bible, we can keep the content and intent of our worship expressions pure before the Lord. We become willing tools in the hands of the Holy Spirit, who always seeks to honor the Lord Jesus and bring glory to His name. But we must seek these things out, examining our worship traditions for what is biblical and searching the Bible for divine revelation. It takes work but those who diligently seek God will find him (Hebrews 11:6). The influences of personality and culture are automatic, affecting us without effort on our part. But the influence of the Spirit of God is attained only upon our initiative as we *obey* the voice of God.

Three Important Questions:

Will I worship to please myself?
Will I worship to please others?
Will I worship to please God?

The Way That Is Right

Jesus said it this way, "I am the way and the truth and the life. No one comes to the Father except through me" (John

14:6). As we discover all the ways we can worship God, we must not forget that Jesus is *the way*. As we thrill to all the wonderful truths the Bible contains on worship, we must remember that Jesus is *the truth*. As we enter the flow of the River of Life from God's throne, we must bear in mind that Jesus is *the life*. We must never let the awesome wonder of time spent with the Father obscure the fact that we have come to the Father through Jesus, the Son. Scriptures about worship from both Testaments will enlighten us but Jesus is at the heart of every verse. His blood is our only qualification. Were it not for Jesus, the presence of the Almighty would consume us; but because Jesus has borne our sins away, God's presence renews us. Jesus is the way that *is* right.

What is it about worshiping God that brings such a powerful response from the Creator's heart? In the words translated "worship" from the Hebrew and Greek, submission is the central idea. Isaiah makes it clear that a submissive heart elicits a loving response from the heart of God. This is what the LORD says: "'Heaven is my throne, and the earth is my footstool. Where is the house you will build for me? Where will my resting place be? Has not my hand made all these things, and so they came into being?' declares the LORD. 'This is the one I esteem: he who is humble and contrite in spirit, and trembles at my word.'" (Isaiah 66:1,2)

With a poor and contrite spirit we must worship the Jesus revealed to us in the pages of the Bible. He is not the Jesus of imagination, created in our own image by the design of our flawed personality. He is not the Jesus of society, marred by the clumsy minds of men. He is the Jesus slain before the foundation of all creation. He is the image of the invisible God by whom all the worlds were made and the virgin-born servant emptied of all but love, who became the Lamb of God, the sacrifice for all sin. He is the preacher to souls in captivity and their avenging hero. He is the conqueror of death, hell, and the grave who rose by the power of the Spirit to new and eternal life. Jesus is the One whose coronation heaven witnessed. He is now seated at the Father's right hand and His name is above every other name. He is the One before whom every knee will bow and to whom every tongue will confess that He indeed is Lord, Master, and Sovereign. Only this Jesus, the Jesus of the Bible, prompts our worship for no other Jesus could. He calls us to enter into His life. When he senses in us a contrite spirit He opens for us all the glory of His presence and all the power and peace of His reign.

"This is what the LORD says: 'Heaven is my throne, and the earth is my footstool. Where is the house you will build for me? Where will my resting place be? Has not my hand made all these things, and so they came into being?' declares the LORD. 'This is the one I esteem: he who is humble and contrite in spirit, and trembles at my word'" (Isaiah 66:1,2).

As we hold His immortal Word in our mortal hands, we tremble. Entering His presence is the greatest privilege life affords. In awesome stillness we lay personality down. In desperate abandon we cast culture aside With trembling hearts we take up His Word. In nearness to Him, our personalities will be reborn in His image. Our souls will be cleansed by repeated exposure to His glory in the same way gold is purged from base metals by fire. In unity of spirit and purpose, and in diversity of reborn personality and reformed culture, the Church will arise blazing as never before with the glory of God. All flesh will witness the entrance of the King as He comes to live and reign in His Church, the People of God.

The Surgery of the Sword

How can we know the difference between the voices within us, those of the Spirit of God, and those of personality and culture? Experience and culture have shaped our souls, giving us the emotions, the memory, the values, and the deep-seated needs we each have. The voice of the soul is emotional, crying from pain of the heart's untended wounds, and desperate in its attempt to satisfy the needs of the hidden self. There is no way to escape the forces of life that shape and injure the soul. We need surgery. We need a physician of the soul who can cut

away the damaged memories, cleanse the neglected lesions of
the heart, and satisfy the deepest needs of the most wounded
and desperate soul.

We have such a one in Jesus. The writer to the Hebrews
presents us a powerful image of how God works in us to help
us sort these things out. "For the word of God is living and
active. Sharper than any double-edged sword, it penetrates
even to dividing soul and spirit, joints and marrow; it judges
the thoughts and attitudes of the heart" (Hebrews 4:12). The
Great Physician's surgery is done with the most powerful and
sure instrument—the Word! He speaks within us from a place
deeper than the soul—the spirit, the God-conscious part of us
that knows without physical evidence and believes before
there is proof. The voice of God's Spirit is reasonable and
quiet, still and small, speaking in a peaceful urgency so unlike
the clamoring of the soul. As we read the Word, the Lord
speaks in our spirit. As we commune with Him in worship, He
speaks. When He helps us see something in our hearts contrary to the Word, the Lord lifts His Sword, ready to do His swift
surgery. If we invite Him, He will change us. As quickly as
our sins were forgiven, His Sword will strike, lovingly healing
the hurt as the offending memory, attitude, or misconception
is swept away by Calvary's love.

It is through the Word of God that we discern the difference between soul and spirit, between reason and passion. It is
the only sword sharp enough. No wonder we tremble before
it. In the Word we find our Savior and our healing as He
causes spirit to rise above soul in True Worship. In all of this,
humility is the key. We are totally dependent upon God, His
revelation, His Spirit, and His amazing love and grace. He
responds to the humble heart. "Blessed are the poor in spirit,"
He said in the first point of His Sermon on the Mount, "for
theirs in the kingdom of Heaven" (Matthew 5:3).

To begin this voyage toward life's highest priority, toward
worship that pleases God, toward a life that is centered upon
God himself, we must leave the excess baggage of personal
preference and cultural conditioning on the pier. This is a

round trip excursion. We will return to our personal feelings, for personality and culture have important roles to play in our worship and witness. But if we allow the Holy Spirit to work His divine craftsmanship, our load will be lighter than before, stripped of the dead weight of ungodly influences. We will be free as never before to engage in our ministry, every believer's ministry, the ministry of passionate and reasonable worship that pleases God. And, we will be free to bring light to the surrounding darkness as never before. All we need for the trip is the map of His Word and a heart set on pleasing God whatever the cost and wherever it may lead.

Chapter Two

APPROACHING THE ALMIGHTY
The Tabernacle/Temple and The Holy Of Holies

Moses

All the artisans were finished. There was no more fabric to be formed into tents, no more wood to be hewn into pillars and furnishings, no more gold to be beaten into altars and capitals. All the work for God's dwelling place was finished. Again the Lord spoke to Moses, "Set up the Tabernacle, the Tent of Meeting, on the first day of the first month" (Exodus 40:2).

Perhaps Moses wondered what would happen when the Tent was assembled. He had been there on the mountain when God manifested His holy presence. He had stood on the rock and had seen the glory of the Lord. He saw the Lord write the Law on the tables of stone. All the people saw was smoke and lightning. Moses heard the voice of God, and the people heard only thunder. The prophet descended Mt. Sinai with the words of Yahweh in his very hands only to find the people worshiping a golden calf of their own making and materials, disgracing themselves in every lewd perversion of worship one could imagine.

But then, these same people, so recently ascended from slavery, had pooled their hard-earned skills and worked together to build this beautiful portable sanctuary and its furnishings. They had given of their new-found riches until Moses had to stop them from giving. Their gold had gone to cover the ark of God instead of a pagan idol. Now the moment had come to see what all their cooperative labor had produced. This collection of poles, clasps, boards, bars, and pillars, and these sections of fabric and animal skins, and all these utensils, garments, vessels, altars, and tables were laid at Moses' feet. It was time to bring order out of chaos. Moses blessed them, and they got to work. These were skillful people, and soon the sanctuary was taking shape. Moses guided them as they assembled the habitation of God in the earth, the place where He would dwell in the midst of them. When the work was finished, the breeze must have stirred the fabric walls and a deep silence sank into each heart as the people and Moses looked at what they had done.

Moses placed all the furnishings in their exact positions and anointed them. He took the oil and anointed everything the people had made, setting this work apart to be God's dwelling place. It was to be the Tent of Meeting. Here man would meet God. Creatures would come before the manifest presence of the Creator to worship. Sins would be confessed, forgiven, and cast away. Healing for diseases of body and soul would be administered. Direction would be found for the elders as they led the people of God. The works and words of God would be recorded and taught to generations to come. This Tent of Meeting would be the center of the camp, the nation, the heart of the people.

So Moses finished the work at last. Now even the breeze was still. No one moved, not even the children. From somewhere a cloud came, not the forbidding storm of Sinai; this was fabric of a friendlier sky. No one shrunk back from this inviting presence. Each face glowed as with an inner fire. The cloud filled the house they had made with their own hands and resources. No one, not even Moses could enter the Tabernacle because of the cloud. God had inhabited their praise. Jehovah was now enthroned upon their offerings of worship. Unlike the worship at the golden calf, no one was debased here. No one was used or abused. All were exalted by the presence of a Holy God, His presence resting upon and within the work of their hands. Eventually the cloud lifted enough for the priests to enter.

For the next generation, when the cloud moved the people moved. When it stayed, they stayed. At night the cloud was a friendly flame reminding them of the indwelling and the sovereignty of their God. It would be so, until they came to the land of their promise. Wander though they might, He would always be there, dwelling in the house they had built for Him.

Biblical Models of Worship

Moses and the people of Israel pleased God with the Tent of Meeting. He received it as an offering of worship. He came to live in it and began to rule from it. As wrong as the people had been at the foot of Mt. Sinai, they were just that correct at the Tent of Meeting. But that Tent was far more than just the form, content, and structure of *their* worship. It was the template for worship for all mankind and for the ages. The Tabernacle in the Wilderness set the pattern for the way God wants man to approach Him. It is the original illustration of the passion and reason of True Worship. It is the first of several biblical models of worship we will study, and in many ways it underlies all the other models.

What is meant by a "model of worship"? To understand this method of studying biblical truths about worship, we must understand the use of models.

The strange thing about standing on the deck of the battleship USS North Carolina while on vacation a few years ago was that it felt familiar to me. I had never been on it or any large naval vessel before, but, in my younger days, I had built several models of World War II battleships. Because my eye had studied the form of a battleship in miniature, the real thing seemed familiar to me, only greater than any of my models could ever have been. Those plastic models coupled with my imagination had somehow bridged the impossible gap of space and time between the high-seas warfare of the 40's and the daydreams of a landlocked boy a generation later.

Models serve as illustrations, helping us understand large realities that are otherwise beyond us. They bridge the impossible gaps between our finite minds and infinite truths. These dictionary definitions will help: Model, 1) a structural design, 2) a miniature representation; also: a pattern of something to be made, 3) an example for imitation or emulation, 4) type, design (Merriam-Webster, 1974).

Worship is such a large truth that the Bible gives several models to help us understand it. In the next three chapters, we will discuss seven biblical models of worship that give an overview of a subject that touches every aspect of life. In doing this, we confidently follow the example of New Testament writers who employ events and objects from the Old Testament as models for New Testament truth. We must remember, however, that each model is only a partial revelation and does not reveal the whole truth about worship. Those who major in one model to the exclusion of the others become unbalanced and ultimately fall short of all that God has for them.

Praise and Worship
In Terms of His Presence

Before we can discuss the models, we must define what we mean by praise and worship. Let us think of them in terms of the presence of the Lord. What is meant by the term "the presence of the Lord"? How can we speak of entering the presence of a God who is everywhere? Let's take a reasoned look at the Scriptures. The Bible indicates that there are three characteristics of God's presence: omnipresence, inward presence, and manifest presence.

The omnipresence of the Lord means He is everywhere at all times, demonstrating His absolute mastery of time and space, which are, after all, His creations. Paul preached God's omnipresence to the Greeks at Mars Hill (Acts. 17:28). It is the most general revelation of God's presence, a natural starting point as we witness to an unbelieving world.

The inward presence of the Lord is His presence within the hearts and lives of His people. Throughout the Bible, God speaks of dwelling with and in His people. For example:

"What agreement is there between the Temple of God and idols? For we are the Temple of the living God. As God has said: 'I will live with them and walk among them, and I will be their God, and they will be my people'" (II Corinthians 6:16).

The manifest presence of the Lord is deeper still. God is present within creation, within His people, and within *the praise* of His people. "But thou art holy, O thou that inhabitest the praises of Israel. Our fathers trusted in thee: they trusted and thou didst deliver them. They cried unto thee, and were delivered: they trusted in thee and were not confounded." (Psalm 22:3-5, AV). In this great psalm, so descriptive of the agony of the Cross, we get an important glimpse of the majesty of the throne. (The throne and the Cross are never far from the True Worshiper's heart.) The Lord inhabits, or dwells in, the praises of His people. Modern translations also say that He is enthroned upon the praise of His people. ("Yet thou art holy, enthroned upon the praises of Israel" RSV.) This little verse is one of the richest veins in the gold mine of Scripture. It will yield more riches when we discuss the Throne Room model. For now let us just say that when God's people begin to express their praise (thanksgiving and exaltation) to God, He responds. He shares with them a deeper sense of His presence.

How does this happen? How does the Lord intensify our awareness of His presence? Jesus gives us the answer when we listen to His conversation with Nicodemus. "Jesus answered, 'I tell you the truth, no one can enter the kingdom of God unless he is born of water and the Spirit. Flesh gives birth to flesh, but the Spirit gives birth to spirit. You should not be surprised at my saying, 'You must be born again'" (John 3:5).

Jesus said that the Spirit of God moves like the wind, unseen and mysterious, yet powerfully obvious in effect. Like the air around us, the unseen omnipresence of God surrounds us and gives us life. We may not be aware of His presence but, just as we would miss air, we would be desperate if His omnipresence were suddenly taken from us. Still we go on, taking the omnipresence of God for granted as we do the earth's atmosphere, giving it little thought. But when the air begins to stir, we notice; a cool breeze refreshes; a mighty wind impresses. When we turn our hearts toward God to be His people, He begins to move in our hearts, like air beginning to stir. This is His inward presence. And when we begin to praise Him, He moves within us like a mighty wind, powerful in its effect, and we experience His manifest presence.

The Presence of the Lord

The Omnipresence — God is everywhere.
The Inner Presence — God is in His people.
The Manifest Presence — God is in the Praise of His People.

He is always faithful to indwell our praise. But are we always faithful to give Him praise?

A Worshiper's Prayer

O God, may the revelation of this truth ignite a passion in our hearts. In the private place of prayer, give us a hunger for the sweet stirring of Your Spirit. In our public worship, let us find no rest until we see the effects of the rushing, mighty wind of Your Spirit moving in our midst! In our daily living, may the joy of your creativity emanate from us like a cool breeze on a hot summer's day. You are always with us and in us, but You long to move in us as we praise You from our hearts.

Now, let us define praise and worship in the light of His presence.

Praise is the expression of thanksgiving to the Lord and the exaltation of the Lord that brings us into His presence.

Praise is the *willful entrance* into the presence of God by speaking forth thanksgiving to God and by exalting God's name, His character, His mighty deeds, and His glory. Praise is a deliberate action of soul and body. We praise God by expressing gratitude to Him and by proclaiming His glory, deeds, and character. Praise is centered on God but is often expressed to others. We tell others how thankful we are or how great God is. The music of praise tends to be horizontal in direction, singing about God.

Worship is the expression of submission to God, adoration of Him, and commitment to Him.

Worship is the *willing response* of our spirit to the revelation of the character of God by the moving of His Spirit in our hearts. Worship is the act of communing with God when we are in His presence. We worship God by expressing love for Him and commitment to Him. Worship is centered on God himself and is primarily expressed directly to Him, although many worshipful expressions of God's glory can be directed to others. The music of worship tends to be vertical in direction, singing directly to the Lord—in other words, songs of prayer. Through praise, we enter the Lord's presence. Through worship we respond to His presence.

Important Reminder: Each model of worship is only a partial revelation and does not reveal the whole truth about worship.

MODEL NUMBER ONE
The Tabernacle / Temple Model

The first biblical illustration we will study is the Tabernacle/Temple model, the Tabernacle of Moses and the Temple of Solomon. We place them together because for the purposes of understanding worship their function is the same. These historical structures illustrate how we may scripturally "come before His Presence" (Psalm 100:3).

Moses' Tabernacle was built just after the Exodus from Egypt with the instructions God gave on Mt. Sinai. It was a system of tents with an open outer court and an enclosed Tent, called the inner court, which housed two rooms, the Holy Place and the Holy of Holies. The outer court had an altar for the sacrifices and a huge basin of water called the laver for washing the priests' hands. The Holy Place had a table for the shewbread, a lamp stand, and an altar of incense.

The Holy of Holies had only the Ark of the Covenant. A massive curtain called the veil hung between the two inner chambers. Here in this secret, secluded place the manifest presence of the Lord dwelt in the earth. Why? Because God longed to dwell with His people, because He could accept the blood sacrifices in anticipation of the cross, and because the Old Testament Tabernacle was built as a praise to the Lord, worthy of His indwelling. "Then the cloud covered the Tent of Meeting, and the glory of the LORD filled the Tabernacle" (Exodus 40:34).

Many generations later, Solomon's Temple, a beautiful structure also built as praise to the Lord, housed the same furniture, sacrifices, and activities. The Bible records the powerful day when the manifest presence of the Lord came to dwell in this structure of praise. "The trumpeters and singers joined in unison, as with one voice, to give praise and thanks to the LORD. Accompanied by trumpets, cymbals and other instruments, they raised their voices in praise to the LORD and sang: 'He is good; his love endures forever.' Then the Temple of the LORD was filled with a cloud, and the priests could not perform their service because of the cloud, for the glory of the LORD filled the Temple of God" (II Chronicles 5:13,14).

These two structures are filled with vivid imagery of Jesus and His work of salvation, but what does the Tabernacle/Temple model tell us about worship? The Tabernacle/Temple model shows the power of sin and the greater power of grace. We also see in the Tabernacle how God wants us to approach Him—the *reason* of worship.

Sin separates from God. Of all the nations of the earth only Israel had the Tabernacle and the Temple. Of all of Israel, only the men could come into the outer court. Of all the men of Israel, only the priests could enter the Holy Place. Of all the priests, only the high priest could pass through the veil into the Holy of Holies and only once a year.

Before Calvary, the only way God could dwell in the earth in His manifest presence was deep within the praise-built walls of the Tabernacle or Temple. The sin of mankind so filled the earth that the *Shekinah*, the glory of the Lord, was seen only in a glow above the Ark of the Covenant. At the Exodus, through God's astounding grace, this one nation had witnessed His clouded majesty at Sinai and now they knew, seeing the fire by night and the cloud by day, that He was in the midst of the Tabernacle. But they could come no closer and had no desire to. Their sin excluded them. Entrance to the outer court and the inner chambers was for a certain few by blood sacrifice only.

Modern man has grown quite comfortable with sin, but God has not. To be True Worshipers, we must see sin in its true colors. We see sin in the somber hues of Almighty God secluded in a little room in a Tent when His heart's deepest longing was and is to dwell in all the earth, in every heart, in the full splendor of His majesty. We see it in the thick darkness of the human heart, groping for light and color, but finding only hell's colorless shadows. It is also seen in the blood red of a Savior, beaten and broken, pierced and pinned to a cross. These are the true colors of sin. There is no beauty here, no joy, no peace. Sin is dark because God is light and sin separates from God. Sin is death because God is life and sin separates from God. We see this in the Tabernacle and the Temple.

But we also see access. Sin is not an unsolvable problem. God has always had a redemption plan. In anticipation of the blood of the one spotless lamb, the Israelite worshiper could come into the outer courts of God's very presence. The priests could come into the Holy Place to burn the incense, exchange the shewbread, and tend the oil lamps. Moses and Aaron, and the High Priests of subsequent generations could enter into the Holy of Holies where dwelt the manifest presence of the Lord. Sin is not the final word. Grace has always abounded in the very face of sin. Grace is the final word.

There is a reasonable, systematic way to "come before His presence." The Tabernacle/Temple model teaches us how the Lord wants us to come into His manifest presence. This is the "reasonable service of worship" referred to in Romans 12: 1,2. The Tabernacle of Moses was the first habitation of God in a structure of human construction. It provides a pattern of worship to which all other models conform. To discern this pattern, we let Scripture interpret Scripture.

The Bible identifies the outer court as the place of thanksgiving and praise. "Enter his gates with thanksgiving and his courts with praise; give thanks to him and praise his name" (Psalm 100:4). The descriptions of the Tabernacle and Temple illustrate that the outer court is also a place of sacrifice, repentance, and cleansing, symbolized by the altar and the laver. Putting all these elements together, we see that before we can enter the Holy Place or the Holy of Holies, we must pass through the outer court. In other words, before our spirits can worship, that is, to respond to His manifest presence, we must first fulfill our definition of praise: give thanks, offer ourselves to Him in humility, and praise His name. Just as the Old Testament worshiper could not barge into the Holy Place and take a seat, we cannot plop ourselves down in the Holy Place or the Holy of Holies and take a few frantic glimpses of His glory and then be on our way! We must approach the Lord in the way He has prescribed. It is only reasonable.

It is important to understand what I am *not* saying here. I am not talking about emergencies. I was traveling up a mountain road on the Island of Luzon in the Philippines with an American missionary at the wheel of our little Japanese truck. Drivers in the Philippines do not have the same attitude toward lanes as we have in the USA. The lanes in the Philippines are more like suggestions than definite paths to take. It is OK in their thinking to pass on a mountain curve. If someone is coming, he will probably get out of the way. This was a challenge to my American driving sensibilities but I was trying to adjust. The American missionary was himself new in the country and was doing his best to drive Filipino style. He slowly started around a big truck on a mountain curve. When we got almost even with the truck a huge red-and-white bus came barreling down the mountain two-lane headed straight for us. At that moment, I did not carefully find my way through the gates of thanksgiving or leisurely linger in the courts of praise or even stop to search my heart at the altar of sacrifice. I went straight into the Lord's throne and yelled, "Jesus, help us!" He did. The bus driver swerved as much as he could, the truck we were passing went faster, my missionary friend slowed down, and somehow we got back into our lane just as a massive red-and-white blur roared by. I am not talking about approaching God in emergencies. We are His children and He wants us to call upon Him in time of need. No gate or outer court is required.

The other thing I am *not* talking about is the occasional sovereign move of God. Sometimes *God just moves.* Analysts cannot determine why. The participants cannot give you a formula they followed. God just moves. These times are wonderful. I grew up in a classic Pentecostal church. Once in a while we would have a great move of God in one of our services. The presence of the Lord would just permeate every-thing that was said and done. Sometimes on these occasions there wouldn't even be a sermon. (I used to wonder how the pastor must have felt when he heard someone say, "My, we had the best service this morning. The pastor didn't even preach!")

Looking back on those occasional moves of God, I have come to a realization: God is sovereign and can do whatever He wants to do. He can establish a system of how something will work and then violate that system and make it work some other way. It is called a miracle. For instance, God devised a system that makes the sun appear to move across the sky but He made the sun appear to stand still for Joshua—a miracle. God can lay out for us a pathway to His presence and then invade our meetings however He wants. We should not form the disciplines of our lives by our behavior in emergencies or by God's sovereign alternatives. We need to find the systems God has designed for us and walk in them daily.

Let's look at the Tabernacle/Temple model in greater detail. In addition to the Psalm 100 interpretation of the meaning of the gate and outer court, let's think of the other furnishings in terms of these frequent scriptural analogies, bread for the Word and presence of God, incense for prayer, and oil for the light and power of the Holy Spirit. We can now see the significance of the Tabernacle/Temple model to our modern worship.

In private devotions and public worship, we can follow this pattern into the very presence of the King. We pass through the gates of thanksgiving before we enter the outer court of praise. We pass through the outer court of praise before we enter the inner court of worship. Praise comes before worship. Spirit precedes truth. Ministry *to* the Lord leads to ministry *from* the Lord. *Ministry to the Lord comes before ministry to man.* Passing through the outer court of thanksgiving, praise, and humility prepares our hearts for the Word, for effectual praying, and for the illumination and regeneration of the Holy Spirit. Time spent in the Word and prayer and in the light of the Spirit prepares us to pass through the torn veil to the Holy of Holies to wait in the stillness of His awesome presence.

THE TABERNACLE / TEMPLE MODEL
The Reasonable Service of Worship

Outer court Thanksgiving (for who He is and what He has done)
Praise (exaltation of His Name and Character)
Offering (giving ourselves to Him in repentance and humility)

Inner court The Table of Shewbread (the Word of God)
(Holy Place) The Altar of Incense (effectual prayer)
The Golden Lamp Stand (The Holy Spirit)

Holy of Holies The Ark of the Covenant (God's Glory) and Promise
God's Manifest Presence
His Righteousness and Holiness

This progression is divine genius. This process helps us center our passions on God himself. Thanksgiving is the logical starting point for it gives the worshiper the proper perspective on life. It is the equivocator of all men. Praise focuses us on God and not ourselves. A contrite heart is the object of the Lord's desire. We, like the elders around His throne, must remove all our earthly crowns and cast them at His feet. We are ready for the inner court only when we have passed the gate of thanksgiving, the court of praise, and the altar of sacrifice. The Tabernacle/Temple shows us these things in vivid imagery. It is important to note that we do not leave the outer court elements there in the outer court. We don't pick these things up and put them back down. We take thanksgiving, exaltation, sacrifice, humility, and worship with us all the way into the Holy of Holies.

The Tabernacle/Temple model instructs us in how to systematically approach God both privately and publicly. Passage through the old Tabernacle and Temple was bought with blood. There is no such thing as praise and worship without the blood of the Lamb. Jesus is all in all: the Beautiful Gate to

THE TABERNACLE / TEMPLE MODEL
and the Worship Experience

Tabernacle/Temple	Private Worship	Public Worship
Outer Court	Thanksgiving	Thanksgiving
(Gate/Outer Court	Praise	Praise
Altar of Sacrifice)	Submitting heart	Submitting heart
		Tithes and offerings
Inner court	Prayers of Petition and	Corporate Prayer
(The Holy Place with	Bible Study in the light	Sermon with the
Altar of Incense and	and power of the Holy	Anointing of the
Table of Shewbread)	Spirit	Holy Spirit
(The Holy of Holies	Waiting in God's Presence	Altar time
With the Ark of His	Receive His Righteousness	Personal and
Presence and Promise)	and Holiness	Corporate Prayer

the outer court; the sacrificial Lamb in the outer court; the Word in the shewbread, the object of the Spirit's light, the effectual fervent prayer of intercession in the incense, the torn veil, and the Ark of the Presence. It is all by Him, through Him, and for Him. Were it not for the blood of Jesus, we could not come before the manifest presence of God. Our sins would isolate us from Him.

The Holy of Holies

The destination of the worship experience as it is seen in this model is the Holy of Holies. In three accounts of Jesus' crucifixion (Matthew 27:51; Mark 15:38; Luke 23:45), a strange happening is recorded. At the moment of Jesus' death the heavy veil in the Temple separating the Holy of Holies from the Holy Place was torn from top to bottom. Once the sin problem was solved by the perfect sacrifice, the manifested presence of the Lord could no longer be contained in that little room. The manifest presence of the Lord burst forth from the old order, to search out the willing hearts of a new order and come to rest there. It was as if the old covenant of His promise exploded into a new covenant of His presence and the veil suffered the force of the blast. Now, instead of one Temple, He would dwell in a multitude of temples, temples of flesh not stone. Through the Church, His glory would fill all the earth.

It is our great and blood-bought privilege to enter the Holy of Holies, passing through the riven veil of His earthly existence. "Therefore, brothers, since we have confidence to enter the Most Holy Place by the blood of Jesus, by a new and living way opened for us through the curtain, that is, his body, and since we have a great priest over the house of God, let us draw near to God with a sincere heart in full assurance of faith, having our hearts sprinkled to cleanse us from a guilty conscience and having our bodies washed with pure water. Let us hold unswervingly to the hope we profess, for he who promised is faithful. And let us consider how we may spur one another on toward love and good deeds. Let us not give up meeting together, as some are in the habit of doing, but let us encourage one another—and all the more as you see the Day approaching" (Hebrews 10:19-25).

"Let us draw near," the writer says. The Tabernacle and Temple show us how. When we realize the magnitude of what Jesus has done for us by opening the Holy of Holies, we *will* draw near. We will set our passions here, on the presence of our Redeemer. Notice in the Hebrews passage the wonderful things that result from time spent in the Holy of Holies: "a sincere heart," "full assurance of faith," "love and good deeds," and "meeting together." Is this not the will of God for every believer? Is this not the pastor's prayer list for his people? Could we not say that purity in heart, consistent faith, love, good works, and faithful attendance to worship are signs of Christian maturity? These things are not found in programs and plans, committees and councils, or rituals and routines. They are found in the presence of the Lord, in the Holy of Holies. If we long to see these things in our lives, we must "draw near." We must worship God, personally, corporately, and passionately, centering our lives on Him. As we do, we pass through the outer court and inner court and gain entrance to the Holy of Holies. The Holy of Holies can be anywhere we choose to make an altar to God. We have access to this chamber at any time. Wherever and whenever, this is a sacred place because of the ways God can minister to us here. What are the characteristics of the Holy of Holies?

The Holy of Holies is a place of exchange. This is the realm of His righteousness, His "right-standing" before God. As we linger there, an exchange takes place: His strength for our weakness, His righteousness for our iniquity, His peace for our turmoil, His wisdom for our confusion.

It is a place of intercession. Here we can feel His heartbeat and know His concerns. His prayers can well up in us by the power of the Spirit and we can join Him in intercession. The effectual, fervent prayer of the one righteous man, Jesus, avails much. His righteousness has now been accredited to our life. With this righteousness comes the power of *our* effectual, fervent prayers, when led and empowered by the Holy Spirit. Passionate prayers make a difference.

This is a place of wholeness. All of our inadequacies are made whole within the realm of the splendor of His holiness. As we worship God privately or publicly, we pass through the veil into the Holy of Holies to wait in His presence, drinking in His completeness and finding wholeness in His holiness.

The Holy of Holies
A place of exchange—my weakness for His strength.
A place of intercession—I pray in power according to God's will.
A place of wholeness—I am made complete in Him.

CONCLUSION

Just as the ancient Hebrews saw the glory of the Lord fill the house they built for Him, we can see the glory of the Lord manifested in our worship and our works today. We are the Tabernacle in the Wilderness. We are the habitation of God by His Spirit. "And in him you too are being built together to become a dwelling in which God lives by his Spirit" (Ephesians 2:22).

With the Tabernacle / Temple, God has given us the blueprint for worship. The passion and reason of worship are clearly seen. The truths illustrated here underlie every other model. Like a divine template, all other truth about worship must conform to God's first revelation of how we may approach Him through the righteousness of His kingdom. At terrible personal cost, God opened up the way to His manifest presence, the Holy of Holies. Not only can we go in, but we must. It is the ministry of every believer and his blood-bought privilege.

The Tabernacle / Temple Model
Hebrews 10:19,22

When I worship God in spirit and truth, I enter the Most Holy Place by the blood of Jesus. I will draw near.

Chapter Three

CELEBRATING THE LORD'S PRESENCE

David's Tabernacle, the Holy-Royal Priesthood, the Living-Sacrifice Of Praise

King David

T he exuberance of the young king was infectious. He had ruled for seven years in Judah and now he was king over all of Israel. Long years of civil war were behind him now. The rhythm of his dance was born in memory of all the young man had experienced: lonely pastoral nights and days as a shepherd; the adulation of a nation for a young champion after Goliath had fallen; the embrace of King Saul and also his unreasoning wrath; the friendship of Jonathan and the loss of him; living as friends among the Philistines who had been and would be again, mortal enemies; being both outlaw and king in his own country; anointed king in Judah and now in all Israel.

There was much cause for a joyful dance. The greatest cause of all was this historic procession—the Ark of the Covenant was on its way to Jerusalem, the City of David. He had ordered the finest new cart his kingdom could produce, and now the Ark rested securely thereupon with Uzza and Ahio, brothers who had been raised with the Ark in their home, marching proudly on either side. Even the oxen pulling the cart seemed to step with a measure of pride previously unknown to the species.

King David, at the head of the procession, danced past the threshing floor of Nachon. He had conquered Jerusalem, a stronghold of the Philistines in the Promised Land and had found there some impressive high ground. That was where they were taking the Ark. David had pitched a Tent there for it. When the Ark was displayed in the Tent on Mt. Zion, all of Israel would be able to see that God's glory had returned. The glory had departed from Moses' Tabernacle years before, during the time of Samuel and Eli the High Priest. In fact, Eli's sons, Hophni and Phineas had so corrupted the worship of Jehovah that God's glory could no longer rest there. In David's view, God had abandoned the tents of Jacob (Psalm 78) and had now chosen David and Mt. Zion as His dwelling and ruling place. Soon the Ark would rest in a Tent on Mt. Zion.

David's rhythmic reverie was overcome by a silence stealing its way toward the front of the procession from the back where the Ark was. Why had the music stopped? Why had the procession halted? Why the sudden, sickening silence? The king hurried back to the Ark. Uzzah, son of Abinadab, lay dead by the Ark. His brother, Ahio, bent over his lifeless form, not yet comprehending enough to weep. The incredible silence which could be no deeper, grew deeper still. A corporate shudder ran through the crowd as Ahio's sudden wail split that silence. The oxen had stumbled at Nachon's threshing floor, and Uzzah reached out to steady the Ark so that it would not fall. Now he was dead, and the mourning of his brother and blank stares of the crowd were all that was left of a young king's victory celebration.

As an artist, King David was subject to depression. Three agonizing months elapsed as David paced in fresh-cut cedar rooms of the new residence in Jerusalem. The Bible says that David was angry with God that day. This soon passed. It also says that David feared God that day. This did not pass. It was necessary for him to fear God to be king of all the people. He had known God as friend when he served as shepherd to his father's sheep on moon-swept Judean hills. He had known God as provider and protector when Saul pursued him. Now, to lead as God's king, he must learn to fear God, his provider, protector and friend.

Sometime during those three months, David consulted the Word of God and learned how the Ark was meant to be transported, on poles through rings on the Ark, on the shoulders of the priests. Bravely, King David tried again, this time with awe and reverence added to his joy and; this time, according to the "due order" of Scripture. And this time he succeeded. Look carefully at what he did next. This man who saw death result from the violation of the due order of Scripture did not place the Ark back in Moses' Tabernacle. There is no reference that he ever did. Instead, David put the ark in the open Tent on Mt. Zion—*David's Tabernacle!* It was the open Holy of Holies with no outer court, no Holy Place, and, except for its dedication ceremonies, no animal sacrifices. For a generation the people, led by great choirs and orchestras and magnificent pageantry, worshiped God at Mt. Zion at the Tabernacle of David. The songs of Zion would become world famous, the envy of God's enemies and everlasting. They would become the first hymnal of the New Testament Church.

MODEL NUMBER TWO
The Tabernacle of David

One character from the Old Testament towers over all the others in the amount of space given to King David's life story. No other figure is like him in skill as an artist, administrator, warrior, and worshiper. He was the Messiah's most important ancestor. He was a man of powerful passions, and he loved the Word of God. His writing chronicled his personal struggles in such a timeless way that the Psalms (more than half are his) have become the companion of the New Testament in every age of Christianity. The Book of Psalms is the most quoted book in the New Testament, its original contributor declared to be the man after God's own heart. All of this is for a reason. King David and his era were precursors of New Testament leaders and times. It is no coincidence that David and his art have always found a home in the hearts of those who follow the Son of David.

For us to understand how the Church Age is foreshadowed in the history of King David and his times, we must understand something about Old Testament prophesy. In his book *Prophetic Light,* Frank M. Boyd explains that Old Testament prophets had a unique vantage point on the future. They described events in sequence that would really take place over wide expanses of time. Boyd's example is the account of Jesus reading from Isaiah 61:1,2) in His hometown synagogue. Jesus stopped reading in mid-sentence, closed the book, and announced, "Today this scripture is fulfilled in your hearing"(Luke 4:21). Had he kept reading, He would have crossed a gap in time that Isaiah had not seen.

Already a gap of almost two thousand years has elapsed since the beginning of "the year of the Lord's favor," and still "the day of vengeance of our God" has not arrived. In other words, the prophet sees both advents as one would look at distant ranges of mountains, the intervening valleys not being visible until one climbed to the top of the nearest range. This is "prophetic perspective."

Paul calls the Church a mystery. The Church Age was unseen by the Old Testament prophets for it is a valley between mountain peaks of prophecy, a parenthesis between the first advent of the Lord and His return.

The Tabernacle of David, is one of the most striking Old Testament pictures of the New Testament Church and an important biblical model for the understanding of worship. During the reign of King David and the early reign of Solomon, between Moses' Tabernacle and Solomon's Temple the manifest presence of the Lord dwelt in Jerusalem on Mt. Zion in a Tent, the Tabernacle of David. It was the most New Testament-like period in Old Testament times.

Here is a brief history. II Samuel 6 and I Chronicles 15 and 16 tell the story of David's Tabernacle. As soon as David had been anointed king in both Judah and Israel, he sought to unify the people around the presence of the Lord by sending for the Ark of the Covenant. He did not send to the Tabernacle of Moses on Mt. Gibeon as years before the Ark had been removed as a sort of good luck charm in battle. The Philistines had captured it but had returned it when it proved to be hazardous to their idols and their health. Israel's first king, Saul, showed no interest in the Ark so it rested in a private residence for more than twenty years. Children grew up around this holy thing taking it for granted.

But Israel's second king, David, was a man with a different heart, one that burned for the presence and truth of God. Longing for the presence of the Lord, he sent for the Ark. He had conquered Jerusalem and a Philistine garrison on a hill there. Something about the site moved the king. This was a place where God should be worshiped. He pitched an open Tent on this hill he called Zion.

David's passion was a proper one. The people needed to know that God was among them; that He was on their side; that He was their God, a loving, approachable God. This was the God David knew. As David watched over his father's sheep night after night, he discovered that the Lord dwells in the praise of His people. David had learned to minister to the Lord with music and experienced the sweet visitation of God as the Lord came to dwell in his humble songs of praise. Anointed by Samuel but pursued by Saul, David found the Lord to be his high tower and strong defense. All the while, David was writing and now he had a quiver full of pointed songs to strike the hearts of the people with revelations about God. He longed for the people to experience the presence of the Lord the way he had. So, he made the best new cart his new kingdom could produce and sent for the Ark. The procession began.

But, as hot as David's passion burned, it was an uninformed passion. He failed to consult the Word of God on how the Ark was to be transported. Without the Lord's presence, the Ark was just a beautiful box, and all could handle it. But when they worshiped God, even with flawed understanding, He returned to the Ark. Without the blood sacrifice, touching it proved a life-consuming violation of divine order. Uzza died by the Ark. But the second attempt, performed according to the due order of Scripture, was successful, and the Ark came to rest in the Tent on Mt. Zion. Truth had to inform passion.

Biblical References to the Tent on Mt. Zion

Scripture	Meaning
Psalm 78:67-72	Asaph teaches history of David's acts. God abandoned Moses' Tabernacle and chose David and Zion
Isaiah 16:5	The Messiah will sit and judge from the Tabernacle of David.
Amos 9:11,12	The Lord will rebuild the Tabernacle of David so that all mankind can seek the Lord.
Acts 15:17-22	James settles the dispute over the salvation of the Gentiles by quoting Amos 9. The establishment of the N.T. Church is the rebuilding of David's Tabernacle.
Heb. 12:19-24	The writer says that New Testament believers have come to Zion not Sinai to worship. The first place called Zion was the Tent on the hill in Jerusalem.

It is important for us to study the Tabernacle of David, the rule of King David, the times of David, and the early part of Solomon's reign. (For a more complete biblical treatment of the Tabernacle of David please see the first article in the Appendix.) During this era, the heart of God was revealed in many of the religious and political systems. Of course, all observations must be reinforced by New Testament truths before we build our ministry systems upon them. Now, let's look for the Church in the reign of King David.

To understand the relevance of this Old Testament era to our worship today, we must carefully observe the times of King David. We need to examine the Tabernacle of Moses as it was in his day. We must see clearly what David did and did not do. He did not place the Ark back into Moses' Tabernacle but placed it in a Tent on Mt. Zion. We must then compare the Tabernacle of Moses with that of David.

Most rewarding is the comparison of the two Old Testament systems of worship with New Testament truths. A three-way comparison of the Tabernacle of Moses, the Tabernacle of David, and the Church reveals the significance of this period of history. I am indebted to Kevin Conner for the idea of the comparison chart. His excellent book *The Tabernacle of David* is a wonderful resource.

Analysis of Comparison Table

In the days of King David, the Tabernacle of Moses had an outer court with a beautiful gate and an altar for personal sacrifice. The Tabernacle of David had no structural outer court or gate, but Psalm 100 calls the gate thanksgiving and the courts praise. In the New Testament Church we combine the two—gates of thanksgiving, outer courts of praise, and altars of humility.

In the old Tabernacle there was a Holy Place with an Altar of Incense, a Table of Shewbread, and a golden Lamp Stand. David's Tabernacle had no such structure but Psalm 24 indicates that the area around the Ark was considered a "holy place". "Who may ascend the hill of the LORD? Who may stand in his holy place?" In the Church we enjoy a Holy Place of prayer and Bible study in the light and power of the Holy Spirit.

COMPARISON TABLE

MOSES' TABERNACLE (in David's time)	DAVID'S TABERNACLE	JESUS' CHURCH
Outer court with Furnishings	No outer court or furnishings	Thanksgiving/praise/ humility
Holy Place with Furnishings	No Holy Place or furnishings	Worship/Word/prayer in the Spirit's light
A heavy veil	No veil	The torn veil
Holy of Holies with no Ark	The Ark of God in an open Tent	The presence of God/ communion with Him
Daily animal sacrifices	Initial animal Sacrifices/daily spiritual sacrifices	One blood sacrifice/ The sacrifice of praise
Old priesthood	New priesthood	The Holy-Royal Priesthood
Old, silent worship	New, vocal worship	Worship in spirit and truth
A few psalms, very little music	Many psalms, appointed choirs and orchestras	Psalms, hymns, spiritual songs/ singers and players
The old covenant	The Davidic covenant	The new covenant
The glory departed	The glory returned	Jesus is the glory
A desolate house	A restored house	A spiritual house
Jews, proselytes only	A vision for all nations	"Whosoever will may come!"

In Moses' Tabernacle there was a heavy veil separating the Holy Place from the Most Holy Place. There was no such veil at David's Tabernacle, and today we see only the remnants of a torn veil. In the tattered old Tabernacle in David's day there was no Ark in the Holy of Holies. David's Tabernacle was made just to house the Ark of God. Today we enjoy ready access to the Presence of the Lord and intimacy with God in the Holy of Holies.

At Moses' Tabernacle there were endless animal sacrifices. Animals were sacrificed only once at David's Tabernacle. After the dedication day, the sacrifice of praise was the only sacrifice given there. Today we minister to the Lord with the Sacrifice of Praise because Jesus was our one-time sacrifice of blood.

At the old Tabernacle there was an old order of priests. David established a new order. Jesus has called us all to be His Holy-Royal Priests. The old order of worship was silent and individual. David's order of worship was loud and corporate. In Jesus' Church our order of worship is "spirit and truth," sometimes silent, sometimes loud, always personal, regularly corporate, and always led of the Holy Spirit.

The old way had very little music if any. David's way was musical, even with appointed singers and players to lead. The Lord wants a Church full of music—psalms, hymns, and spiritual songs—and He has appointed singers and players to lead. There was an Old Covenant, then a Davidic Covenant, and now we have a New Covenant. In the old Tabernacle the glory had departed. In David's Tabernacle the glory was restored. In the Church Jesus is the Glory.

The old worship was for male Jews and proselytes only. David's Tabernacle was open to all Israel. The Church of the Lord Jesus Christ is for "whosoever will."

David's Tabernacle bears a closer resemblance to the Church Jesus established than it does to the Tabernacle of Moses that preceded it or the Temple of Solomon that came after. Thus, this unique period of time when God ruled both in the hearts of men and in the political structure becomes a striking illustration of "His kingdom come, His will done on earth as it is in heaven." This is the very thing Jesus instructed us to pray for every day.

David centered his life on God himself. He never confused God's blessings with God. Psalm 103 makes a distinction between blessing God with all that is within us and seeking his benefits. The Tabernacle of David teaches this focus. Just as the Tabernacle of Moses calls us to individual piety, the Tabernacle of David calls *the Church* to center upon God. King David's goal was to center the nation of Israel on God. King Jesus longs to do the same thing today with the Church.

THE TABERNACLE OF DAVID MODEL
Praise and Worship as described in Psalms

Model(Psa. 24:3)

Ascend the Hill of the Lord

Stand in the Holy Place

Worship Order

Come Before His Presence with Joyful Songs (100:2)
Give Thanks (18:49)
Celebrate (145:7)
Worship and Bow Down (95:6)
Receive the Word (19:7-14)
Wait on God (62:1)
Pray (61:1,2)
Seek God's Face (24:6)

Truths from David's Tabernacle

Here we see the spiritual, joyful, and personal nature of worship. David teaches us that worship that pleases God is not the physical sacrifice of animals but the spiritual sacrifice of the heart. Instead of a deadly thing, worship is a living thing of joy! It is not blood He is after. He wants *us!* Samuel first expressed that obedience was better than sacrifice. David heard what he was saying. He knew that God longed in His heart for a relationship with His creation. As we learn obedient praise we learn how to enter into that relationship. The open Tent on Mt. Zion was the most powerful invitation God made to man before the Cross was lifted against the sky from another mountain, Mt. Calvary. In fact, Psalm 68:17 tells us that God has made His way from the old mountain where His presence was hidden to the new one where His presence is revealed, "the Lord has come from Sinai into his sanctuary." On His journey from Sinai to His sanctuary, the Lord had to take the road that led to the cross. Today, because of Mt. Calvary our worship is spiritual, joyful, and personal like the worship they enjoyed on Mt. Zion. Through the worship described in the Psalms we learn to passionately and obediently celebrate the Lord's presence.

David's Tabernacle illustrates the priesthood of the believer in corporate worship. In Moses' Tabernacle and in Solomon's Temple, much of the worship was shut away from public view, performed by the select priesthood of Levi's house. Though David was of the Tribe of Judah, he had learned that God would respond to his praise also. He led the whole nation in corporate worship at Mt. Zion, foreshadowing a day when every believer would be a priest and king unto the Lord. Today we stand in His presence, a mighty kingdom of priests ministering unto Him the sacrifice of praise!

The Book of Psalms is the first songbook of worship. More than half the Book of Psalms dates from this period of history. Most of the others were inspired by this great era of worship. Three times the New Testament tells us to sing psalms in our worship. Therefore, not only do we sing these great masterpieces, but we read them, memorize them, preach from them, and follow their instructions in worship. Surely worship, as instructed in Psalms, is worship that pleases God.

Ministry to the Lord is excellence in honor of the King. One cannot read the Psalms or study the history of David's rule without seeing the emphasis on excellence. Leaders were chosen because of their skill. Professional singers and instrumentalists were employed to make much of the music of the kingdom. Everything was done as if it was done for God himself because . . . it was! Happily, this attitude is returning to the kingdom today. Mediocrity and church music should not be synonymous. True worship brings with it a proper attitude toward skill that focuses our ministry on God himself—excellence for the sake of the King.

David's people enjoyed a unity of generations. Many cultures surrounded Israel in David's day. Leaders had the same challenge we have today to keep hearts and lives pure in spite of hostile cultures. However, there is no record of a youth culture in David's time. Consider the instruction given to the music teachers. Heman's family, fourteen sons and three daughters, is the example given in I Chronicles 25.

"All these were sons of Heman the king's seer. They were given him through the promises of God to exalt him. God gave Heman fourteen sons and three daughters. All these men were under the supervision of their fathers for the music of the Temple of the LORD, with cymbals, lyres and harps, for the ministry at the house of God. Asaph, Jeduthun and Heman were under the supervision of the king" (1 Chronicles 25:5,6).

This was the case for all the leaders.

Along with their relatives—all of them trained and skilled in music for the LORD—they numbered 288 (I Chronicles 25:7).

Student musicians played along side the adults in an orchestra of two hundred eighty-eight players. The implications of this are sobering for the contemporary church music program. Have we unknowingly bought into the world's system when we isolate teens from adults in music and worship ministry? Have we supported the enemy's efforts to divide children from parents? Can we look at how few young singers and players graduate from youth choirs and orchestras into the adult programs and say that recognizing a separate youth culture is God's plan? It may be that David's Tabernacle points us to a better way. As soon as voices change and instruments are sufficiently mastered, let the young people minister *with* the adults. Surely God intends that True Worship bridge the barriers Satan erects between people. Churches that have traditionally blended together youths and adults have generally seen a greater graduation rate of youthful singers and players into adult singers and players.

It is reasonable to believe that True worship can be the unity underlying the diversity of worship. Cultural differences will not disappear. Far from it. God loves the variety of musical styles His people produce just as He enjoys the variety in all His creation. In True Worship, culture becomes the flavoring, not the nourishment. It is the localized expression of universal truths. True worship transcends cultural barriers and unifies the church, not stylistically, but substantially, at the content level.

Just as the Lord loves the variety of ways in which we make music, surely He abhors music that is not made for His glory or for the refreshment of the heart of man. It is flavoring without meat. When we can see the difference between style and content, we are on our way to a unified culture: youth with age; black with white; oriental with occidental; east with west; each expressing the glory of God in his own cultural language to the delight of his Lord and to the edification of his brethren. This millennial vision, firstborn at David's Tabernacle, is reborn in the Church, and will be fully realized when Jesus reigns on earth for a thousand years of peace.

We should seek a worldwide revelation of God's majesty. Evangelism's first fires were stoked around David's Tabernacle. Prior to this time, it seems only God expressed interest in reaching the rest of the world. The Jews either developed a hatred of other races or were in danger of being swallowed up by them. Their national identity was so weak they could not influence other nations to worship the One True God. King David's vision was different. He conquered the surrounding nations but he had also lived among them. He knew they were enemies of God because they needed God. His vision was that the kings of all the nations would come to Mt. Zion, to David's Tabernacle, to worship the Almighty One of Israel. This is such New Testament thinking! No wonder we identify so with David's songs. Centuries before Calvary David heard the Lord's heartbeat for souls. When James set-tled the argument about how to treat the Gentiles who came to know Jesus, he pronounced the beginning of the fulfillment of David's dream. The Tabernacle of David stands as a most instructive and revealing Old Testament portrait of the New Testament Church.

Like King David, we must be passionate for the ways of God. Revivals will destroy our comfort zones and stretch us into new arenas of thinking and doing. David discovered that his best new cart would not carry God's presence. Neither will your's or mine. We must seek out the due order, just as King David did. Too many Uzzahs have died trying to steady the shaky devices of unscriptural leaders.

Also, we must hunger for the presence of the Lord as King David did. Without God's presence all our impressive buildings and elaborate organizational structures will be just so many beautiful boxes, like the Ark of the Covenant in the land of the Philistines. However, when surrounded by and permeated with the praise of the Almighty, as was that Tent on Mt. Zion, these same houses and structures will be known for the sweetness of God's presence. These are the lessons of David's Tabernacle.

The Tabernacle of David
Psalm 145:7
When I worship God in spirit and truth,
I celebrate His abundant goodness
and joyfully sing of His righteousness.

MODEL NUMBER THREE
The Holy-Royal Priesthood

At David's Tabernacle, the great worshiper-ruler established a new order of priests. "David told the leaders of the Levites to appoint their brothers as singers to sing joyful songs, accompanied by musical instruments: lyres, harps and cymbals" (I Chronicles 15:16).The purpose of this new order was joyful praise: They were to praise the Lord with vocal and instrumental music made unto the Lord. "He appointed some of the Levites to minister before the Ark of the LORD, to make petition, to give thanks, and to praise the LORD, the God of Israel" (I Chronicles 16:4). These three things made up their job description: to make petition (some translations have "to commemorate" or to bring to memory and to celebrate great events and truths), to thank God, and to praise God.

This new order of the Old Testament priesthood has a decidedly New Testament ring to it. Look at Peter's description of the New Testament Church in I Peter 2:4-9:

> *As you come to him, the living Stone—rejected by men but chosen by God and precious to him—you also, like living stones, are being built into a spiritual house to be **a holy priesthood** offering spiritual sacrifices acceptable to God through Jesus Christ. But you are a chosen people, **a royal priesthood**, a holy nation, a people belonging to God, that you may declare the praises of him who called you out of darkness into his wonderful light.*

In the same way that King David established a new order of priests for his day, David's greater son, King Jesus, has established us a new order of priests to minister unto Him. Peter's words contain a wealth of truth for teaching and texts for preaching.

We form a spiritual house. Our dwelling with God is essentially spiritual in nature, not soul-ish or physical. **We are a holy priesthood.** Through the application of Jesus' blood to our lives we can stand in the presence of the Most High. **We are a chosen generation,** chosen as was Levi's line. We are chosen by the Lord to be close to Him, to know His heart and to do His work. **We are a royal priesthood.** We are set apart for the King. We minister to Him in His Throne Room. We represent His rule. We extend His kingdom, ministering for Him. **We are a holy nation.** He is our sovereign. We are His subjects. He rules over us. His law is our civil code. His truth forms the borders of kingdom. **We are His own special people** (NKJ) "a people belonging to God" (NIV), "God's own purchased, special people" (AMP). We are bought with a price, with a special place in His heart. He has called us out of darkness so that we might "Shew forth the praises of Him" (AV), "proclaim the praises of Him" (NKJ), "declare the praises of Him" (NIV), "set forth the wonderful deeds and display the virtues and perfections of Him" (AMP), "proclaim the excellencies of Him" (NAS). The purpose of the Church, then, is to proclaim and display the perfections of our Lord. Our purpose is His praise!

The term, "Holy-Royal Priesthood" sums this up for us, showing us who we are in God. We are made holy by His righteousness and regal by His majesty. We are holy by His blood and royal by His decree. It follows then that our whole lives should reflect Him in every detail from our speech to our conduct, from our goals to our methods, from the pronouncements of our lips to the products of our hands.

To illustrate the difference between "holy" and "royal" I'll tell you about my old car, a Volkswagen Rabbit. It was a diesel. To make matters more challenging, I bought it used when I already had one diesel car, an Oldsmobile Cutlass. I bought the Olds many years ago when the buyer usually paid an extra $1,000 because the car had a diesel engine. By the time it was paid for, the same car was worth $1,000 less because it had a diesel engine. Well, having one of these masterworks wasn't enough for me, I bought a second one, a diesel Rabbit. Shortly after I bought it, we moved from Kansas to North Carolina, halfway across the North American continent. The Rabbit was never the same after that grueling trip. What was a tight little car when I left Wichita was a loose little buggy when I got to Winston-Salem.

At the church in Winston-Salem, we were building a major new facility but I didn't have any money to give to the project. One Sunday morning I was leading worship in the second service. The Lord spoke clearly to my heart, "Sell the Rabbit and give the money to the building project." Naturally, I thought He was kidding. I needed that car, loose as it was after its recent trip through the Smoky Mountains. The next Sunday—same time, same channel—the Lord spoke the same thing again. This time I knew it was really Him so I sold the car and got about $750 for the building fund. One of the players in our orchestra heard about what we had done and gave me a much bigger car he wasn't using. Why did I sell my car and give the money to the building fund? Because that was not just any Volkswagen Rabbit; *it was a Royal Rabbit.* It belonged to my King! He had every right to the equity in it. He also provided another car for me and for my family. That's what it means to be "royal"—set apart for the use of the King! We are made holy by what Jesus has done for us. We are made royal when we accept His invitation to be completely His.

Being His Holy-Royal Priest is the self-esteem program of the kingdom of God. The Lord wants us for who we are, not what we can do. He has chosen us, as would an ancient king, as His friend and confidant; His worthy (holy), personal (royal), priest. He wants to be with us. We bring joy to His heart as we honor Him, listen to Him, and obey Him. The Holy-Royal Priesthood teaches us that our chief function in life is the same as that of the Church, to minister to the Lord. Our ministry within God's kingdom and to the outside world flows from our personal intimacy with the King.

When age, illness, tragedy, or circumstance remove our ability to *do* all the things we have spent a lifetime learning to *do,* we will still have our full value in the eyes of our King. He loves us simply because we *are His* and not on the basis of what we can do for Him. We are His holy-royal priests forever. Infirmity cannot strip this priestly garment from us. Age never calls upon us to step aside. No retirement banquets are ever planned for the holy-royal priest. Death itself will only increase our intimacy with our Sovereign Lord.

Seeing ourselves as His Holy-Royal Priests will revolutionize our personal worship. We do not come just to ask Him for favors. We come with humility, thanksgiving, and praise into the courts of our King. We minister to Him with our love and devotion. We hear His voice and feel His heartbeat. Having done this, we can pray and intercede in His power. When the Church gathers together, we form a special group of people, the Holy-Royal Priesthood. The focus of the meeting should be ministry to the Lord. When we learn to minister to Him by corporately proclaiming, declaring, and displaying His excellencies, He will minister to people through us. Do we really think *we* minister to people? Arrogance and pride tell us that we do but *we* have no more power to minister to man than the Old Testament priests did to forgive sins. Our power is in letting *Him* flow through *us. He* does the work; *we* are His agents. Touching God is the only way to effectively touch man. This thinking will transform public worship from dull, predictable routine into the *"power and demonstration of the Spirit"* of which Paul speaks.

THE HOLY-ROYAL PRIESTHOOD MODEL
Illustrates our relationship with God

Model	Application
We are Holy Priests (1 Peter 2:4,5)	Carry the Ark of His Presence (I Chronicles 15:2)
	Minister to the Lord (1 Chronicles 16:4-6)
	Offer Spiritual Sacrifices (I Peter 2:4,5)
We are Royal Priests (1 Peter 2:9)	Called to be with Him (Mark 3:13)
	Called to be His friend (John 15:12-17)
	A Chosen Generation (family line) / A Holy Nation /A Purchased People / To proclaim and demonstrate His excellencies (1 Peter 2:9)

The primary function of the Holy-Royal Priesthood model is one of identification, transforming our vision of who we are individually and corporately. Like the disciples, Jesus has called us and qualified us first just to be with Him and, after that, to do things for Him. "He appointed twelve—designating them apostles—that they might be with him and that he might send them out to preach" (Mark 3:14). God's primary call upon our lives is a call to relationship. The impact of our lives upon others flows from our passion for God and from His truth flowing from us. Therefore the ministry of the believer to others begins with ministry to the Lord.

The Holy-Royal Priesthood
Revelation 1:6
When I Worship God in spirit and truth, it is because he has made me His Holy Priest by His Blood and because He has called me to His palace to be His Royal Priest.

MODEL NUMBER FOUR
The Living Sacrifice Of Praise

In addition to establishing a new order of priests, King David also instituted a new order of worship, the sacrifice of praise, as the function of the new priesthood. We see from the Old Testament priesthood that our ministry to God is worship and our ministry to man is that of reconciliation to God.

A Living Sacrifice
Romans 12:1,2

We Minister to God with the Living-Sacrifice of Praise. The initial aspect of this ministry is the presentation of ourselves to Him. "Therefore, I urge you, brothers, in view of God's mercy, to offer your bodies as **living sacrifices,** holy and pleasing to God—this is your spiritual act of worship. Do not conform any longer to the pattern of this world, but be transformed by the renewing of your mind. Then you will be able to test and approve what God's will is—his good, pleasing and perfect will" (Romans 12:1,2). The King James Version of this passage emphasizes our value to God in the "service" we render Him. But the original language is more inclusive. The original words refer to the service of God as was done at the Tabernacle of Moses, having a strong worship connotation. Strong's definition includes this: " . . . ministration of God, i.e. worship:—divine service . . . to minister(to God). i.e. render religious homage:—serve, do the service, worship". So the original words Paul used were concerned with both service and worship. Thus the modern translations: "your spiritual worship" (NIV), "your spiritual service of worship" (NAS), "an act of intelligent worship" (Phillips), and "your reasonable (rational, intelligent) service and spiritual worship" (AMP).

This passage deals with more than the daily routine of serving God by serving man. It has to do with presenting ourselves to Him in worship. Worship that pleases God is both an event and a process.

First let's look at some worship events. When we kneel for private prayer, our Bibles open before us, we present ourselves to Him. When we gather with the family around the family altar to share, pray, and read the Word, we present ourselves to Him. When we take our place among the redeemed of the Lord in public worship, we present ourselves to Him. When we lift our voices, our hands, and our faces to Him in thanksgiving, praise, humility, adoration, and exaltation, we are presenting ourselves to Him. When singers and instrumentalists gather to rehearse, they are presenting their bodies to Him as living sacrifices. When volunteers gather for a workday at the church, they do the same. Service to man is the other side of the same coin. When we go into the world to represent Him as our King, to shine as lights in the darkness of our day, to speak His truth, and to stand for Him steady upon the rock of His Word while society's storms rage around us, we also are presenting ourselves to Him.

The sacrifice of the Holy-Royal Priesthood is also a process, something that is done "continually". Let's think about that for a moment. What activities in our lives can we say are continuous? Mostly we start doing something, keep doing it for a while, and then stop doing it. It is not continuous. What is? The life functions of the body are continuous. Breathing, digesting, and pumping blood are continuous activities. This is the role worship plays in the body of Christ. It is a continuous activity through which spiritual oxygen, nourishment, and life-giving blood reach the extremities of the Body. This is a "living" sacrifice, brimming with the vibrancy of passionate worship and the truth of effective service.

A Sacrifice of Praise
Hebrews 13:15,16

True worship involves the sacrifice of praise, vocal in nature, as we see in the summation of Hebrews, the great treatise on the New Covenant. "Through Jesus, therefore, let us continually offer to God a sacrifice of praise—the fruit of lips that confess his name. And do not forget to do good and to share with others, for with such sacrifices God is pleased" (Hebrews 13:16). The Living Sacrifice of Praise is holy, consistent, daily living, "to do good and to communicate, forget not." But it is also vocal expression, "the fruit of our lips." Neither vocal expression nor consistent living can alone make up the sacrifice of the Holy-Royal Priesthood. This priesthood is one of worshiping servants.

Let's reason this out. We cannot silently go about serving God. We must minister to the Lord with our voices. We must not sing great songs or shout great shouts if we do not live lives of great integrity. There is always a danger that vocal praise will be supplanted in importance by service. There are many reasons for this. One is that vocal praise seems less productive than service. We cannot see measurable results. Our ministry to God may never be as measurable as our ministry to man, but it must never be allotted a secondary role. Since the Living Sacrifice of Praise is vocal, no amount of service rendered to man can ever take the place of love and devotion expressed to God. The Bible truth is this: when we are worshiping God we are serving Him and when we are serving God we are worshiping Him. The opposite danger must also be avoided; those who participate in extensive worship "activity" but who never lift a hand to serve. True worship involves both the heart and the hands.

THE LIVING SACRIFICE OF PRAISE MODEL
Ministering to the Lord as His Holy-Royal Priest

Model	Application
The Living Sacrifice (Romans 12,1,2)	The presentation of the body (attendance to worship) The reasonable service of worship (praise-leads-to-worship sequence) The renewing of the mind / Breaking the world's mold / Proving the will of God
The Sacrifice of Praise (Hebrews 13:15,16)	Continual ministry (expressed in all of life) / A life-giving process: The fruit of lips giving thanks to His name (vocal) Do good and share with others(action)

Results of the Sacrifice of Praise

The Living Sacrifice of Praise demands obedience to the Word of God. Many are reactive, not proactive in their praise. Out of fear of moving in the flesh, they praise God only after they feel the Spirit of God moving. We must learn to be pro-active in our praise, entering into praise regardless of circumstances or of how we feel. This proactive praise removes the danger of emotionalism. The Living-Sacrifice of Praise is a matter of obedience to the unchanging command of Scripture not the occasional pull of emotion. Floods of joy may flow from the Sacrifice of Praise, but it is given out of sheer obedience to the Word and thanksgiving to God for who He is and what He has done. We must not wait until the "atmosphere" is right to praise God. We need to praise Him and change the atmosphere. We praise Him because He is worthy and because it is commanded, regardless of how we feel. When we learn these reasons for worship, we are on our way to knowing Him in intimacy and power.

The Living-Sacrifice of Praise brings God Near. Praise is the starting point of our private devotions and our public worship. If we will be faithful to present ourselves to Him and to vocalize our praise, *He will always faithfully inhabit our praise.* Just as He moved into the Tabernacle of Moses, David's Tabernacle, and Solomon's Temple, He will occupy our praise.

The Living Sacrifice of Praise brings people to God. True worship is evangelistic. Lives lived as praise to the Lord shine as lights in the darkness and function as salt to the earth. A worshiping fellowship of such people shines like a city upon a hill.

The Living Sacrifice of Praise
Romans 12:1,2 / Hebrews 13:15,16

When I worship God I am serving Him.
When I serve God I am worshiping Him.
In the heart of God these are not
two things but one.

One ministry of the priesthood in David's time was to bear upon their shoulders the presence of the Lord, the Ark of the Covenant. Today it is the same for the Holy-Royal Priesthood. *We* bear the presence of the Lord with us into the marketplace, the office, the classroom, the factory, the shop, and the home. As we minister the Living Sacrifice of Praise to the Lord with our voices and our lives, we are witnesses to the world of His majesty and grace.

CONCLUSION

The Heavenly Father has called us to himself. Through the gift and sacrifice of His Son, He has broken the sin barrier and imparted to us His righteousness. He has illustrated that call to us through the wonderful picture of David's Tabernacle, inviting us to passionately celebrate and enjoy His presence with excellence. He has called us to be with Him as His Holy-Royal Priests. He has called every believer to minister to Him with the reasonable Living Sacrifice of Praise.

How does our worship minister to God?

Our youngest daughter, Jennifer, demonstrated this to me once when I was away teaching at another church. I found a note she had left me. There were the usual lines a six- or seven-year-old might write to her Dad, but it ended with this gem. "Daddy, I love you more than anything in my room."

Her room was her domain but she put her love for me over everything in her world. That is the kind of love our Heavenly Father wants from each of us. And we present our love to Him as we minister to Him with the Living Sacrifice of Praise!

> **We must not wait until the "atmosphere" is right to praise God.**
> **We must praise Him and change the atmosphere.**

Chapter Four

LIFE FROM THE THRONE ROOM

The Throne Room, the Office Place, and the River of Life

King Uzziah and Isaiah

King Uzziah slowly paced the deepest recesses of the Outer Court, the way a confined animal paces its cage. He was Israel's king but he could legally go no farther toward the Ark of the Presence. He had seen priests go past this point, into the Holy Place many times. They were of the house and line of Levi. They could go in before the veil that hid the Ark. They could burn incense before the presence of the Lord. But, Uzziah the king could go no closer than the Outer Court, as if he were just another common man.

But he knew deep inside that he was no common man. He may have started out that way, but no one could say that now. He had become king when he was only sixteen years old. Could anyone have expected anything much? Well they got much and more. Uzziah did right in the Lord's eyes according to all his father Amaziah had done. He sought the Lord and with the aid of Zechariah the prophet always had a clear vision of what to do. He had made many successful forays against the Philistines and other heathen nations. Even the Ammonites brought tribute to Him. King Uzziah's fame stretched all the way to the borders of Egypt. He had fortified Jerusalem with towers. Even the desert was armed with watch towers Uzziah had built and watered with the wells he had dug. His love of the soil had inspired farmers and vine dressers as far away as the mountains and in Carmel. He had organized a massive army and fortified the soldiers with new weapons of destruction. He had even encouraged the creativity of the people. Now after fifty-two years of such excellent leadership the land was secure. Of course there were those high places where some of the people sacrificed to idols. But these cost the government so little and they bought so much civil peace, surely Jehovah was not concerned over these minor infractions of worship law. He didn't *seem* to mind. The high places had been there as long as Uzziah could remember seemingly with no ill effect.

He was a good king. Surely this counted for something. It did in the city and in the provinces. Everyone waited on him. His desires mattered. After fifty-two years, who could remember anyone else as king? Uzziah had obviously been blessed by Jehovah for his outstanding leadership. That young writer, what was his name?—Oh yes, Isaiah, was busy writing the story of Uzziah's triumphs. Soon all Israel would be able to see the scope and detail of Uzziah's excellent reign. Surely this counted for something here, in the Temple.

There was a time during the reign of his ancestor, King David, when all could come right up to the Ark. But Solomon had moved it inside to the Holy of Holies in the Temple. Of course it had to be. It couldn't really be any other way. It was just that Uzziah had never seen the Ark. He had never seen the Altar of Incense, the Table of Shewbread, or the Golden Lamp Stand in the Holy Place. He could understand about the Holy of Holies, but the Holy Place, why couldn't the king go in there?—especially a good king, one who was so obviously blessed by Jehovah.

No one was watching, no prying priests nosing about. Who was to prevent him from going inside, into the Holy Place? His sixty-eight-year-old heart was pounding like that of a youth in his first battle. Now he was going to see for himself what the priests enjoyed. He gently drew back the curtain that led to the Holy Place. The light was so faint, compared to the bright sunshine outside, that he could see only shapes at first. He stood there holding the curtain open for a moment, then realizing his vulnerability in that position, he quickly planted himself a step inside and closed the heavy curtain behind him. As he waited for his eyes to adjust, his heart tried its best to leap from his chest. Jehovah had not stopped him! Surely, this was no more an affront to him than those high places. Surely God would welcome so important a worshiper as a godly king. Soon he could make out by the flaring lamplight the Table of Shewbread. It was rather plain to his tastes. There were much nicer tables in the palace.

Quickly his gaze settled on the Altar of Incense. A thin trail of smoke snaked upward from the bowl on the Altar. How can one's heart pound so when one is scarcely breathing at all? If Jehovah liked this aromatic offering, surely *more* incense would be *more* pleasing to Him. He gingerly stepped forward as if the floor might drop from beneath him if he weren't careful. Soon he was standing where the priests had stood and he slowly added more incense to the flame. For a moment the flame was overcome. It dimmed and hid its light. Uzziah's racing heart suddenly stopped, and his breath completely forsook him. After a moment, the flame accepted the new fuel and flared again, sending a new circle of smoke toward the heavens.

Uzziah had just enough time to restart his heart and lungs when, a clamor arose behind him. The sound of clanking armor was a friendly one to a king on a battlefield, but was foreign to this little worship room. Azariah the priest and eighty valiant Temple guards were standing silhouetted against the bright light of day that streamed into the Holy Place from the Outer Court. They blocked the king's escape. The king was used to being in authority but here he knew he had no power. In the stillness of the standoff the priest spoke with equal measures of quiet rage and soul-deep pain, "It is not for you, Uzziah, to burn incense to the Lord, but for the priests, the sons of Aaron, who are consecrated to burn incense." Uzziah did not move. "Get out of the sanctuary!" The rage of the priest was winning out over the pain and was no longer quiet, "You shall have no honor from the Lord God."

The fury of the priest was matched by the fury of the king. Who were these sons of Aaron? Who was he but a son of David? David had stripped away the kingly garment and worn only the linen of the priests to dance before the Lord. Uzziah held the censer in his hand fully intending to continue this defiant act of "worship."

Amid the angry furrows of his brow a sudden explosion of white tissue broke out—leprosy! With horror demanding they watch their king, the priests looked on as the leprosy covered the forehead of King Uzziah. When the king realized the sudden pain above his eyes matched the spot of the fixed attention of the men in front of him, he turned the golden censer to see his reflection there. The hardened vessel of his single-minded anger splintered into a thousand shards of fear, each an individual knife piercing his rebel heart. He ran for the curtain. The soldiers let him through and then chased him out of the Temple. He did not die right away but finished his days in an isolated house, a boy turned king and seeker of God turned proud man, turned profane burner of incense, turned leper.

The news of Uzziah's transgression and death struck the young Isaiah a harsh blow. He had enjoyed his hours with the king, interviewing him for the biography he was writing. Each chapter glowed with wisdom, success, victory, and accomplishment. Who could have foreseen this last chapter? Now Uzziah was dead, his son Jotham reigning in his place and doing well actually. But Isaiah was not doing well. The death of Uzziah had shaken all his props. If Jehovah would punish so great a man for such a small violation when one could almost make a case for it from other kings, who could know whom to seek out, whom to follow? Young Jotham was only twenty-five years old, younger even than Isaiah. How could he ever attain the place in Isaiah's heart his father had known? Who was worthy of the devotion Isaiah longed to give? Whose story was worthy of the skill of Isaiah's practiced pen?

Isaiah does not tell us where it happened, only that, "In the year that King Uzziah died I saw the Lord sitting on a throne, high and lifted up, and the train of His robe filled the Temple" (Isaiah 6:1). Later he would say, "I have seen the King, the Lord of Hosts!" His life was changed by this vision of God in His Throne Room. The historian became a prophet. The skillful writer found a story to tell worthy of his talents. "Whom shall I send, and who will go for Us?" the Lord asked. "Here am I! Send me!" Isaiah replied.

MODEL NUMBER FIVE
The Throne Room of the Lord

Submission to God is the heart of worship. Uzziah's error was in losing the humble heart that God had used to make him an effective leader. His pride became his undoing. "But after Uzziah became powerful, his pride led to his downfall. He was unfaithful to the LORD his God, and entered the Temple of the LORD to burn incense on the altar of incense" (2 Chronicles 26:16).

Pride is the enemy of worship. Humility is the essence of worship. When we cast our crowns at His feet, His kingdom begins to come in our lives. Our lives are centered upon Him. The passion of our worship springs from the truth of our humility. Thus is He enthroned upon our worship. "Thy kingdom come, Thy will be done, on earth as it is in heaven." These words in the Lord's Prayer are so familiar to us we may never have spent time really thinking about them.

Consider what it would be like—God's kingdom here and now on this earth as it is in heaven. Three words would be necessary to describe the kingdom of God: righteousness, peace, and joy! The Lord desires to do more than just visit us with His Presence; He wants to establish His kingdom in us. He longs for the church to become His capital city. Kingdoms of the world all have a center of power, a capital. The Roman Empire stretched across the breadth of the western world but always at the center was Rome itself, the seat of power, and somewhere in the capital, the palace and Caesar's throne. If we are to pray every day the Lord's kingdom come and His will be done right here with us, what we are really seeking is the center of His authority, the seat of His power—the Throne Room of Almighty God. Our personal altar, our house of public worship, indeed, our very hearts, can become His Throne Room, an extension of the kingdom of God. His throne may be established in these places through our praise, adoration and obedience. How do we recognize His Throne Room when it comes to us?—by the witness of the Spirit and the Word. Let us look to the Scriptures to guide our reasoning.

Psalm 22:3

But Thou art holy, O Thou that inhabitest the praises of Israel. (KJV)
Yet thou art holy, enthroned upon the praises of Israel. (RSV)

In this important Messianic psalm, we find one verse whose full translation is an amazing key to the understanding of our relationship with God. Both of these translations are correct. Consider these definitions:

STRONG'S, *yashab* - "to sit down (specifically as judge . . .); by implication to dwell, to remain;"
WILSON'S - "to sit down; to dwell in, inhabit . . . frequent. Gesenius understands the word of kings sitting on thrones."

Using the models, let's reason this truth out. First, we know that the Lord inhabits our praise. This is illustrated in the first models, God's dwelling places: the Tabernacle/Temple with the Holy of Holies, and the Tabernacle of David. Next we see that He is enthroned upon our praise. We see this in the Throne Room model. Because we have been brought into relationship with Him (the holy-royal priesthood), our obedience in praise and worship (the living sacrifice of praise) prompts in us His presence (His habitation) and His power (His rule). In its most basic sense, to worship as it pleases God establishes His throne in us, and in our place of worship, honoring His presence and submitting to His rule.

THE THRONE OF GOD AND OF THE LAMB MODEL
God's Response to our Praise and Worship

Scripture	Application
Psalm 22:3	God takes our praise to be His Dwelling and Ruling Place (Mt. Zion)
Isaiah 6:1-8 / Revelation 4,5	The Throne Room is a place of -Praise and Worship -Revelation of God -Awe and Wonder -Submission to God -Service to God
Romans 14:17	The Kingdom of God is -Righteousness -Peace -Joy in the Holy Spirit

---

Is there a difference between His rule and His presence? An earthly ruler may visit a foreign country receiving the full honors due a dignitary, but he still would not rule. Yet in his own country, with the amenities comes the authority of his reign. We speak in glowing terms of the Lord's visitation and well we should. But He longs for more than our respect; He wants our obedience. He wants to do more than visit us (inhabit our praise); He wants to rule over us (be enthroned upon our praise). He wants us to center our lives on Him. He longs to be the object of our passion. When we begin to praise and worship Him with all our hearts and with obedient lives, He begins to establish His Throne in us. In effect, indeed in powerful effect, our place of worship becomes His Throne Room. Our Savior becomes our Sovereign. His kingdom begins to come, and His will begins to be done in earth as it is in heaven. How many times do we leave the Lord waiting for our words of praise to deepen into words of invitation, words that make Him our king?

The Throne Room of God

We are given two major visions of the Throne Room of the Most High: Isaiah's experience in his sixth chapter, and John's vision in Revelation beginning at Chapter Four. The most striking thing these men of God saw was the majesty of the One who sat upon the throne. What they *heard* was worship. And so it is for us. When His majesty is revealed in our praise, when His sovereignty is seen in our lives by personal praise and obedience, and in our public services through concerted, passionate praise, worship will be the result and the sounds of heaven will echo around us. The revelation of God is the essential prerequisite for worship. If there is little worship in our lives it is because we have an insufficient revelation of who God is. To receive a vision of His majesty is to respond in humility and worship. It was for Isaiah and John and it will be for us. Let us take a brief look at the Throne Room as revealed in these two passages of Scripture.

The Throne Room is the place of his majesty. "In the year that King Uzziah died, I saw the Lord seated on a throne, high and exalted, and the train of his robe filled the Temple" (Isaiah 6:1). "And the one who sat there had the appearance of jasper and carnelian. A rainbow, resembling an emerald, encircled the throne. Surrounding the throne were twenty-four other thrones, and seated on them were twenty-four elders. They were dressed in white and had crowns of gold on their heads" (Revelation 4:3,4).

Each of us needs a vision of the majesty of King Jesus. This can only be found in His Throne Room. The Christmas story gives us a vision of the incarnation. The Easter story gives us a vision of the atonement and of His resurrection. Worship is intended to give us a vision of His mighty rule, at the right hand of the majesty on high. The apostles changed the world because they had a complete vision of Jesus, Virgin-born Son, Suffering Savior, Resurrected Lord, and Ruling Sovereign. The more we come before the Throne of God and of the Lamb, the greater our vision of His majesty will grow.

The Throne Room is the place for his servants. "Above him were seraphs, each with six wings: With two wings they covered their faces, with two they covered their feet, and with two they were flying" (Isaiah 6:2). "Surrounding the throne were twenty-four other thrones, and seated on them were twenty-four elders. They were dressed in white and had crowns of gold on their heads. Also before the throne there was what looked like a sea of glass, clear as crystal. In the center, around the throne, were four living creatures, and they were covered with eyes, in front and in back. Each of the four living creatures had six wings and was covered with eyes all around, even under his wings. Day and night they never stop saying: 'Holy, holy, holy is the Lord God Almighty, who was, and is, and is to come'" (Revelation 4: 4, 6, 8).

Gathered before the Throne of God and of the Lamb are the servants of the Most High. There are no rebels here, no hidden agendas lurking beneath a facade of false humility. Nothing here is false, nothing hidden. We, angel and believer alike, are here because He has called us to himself and made us for himself. He takes pleasure in us. It is our joy to serve Him or to stand and wait. Servanthood of God outside the realm of His sovereignty is not really service to Him at all, but a dedication to personal kingdoms.

The Throne Room is the place of his praise. "And they were calling to one another: 'Holy, holy, holy is the LORD Almighty; the whole earth is full of his glory'" (Isaiah 6:3). "Each of the four living creatures had six wings and was covered with eyes all around, even under his wings. Day and night they never stop saying: 'Holy, holy, holy is the Lord God Almighty, who was, and is, and is to come'" (Revelation 4:8).

The sound of the Throne of God and of the Lamb is the sound of praise and continual worship unto the Holy One.

This is the glory due unto His name. If we want to have the righteousness, peace, and joy in the Holy Spirit that characterize His kingdom then we must be people of praise, for it surrounds His Throne. If we want our church to be a place where Jesus reigns, then we must make it a place of praise. Each service is a coronation service. Every time we meet we must cast our crowns at His feet. We must relinquish our thrones and bow to His. This is only reasonable. Without an atmos-phere of praise, we cannot be near His Throne for it is sur-rounded by the praise of His creation.

The Throne of God is the place of the revelation of his power and Glory. "At the sound of their voices the doorposts and thresholds shook and the Temple was filled with smoke" (Isaiah 6:4). "From the throne came flashes of lightning, rumblings and peals of thunder. Before the throne, seven lamps were blazing. These are the seven spirits of God. Also before the throne there was what looked like a sea of glass, clear as crystal. In the center, around the throne, were four living creatures, and they were covered with eyes, in front and in back" (Revelation 4:5,6).

The first-century disciples changed their world because of two things. They had a REASON—a vision of the power and glory of God— and they had a PASSION—a power and glory flowing in their lives through the Holy Spirit. Today, if the church needs anything, we need a new vision of who God is. This can only be found in the Throne Room of God. Isaiah was never the same after he saw, "the king". Saul was never the same after the King interrupted his journey to Damascus. The disciples were never the same after the resurrection. We need to get through the outer court and into the place where the glory is revealed, where God's power touches us in a way that changes us forever. Some call it a "power encounter", but whatever the terminology this revelational encounter is essential if we want to rise above the ritual and routine of mundane service and enter the realm of power and glory we read about in the lives of first century believers. At God's Throne we can move from impulse and ambivalence to reason and passion.

The Throne Room is the place of the servant's humility. "Above him were seraphs, each with six wings: With two wings they covered their faces, with two they covered their feet, and with two they were flying. 'Woe to me!' I cried. 'I am ruined! For I am a man of unclean lips, and I live among a people of unclean lips, and my eyes have seen the King, the LORD Almighty.'" (Isaiah 6:2,5). "Whenever the living creatures give glory, honor and thanks to him who sits on the throne and who lives for ever and ever, the twenty-four elders fall down before him who sits on the throne, and worship him who lives for ever and ever. They lay their crowns before the throne and say: 'You are worthy, our Lord and God, to receive glory and honor and power, for you created all things, and by your will they were created and have their being'" (Revelation 4:9-11). "All the angels were standing around the throne and around the elders and the four living creatures. They fell down on their faces before the throne and worshiped God" (Revelation 7:11).

This is the place where the poor in spirit receive the kingdom of Heaven. Here the Lord dwells with those who are humble. Here He esteems those who tremble at His Word. The mighty angels cover their faces. Isaiah was flooded with shame for his sins and those of his people. The elders fall down and disclaim all their life's achievements (cast their crowns) before the One. A proud spirit is a sure sign of one who is nowhere near the Throne of God and of the Lamb. The soul lifted up with vanity cannot be prostrate before its Maker. At the Throne of God and of the Lamb humility is the norm, not the exception. In today's church circles, pride is too often the norm and humility the noteworthy characteristic. We are so far from the Throne of God and of the Lamb.

The Throne Room is the place of worship. "And they were calling to one another: 'Holy, holy, holy is the LORD Almighty; the whole earth is full of his glory'" (Isaiah 6:3). "Day and night they never stop saying: 'Holy, holy, holy is the Lord God Almighty, who was, and is, and is to come.' The twenty-four elders fall down before him who sits on the throne, and worship him who lives for ever and ever. They lay their crowns before the throne and say: 'You are worthy, our Lord and God, to receive glory and honor and power, for you created all things, and by your will they were created and have their being'" (Revelation 4:9-11). "Then I looked and heard the voice of many angels, numbering thousands upon thousands, and ten thousand times ten thousand. They encircled the throne and the living creatures and the elders. In a loud voice they sang: 'Worthy is the Lamb, who was slain, to receive power and wealth and wisdom and strength and honor and glory and praise!' Then I heard every creature in heaven and on earth and under the earth and on the sea, and all that is in them, singing: 'To him who sits on the throne and to the Lamb be praise and honor and glory and power, for ever and ever!' The four living creatures said, 'Amen,' and the elders fell down and worshiped" (Revelation 5:11-14).

We can only wonder how day and night pass before the Throne of God and of the Lamb, but that is the testimony of John. Throughout each day and night the worship never stops. This is the glory due His name. This is the "continual" sacrifice of praise of the servants of God. Our concept of worship must expand beyond an activity that somehow starts and stops. As New Testament believers we have the joy of living life as worship unto the Lord. Like the worshipers in heaven, we can pass each day and night in worship unto the Lord. "And whatever you do, whether in word or deed, do it all in the name of the Lord Jesus, giving thanks to God the Father through him. Whatever you do, work at it with all your heart, as working for the Lord, not for men" (Colossians 3:17,23). According to this Colossians credo, we can do "whatever" (without doubt this means whatever is pleasing to the Lord) in these three ways: in the name of the Lord Jesus with thanks-giving, heartily (with our whole life-force) and as unto the Lord and not unto men. This transforms the "whatever" of living into praise and worship. And, we can know that God responds with His presence and with His sovereignty—right there at the workbench! The worship that surrounds the

Throne of God is both the life-changing event and a life-enriching process. If our lives are not filled with worship, we live them far from the Throne of God. If they are so filled, we carry about on our shoulders, like the Old Testament priests bearing the Ark, the kingdom, power, and glory of God.

The Throne Room is a place of forgiveness, redemption, and change. "Then one of the seraphs flew to me with a live coal in his hand, which he had taken with tongs from the altar. With it he touched my mouth and said, 'See, this has touched your lips; your guilt is taken away and your sin atoned for'" (Isaiah 6:6,7).

"Then I saw in the right hand of him who sat on the throne a scroll with writing on both sides and sealed with seven seals. And I saw a mighty angel proclaiming in a loud voice, 'Who is worthy to break the seals and open the scroll?' But no one in heaven or on earth or under the earth could open the scroll or even look inside it. I wept and wept because no one was found who was worthy to open the scroll or look inside. Then one of the elders said to me, 'Do not weep! See, the Lion of the tribe of Judah, the Root of David, has triumphed. He is able to open the scroll and its seven seals.'

"Then I saw a Lamb, looking as if it had been slain, standing in the center of the throne, encircled by the four living creatures and the elders. He had seven horns and seven eyes, which are the seven spirits of God sent out into all the earth. He came and took the scroll from the right hand of him who sat on the throne. And when he had taken it, the four living creatures and the twenty-four elders fell down before the Lamb. Each one had a harp and they were holding golden bowls full of incense, which are the prayers of the saints.

"And they sang a new song: 'You are worthy to take the scroll and to open its seals, because you were slain, and with your blood you purchased men for God from every tribe and language and people and nation. You have made them to be a kingdom and priests to serve our God, and they will reign on the earth.'" (Revelation 5:1-10)

In no other court of any other king can sins be washed

away. There is no other throne where forgiveness can be found. Only the Lamb upon the Throne has prevailed to open the Book of Life. Only the fires from the altar before this Throne can purge the sin from the lips of a humanity born in rebellion and iniquity. Only the Blood of that Lamb can erase the record of my guilt and yours and record in its place "The Righteousness of Christ."

Do you see why it is so important for us to worship God? When His Throne has come to us, people we have brought to Him can receive the forgiveness and restoration they must have. If there is no True Worship, His Throne of Grace is far removed from us. Our adoration and gratitude—our passion—brings us near to His Throne where all we need awaits us in the friendly, truthful fires of His glory.

The Throne Room is the place of service and obedience. "And with two they were flying" (Isaiah 6:2). "Then I heard the voice of the Lord saying, 'Whom shall I send? And who will go for us?' And I said, 'Here am I. Send me!' (Isaiah 6:8). "After this I looked and there before me was a great multitude that no one could count, from every nation, tribe, people and language, standing before the throne and in front of the Lamb. They were wearing white robes and were holding palm branches in their hands. Then one of the elders asked me, 'These in white robes—who are they, and where did they come from?'

"I answered, 'Sir, you know.' And he said, 'These are they who have come out of the great tribulation; they have washed their robes and made them white in the blood of the Lamb. Therefore, they are before the throne of God and serve him day and night in his temple; and he who sits on the throne will spread his tent over them" (Revelation (7:9,13-15).

With four of their six wings, the living creatures around the Throne of God and of the Lamb covered their eyes and feet in extreme humility and worship. But with the remaining two wings they *flew*. Surely when two-thirds of our energies are fully engaged in worship of the One True God, with the other third we are going to *fly!* What do I mean by that? I mean we are going to serve God. He will send us and we will go. He will lead us and we will follow. He will empower us and we will obey. Isaiah went from a moment of revelation to a lifetime of service. The great multitude of worshipers around the Throne in John's vision are the ones who stand before the Throne of God and serve Him day and night in His Temple. When God's sovereignty is established He then calls us to serve Him in particular ways. When we serve Him, always before His Throne, He empowers us to accomplish the work. Like the living creatures, we fly! If it seems that God is no longer calling people into the ministry, it may be because we are not coming before His Throne in True Worship. It is here, from the Throne of God and of the Lamb, that life-long commissions and urgent orders originate.

We can see now why it is so important to set our affections, our passions, on things above, that we begin to love the Throne Room of our Lord Jesus. Listen to Paul's words: "Since, then, you have been raised with Christ, set your hearts on things above, where Christ is seated at the right hand of God. Set your minds on things above, not on earthly things. For you died, and your life is now hidden with Christ in God. When Christ, who is your life, appears, then you also will appear with him in glory" (Colossians 3:1-4).

This is the direction Jesus was pointing us when He told us to pray that God's kingdom would come and His will be done each day. Jesus came to tell us about the kingdom of heaven. He knew that by the tearing of His own body, He would open up the way for us to enter His very Throne Room; to behold His majesty; to be near His Throne; to join the chorus of angels and saints; to behold His power and glory; to bow before Him, casting all our crowns at His feet; to worship Him as heaven does; to be forgiven, restored, and called into service; and to be sent forth from the Throne of the Most High with eternity's work to do.

We need to set our passion here in the Throne Room for this is where our Savior dwells and *rules*. In this place His priorities become our priorities, His truth, our reasoning. In

the Throne Room we are changed into His likeness as we behold (contemplate, NIV footnote) His glory. "And we, who
with unveiled faces all reflect (contemplate) the Lord's glory,
are being transformed into his likeness with ever-increasing
glory, which comes from the Lord, who is the Spirit" (II Corinthians 3:18). Sometimes great things come from God in a
flash of astounding grace. But clearly the emphasis in this
passage is a continuing process of beholding, of contemplating, the glory of the Lord, of time spent reviewing and rehearsing the truth from the Word until a beam of His glory
splits the shadows of our existence and illumines us. Then, we
are changed.

Today we are summoned before the Throne of the Most
High by the overwhelming evidence of Scripture. He has for
us a coal of fire from the altar of worship before Him that will
cleanse our lives. He wants us to hear the worship of the angels, *"Holy," "Worthy," "Alleluia,"* and join them. He wants to
show us the eternal insignificance of our petty crowns by revealing the eternal majesty of His own. May all our crowns
rest uneasy on our heads until we remove them and cast them
at His footstool. He wants us to hear the still, small voice of
the ministry's call. He wants to send us out with a royal commission.

The Throne of God and of the Lamb
Hebrews 12:22-24
*When I worship God in spirit and truth, I come
to Mt. Zion, God's dwelling and ruling place.*

All of these benefits of His kingdom come and His will
done are ours because He is enthroned in our lives, truly
enthroned upon our praise-filled, passionate obedience. He is
always faithful to be enthroned upon our praise. The question
remains: Are we always faithful to give Him our praise to be
His throne?

MODEL NUMBER SIX
The Lord's Office-Place

Acts 13 tells of one of the most important prayer meetings in all of history. The evangelization of Europe and the Western Hemisphere is traceable to this prayer meeting. This passage is also a key to understanding worship that pleases God. "In the church at Antioch there were prophets and teachers: Barnabas, Simeon called Niger, Lucius of Cyrene, Manaen (who had been brought up with Herod the tetrarch) and Saul. While they were worshiping the Lord and fasting, the Holy Spirit said, 'Set apart for me Barnabas and Saul for the work to which I have called them'" (Acts 13:1,2). The King James Version and New American Standard version have "ministered" or "ministering" to the Lord instead of "worshiping." The word used for "ministered to the Lord " is *leitourgeo*, which in classical Greek, signified at Athens to supply public offices at one's own cost, to render public service to the State; hence, generally, to do service. In the New Testament it is used (a) of the prophets and teachers in the church at Antioch, who "ministered to the Lord" Acts 13:2 (Vine's, p. 755).

They "ministered to the Lord" ("worshiped the Lord" NIV) and they fasted. Fasting is a spiritual exercise used to humble our hearts and to center our hearts on God. We can see what these believers did when they needed direction. Look at their reasonable passion: they touched God with their worship; they established His throne with their praise; and they humbled their hearts through fasting. They centered their lives on God himself. In doing this they provided the Almighty with a place on earth where He could do His work, *an office-place,* and He set apart Barnabas and Saul for that work.

This definition gives us an important insight into the mind of Christ and shows us something very important about our worship. Jesus is looking for people who will give Him their lives as His working place. He is looking for churches that will meet together and focus on Him with their corporate expressions of thanksgiving, exaltation, adoration, and communion.

The Father is still looking for those who will worship Him in spirit and in truth for in that place He will rule and do the work of His kingdom. Add fasting as spiritual warfare against the enemy to this "ministry to the Lord", and the way is cleared for the King's work to be done.

What is that work? Early in His ministry Jesus declared himself to the people gathered in His hometown synagogue. He read from Isaiah and proclaimed that He was the fulfillment of the prophecy. Luke 4:18,19 KJV, reveals to us the office work of the Messiah:

The Spirit of the Lord is upon me, because
He hath anointed me to preach the gospel to the poor;
He hath sent me to heal the broken hearted,
To preach deliverance to the captives,
And recovering of sight to the blind,
To set at liberty them that are bruised.
To preach the acceptable year of the Lord.

Since Jesus is the same yesterday, today, and forever, this is still His ministry. When we are faithful to minister to the Lord with our worship, He will rule among us. When He rules among us He flows through us to do these things for people. Through us He will preach the gospel (to declare the full-strength good news, undiluted by man's ideas). He will use our hands to heal the broken hearted (to "bind up" those who need to experience His healing love). He will speak through us to preach deliverance to the captives (to declare the freedom of those in prisons of all sorts). We will hear Him preach through us the recovery of sight to the blind (to announce the healing of ruined vision and the entrance of pure light). We will see Him set at liberty those who are bruised (to break shackles that bind and bruise the souls of men).

THE CHURCH IS THE LORD'S OFFICE-PLACE.

**Through us He will preach the gospel to the poor.
He will use our hands to heal the broken hearted.
He will speak through us to preach deliverance to the
captives and the recovery of sight to the blind.
We will see him set at liberty those who are bruised.
Through us He will also preach the acceptable year of
the Lord.**

THE OFFICE-PLACE OF THE LORD MODEL
The Healing and Restoration Ministry of Jesus through Worship

Scripture	Application
Acts 13:2	When we minister to the Lord by worshiping Him in Spirit and Truth, centering our lives on Him, our worship becomes His Office-Place.
Luke 4:18, 19	The Lord's Office Work: -to preach the gospel to the poor; -to heal the broken hearted, -to preach deliverance to the captives, -recovering of sight to the blind, -to set at liberty them that are bruised. -to preach the acceptable year of the Lord

---

Through us He will also preach the acceptable year of the Lord (to declare the opportunities afforded us in this age of grace and to warn of His coming to this earth).

He searches each Lord's Day for a people who will provide Him a Throne of praise. When He finds such a church, there He will set up His Office-Place. His Spirit will direct hurting, captive, blind, and bruised people to this place for this local body of believers has become His Office-Place. He can touch hurting people here through the anointed hands and voices of True Worshipers. A church that does not effectively worship cannot effectively touch the world around it with the fullness of the Lord's ministry. A worshiping church will become the Lord's Office-Place just as if a great king had come to conduct the business of His kingdom among them. Indeed, He has.

And the King is in! His office is never closed. The office hours read "Now." Our appointment is our adoration of Him, our passion for Him. Whatever we need from Him is found here. If all we need is to be held by Him, this is the place. If we need a touch, deeper than the hands of man can reach, He will touch us here. If we need to hear His voice, He speaks His truth here in still tones in the hush of His nearness. When we need correction, He calls us into His Office and deals with us, calling us ever upward away from the destructive past toward the future's promise. Though thousands come, His Office is never crowded. Amid the myriad of voices calling to Him, He will not fail to hear our voice. It is only reasonable that He welcomes us to His office because He suffered, died and rose again for what He can do for us here. How He treasures this relationship! How He longs for us to return—and soon!

The Lord's Office Place
Psalm 103
When I worship in spirit and truth, I come into His Office Place where he meets all my needs.

MODEL NUMBER SEVEN
The River of Life

The final biblical illustration we will discuss reveals how the Lord works in His Office-Place. From Psalm 1 through Revelation 22, the Bible refers to the flow of God's blessings as a river, the River of Life. Throughout Scripture, water is consistently used to symbolize the flow of God's Spirit through His people. By focusing on the passages that mention the single image of a river we see a wonderful composite picture of the flow of God's life. Considering how much the Bible has to say about the waters of life, sometimes as springs, wells, fountains, and streams, we must ponder this major biblical picture of the flow of God's life, the Holy Spirit, through His people.

The River of Life is the obedient believer's source of life. "Blessed is the man who does not walk in the counsel of the wicked or stand in the way of sinners or sit in the seat of mockers. But his delight is in the law of the LORD, and on his law he meditates day and night. He is like a tree planted by streams of water, which yields its fruit in season and whose leaf does not wither. Whatever he does prospers" (Psalm 1:1-3).

Worship is the source of our life in God. Psalm 1 makes this clear. Our effectiveness as human beings is the overflow of our relationship with God. Like a tree planted by rivers of water, we will produce and prosper, strengthened as life rolls by because the Spirit of God is our source. Through our natural birth we enter into the river of natural life; we breathe, our heart beats, we live and move and have our being. But the individual who has had a second, *spiritual* birth enters into a spiritual river of life. He is like a tree whose roots penetrate into the living stream at the deepest levels. The spiritual life comes coursing up the roots and stems, trunk and limbs to burst forth into supernatural fruition and perpetual foliage— life of the highest order.

The River of Life is the source of the believer's satisfaction in life. "They feast on the abundance of your house; you give them drink from your river of delights. For with you is the fountain of life; in your light we see light" (Psalm 36:8,9).

There is no shortage of provision in the House of the Lord. With the Lord is the fountain of life. He invites us to drink from this fountain, this abundant supply. There is delight in these waters, refreshing in this flow, satisfaction in this stream. In stark contrast to the writer of Ecclesiastes who saw life as endless frustration and vanity, the Psalmists saw life by the river of God as a satisfying thing. The Spirit of God is the only source of satisfaction in life. Only He can quiet the soul's storms, heal the soul's diseases, ease the soul's pain, and bring rest to the soul's weariness. As Jesus said, to drink from these waters is to thirst no more.

The River of Life makes the whole community of believers, the city of God, glad; and that gladness is their strength and defense. "There is a river whose streams make glad the city of God, the holy place where the Most High dwells. God is within her, she will not fall; God will help her at break of day" (Psalm 46:4,5).

Joy is such an elusive thing. Sometimes as we are trying to do great things for God, our joy can evaporate like water on a hot day. Gladness and joy are found in the presence of the Lord. Our worship can bring joy that will last us through the toughest and longest day. It can be renewed each day and often through the day. Life itself may act as a drain, constantly pulling our joy from us, but worship acts as a faucet, constantly filling us with joy, and therefore, with strength.

As individual believers become tributaries of the River of Life, the combined effect of all these streams flowing together is irresistible. Notice that the source of the stream is "the holy place where the Most High dwells." The People of God are secure and joyful. They know that God's dwelling and ruling place is within them and in their company. Tomorrow will bring nothing outside the realm of His sovereignty or beyond the reach of His presence. There will be gladness in the city of God. Coming together to worship should be a joyful celebration. Public worship should make glad the city of God. When the river flows, it is joyful and uplifting. Remember, the joy of the Lord is our strength; in our gladness is our defense.

The River of Life flows progressively deeper as the believer enters it. "The man brought me back to the entrance of the Temple, and I saw water coming out from under the threshold of the Temple toward the east (for the Temple faced east). The water was coming down from under the south side of the Temple, south of the altar. As the man went eastward with a measuring line in his hand, he measured off a thousand cubits and then led me through water that was ankle-deep. He measured off another thousand cubits and led me through water that was knee-deep.

"He measured off another thousand and led me through water that was up to the waist. He measured off another thousand, but now it was a river that I could not cross, because the water had risen and was deep enough to swim in—a river that no one could cross. He asked me, 'Son of man, do you see this?' Then he led me back to the bank of the river" (Ezekiel 47:1, 3-6).

Ezekiel experienced four levels of depth in the river. As we enter the flow of God's life, we do so in an ever-deepening process. This has many applications. Here are some: the progress we make in our Christian walk from our first days to an ever-deepening, relationship with God; the progress we make in our study of the Word from the basics to the ever-deepening unfolding of God's heart; and the progressive relationship we enjoy with God as we begin knowing little about Him and progress into an ever-deepening friendship. We are concerned with these life processes and also with the worship event. The progressive ever-deepening flow of God's River is also a manifestation of the worship event as we shall soon develop.

The reasonable progression of worship we discussed in our presentation of the Living-Sacrifice of Praise model is reinforced here. We can identify four corresponding levels of our response to the presence of the Lord:

	Ezekiel's experience	Worship Level	Results:
PRAISE	ankle deep	thanksgiving	refreshing
	knee deep	exaltation	awe / wonder
WORSHIP	waist deep	adoration	renewal
	over the head	communion	change

Notice that Ezekiel passes through the first three levels but the fourth was a river he could not cross. If we do not know the fullness of the life available from the river, surely it is because we do not get out into the deep water. We are refreshed by thanksgiving. We are impressed by the majesty of God as we exalt Him. We are renewed by His presence and we think that is all. Really, we have only waded into the river to the waist deep level. We need to let go of the riverbed and launch ourselves into His presence. When we begin to *commune* with God, that is, to "swim" in waters over our head, we will not be able to exit the river at the same spot we entered; we will be changed. The River of Life will have carried us downstream, deeper into the will of God for us. If our worship is not life-changing, it is because we tend to dwell in the areas Ezekiel passed through, accepting refreshing, awe, and renewal rather than seeing the real change in our lives that only comes through communion with God.

Characteristics of the Flow of the River of Life

The River of Life flows from a wellspring in the heart of the believer. "Jesus answered, 'Everyone who drinks this water will be thirsty again, but whoever drinks the water I give him will never thirst. Indeed, the water I give him will become in him a spring of water welling up to eternal life'" (John 4:13,14)

We don't have to wonder about the source of the River of Life; Jesus makes it clear. The river flows from within the heart of the believer. We do not have to create the river or coax it to flow. This flowing stream is the result of the residence of Jesus in our lives. We see this in new converts. For a while they share Jesus with everyone who will listen. *He just flows from them.* What happens as these newborn followers of Jesus become veterans? In many cases, the spring in them is clogged by lesser concerns of life, as leaves and branches clog a spring of water. Worship, both private and public, cleans the spring so that Jesus can flow out of us no matter how long we have been saved. Passion unclogs reason. Springs must be tended if they are to flow freely. The River of Life flows from a spring in the heart of each believer. We don't have to make it flow; it just does! I love the old song that says:,

> *Drinking at the springs of living water,*
> *Happy now am I, My soul they satisfy.*
> *Drinking at the springs of living water,*
> *O wonderful and bountiful supply.*
> © 1950, Renewed 1978, by John W. Peterson Music Company.

The River of Life is actually the flow of the Holy Spirit. "On the last and greatest day of the Feast, Jesus stood and said in a loud voice, 'If anyone is thirsty, let him come to me and drink. Whoever believes in me, as the Scripture has said, streams of living water will flow from within him.' By this he meant the Spirit, whom those who believed in him were later to receive. Up to that time the Spirit had not been given, since Jesus had not yet been glorified" (John 7:37-39).

What flows? What is the nature of the river? It is the life of God, the Holy Spirit. The words translated "Holy Spirit" mean literally the "life" of God, His life force. This is why the image of a flowing river is so powerful—the life of God really does flow down to us and out through us. In the same way that a river flows in the natural world, God's life flows in the supernatural world. A river is inexorably pulled toward the sea by the force of gravity. Just so, the love of God pulls His life toward us. The Holy Spirit is constantly calling to us. When we were in sin, He called to us about our wickedness, our need for forgiveness, and the judgment that we must someday surely face. When we are following Jesus, the Holy Spirit is constantly calling us up higher in the knowledge of the holy, deeper into the love of God and broader into a greater love for mankind. When we come to Jesus we drink from these waters of life. When we believe in Jesus (seek to submit to Him and to follow Him) that drink becomes a spring in us and a river through us. We become a source of blessing to those around us. God flows through people to get to people by the inexorable force of His love, like a river touching every shore and island on its way to the sea.

When we speak of the overflowing life of service or of the flow of a service, we speak well. Everything God has created flows: the human body with all its complimentary systems; the earth and all its geologic and ecological systems; the universe itself with the delicate, cosmic balance of galaxies and planetary systems. Why?—because all creation is telling us about God. It is His nature to express the beauty of form and function, to flow in beauty and usefulness. The flow of the river of life will bring to the believer and to the Church the beauty of the excellence of our King, beauty and fruition, passion and reason, flowing together in perfect harmony. It is the reasonable way of the Spirit of God.

The River flows from the Throne of God. "He said: 'Son of man, this is the place of my throne and the place for the soles of my feet. This is where I will live among the Israelites forever. The house of Israel will never again defile my holy name—neither they nor their kings—by their prostitution and the lifeless idols of their kings at their high places'" (Ezekiel 43:7). "Then the angel showed me the river of the water of life, as clear as crystal, flowing from the throne of God and of the Lamb" (Revelation 22:1).

The Bible makes it clear that the River of Life flows from the Throne of God and of the Lamb. This is not just for some day in the future; it is for today. When we pray each day for His kingdom to come and His will be done, we are seeking the waters of life. The believer has a spring of water in his heart because Jesus has come in and set up His throne there. Beneath the Throne of God and of the Lamb can be found a spring bubbling with the life of God. This spring is the fountainhead of the River of Life.

The river's flow brings fruitfulness. "He is like a tree planted by streams of water, which yields its fruit in season and whatever he does prospers" (Psalms 1:3).

THE RIVER OF LIFE MODEL
Entering the flow of the Holy Spirit

BIBLICAL ILLUSTRATION	SPIRITUAL REALITY
(Ezekiel 47:1-11)	
Water Flowing from the Throne in the Temple	The Holy Spirit flows from the Throne of God and of the Lamb. (Rev.22)
ankle deep water(passed through)	Thanksgiving
knee deep water(passed through)	Praise ,Exaltation
waist deep water(passed through)	Worship , Adoration
over-the-head water (a river that cannot be crossed)	Communion with God
The river flows to the Dead Sea.	The Holy Spirit flows toward Human need.
The Dead Sea is healed and springs to life.	Human need is met by the Lord Jesus.
The marshes are not healed Trees and fisherman at the river	The healing is in the deep flow. "Where the river goes everything will live" (Ezekiel 47:11).

"Fruit trees of all kinds will grow on both banks of the river. Their leaves will not wither, nor will their fruit fail. Every month they will bear, because the water from the sanctuary flows to them. Their fruit will serve for food and their leaves for healing" (Ezekiel 47:12).

". . . down the middle of the great street of the city. On each side of the river stood the tree of life, bearing twelve crops of fruit, yielding its fruit every month. And the leaves of the tree are for the healing of the nations" (Revelation 22:2).

Jesus said the test of the flow of God's life in us in fruitful-ness—the Father would be glorified when we bring forth fruit (John 15:8). In the Psalms, Ezekiel, and Revelation, the river is seen as the source of fruition. "In his season," the Psalmist

says. "According to his months," Ezekiel says. "Twelve manner of fruit, and yielded her fruit every month," John says. In
the natural, fruition is seasonal, but by the river of life there is
a perpetual season of fruition; it is supernatural. The child of
God can be instant in season and out of season for the river
always flows.

When the life of God is coursing through a person, that
person will be productive. I love to look at rivers from air-
planes. From such great heights I can see the effect the river
has on the land. Stretching for miles on either side of the great
Mississippi River are the fruitful fields of the delta, the land of
my birth and upbringing. This is a picture of the life of the
believer in Jesus. He causes life to spring up wherever he goes
because in Him is the throne, the spring, the river. One can
also see how many turns the river takes on its way to the sea.
These bends and oxbows harness the energy and make it more
available to the thirsty land. Man sometimes digs canals
straight from point to point. From the air they are boring to
look at offering none of the diversity and design of the river
on its meander toward the sea. The twisting path of a river is
like the delays we experience in life. We might get through life
faster without all the twists and turns life takes but in the
process of following the route of the river, we bless more lives
than a direct path would afford. The energy of God's life
flowing in us seeps into the people around us when we are
delayed by bends in the flow of the river. The result God
wants is fruitfulness, not a record time to the sea.

**The river's flow brings supernatural strength and endur-
ance.** "Whose leaf does not wither" (Psalm 1:3). "Their leaves
will not wither, nor will their fruit fail" (Ezekiel 47:12).

In this perpetual season of fruition, the leaf does not
wither. Let us reason this out. The True Worshiper is an ever-
green oak, strong and productive throughout the year. Worship connects us to the source of the strength life demands.
Drought brings disaster in the natural world, so dependent is
that world upon water. In the spiritual world, too, drought is
disaster for the waters of life bring not only fruitfulness, but

strength. The Spirit-filled Christian is capable of amazing feats of ministry. This supernatural strength is not ours to waste on selfish pursuits. The power of the river is in its flow. When we are in line with that flow, that power is flowing through us. If we take off in our own direction we leave the river and its power behind .

The river brings healing. "Their fruit will serve for food and their leaves for healing"(Ezekiel 47:12). "And the leaves of the tree are for the healing of the nations" (Revelation 22:2).

The River of Life is a healing stream, not just physical healing, but every type of pain known to man can be swept away by these waters. God wants to ease our pain. He wants to break the shackles on our wrists and heal the deep bruises they have caused. He wants to set us free from diseases of body, soul, and spirit. The leaves of the trees, the fruit of the lives touched by the river, are for healing. Ezekiel and John both saw the river, and the leaves of the trees by the river have a healing effect on the land through which the river flowed. Our time with the Lord is a healing time. Our public worship, when the river of life is allowed to flow in its fullness, will become a great healing service. Sin's diseases, discourage-ment's scourges, and plagues of untruth can be healed in this stream. Even physical ailments can be washed away as the healing stream flows into dry, barren lives. But there is a heal-ing flow only in the deep places. The swamps and marshes, where there is no depth or flow, will not experience healing. The healing is in the deep flow of life. "But the swamps and marshes will not become fresh; they will be left for salt" (Ezekiel 47:11).

The river of life flows toward human need. "He said to me, 'This water flows toward the eastern region and goes down into the Arabah, where it enters the Sea. When it emp-ties into the Sea, the water there becomes fresh'" (Ezekiel 47:8).

The sea that pulls the River of Life on its journey is the Dead Sea, the lowest point on earth except for ocean floors. In Ezekiel's vision the Dead Sea is healed! The waters of life have such power in them they can reverse the effects of centuries of concentrated evil. Think of the salt waters of the Dead Sea being healed by the inflow of the waters of life. Your home, your workplace, your school, or your city is like that Dead Sea. It may seem that you are in the lowest spot on earth. But God's healing waters flow into that Dead Sea through you, through your passionate and reasonable witness! Soon you will see the waters healed!

The river of life always flows toward human need. In the last flood tide John describes in Revelation 22, all human misery is wiped away forever. Until then, the river flows from the throne of God in our hearts toward the needs of mankind. Ezekiel saw this. He describes the flow of the river in graphic terms on its journey to the Dead Sea. "Swarms of living creatures will live wherever the river flows. There will be large numbers of fish, because this water flows there and makes the salt water fresh; so where the river flows everything will live" (Ezekiel 47:9). How important our worship is to the world around us! We are the channels of the waters of life. There are twin currents in the river of life: True Worship and biblical truth, spirit and truth. This composite flow will bring His healing life to the nations. Wherever the river goes there is life!

The River of Life
Ezekiel 47:1-11
When I worship God I enter the flow of God's life.
Wherever the river goes, everything will live!

CONCLUSION OF BIBLICAL MODELS

History speaks to us of the importance of worship. *The Tabernacle/Temple* teaches of the sin barrier and of our individual responsibility to bring our personal sacrifice of praise, humility, and worship to the Lord. Here we discern the pattern by which all times and cultures approach the Holy Presence—Praise precedes Worship. Here we experience the awesome stillness of the Holy of Holies wherein His strength is made perfect in our weakness as we center our lives on Him. *The Tabernacle of David* teaches us to celebrate the goodness of the Lord. This is New Testament worship as it is described in the Psalms. Here we learn the power of corporate worship. Through these historical places we understand how to worship God in the ways that please Him, with passion and reason.

The Bible shows us our relationship with God and our duty toward Him. *The Holy-Royal Priesthood* identifies us as servants of the Most High who have been called into special relationship with Him. We are holy by His blood and royal by His decree. We and everything we own are His. Our value to Him is based in His love for us and not in our achievements. We minister to the Lord with *The Living Sacrifice of Praise*. It is the fruit of our lips and of our lives. It is both a blessed event and a continuing process. He has called us into a special relationship with Him and we please Him with our expressions of praise and our loving obedience. The passion of our praise is the reasonable result of our relationship with Jesus.

Today we extend God's kingdom into our lives with our praise and obedience. We have the awesome privilege of dwelling in *His Throne Room.* We also visit *His Office-Place* where the healing work of His kingdom is done. And, we live fruitful, joyful lives by **The River of Life.** As we worship-serve Him, He flows through us to the healing of the nations. No wonder worship with passion and reason is the ministry of every believer.

These seven truths must become tests of how well we lead worship and goals to strive for in our worship. They are the reasoning basis of all the truths dealt with in this study. They speak to us of who we are in Christ Jesus and through them we see what the ministry of each believer is—to love with passion: to love the Lord our God with all our heart, soul, mind and strength and to love our neighbor as our self. Through this vision for worship we can see how to center our lives and our churches on God himself. They illustrate for us our "righteousness in Christ Jesus." For, indeed, His kingdom is Righteousness!

Chapter Five

PERSONAL RIGHTEOUSNESS
The Heart of the True Worshiper

The Seventh Son of Jesse

W hat was the old man looking for? What was God looking for? It wasn't every day that the prophet of God, Samuel, came to visit. Something was said in the village about a sacrifice. But everyone knew that King Saul was in trouble. It was even rumored that Samuel had pronounced the end of Saul's reign. Samuel could do that—depose kings, anoint kings—such was the power of the old man.

Now the sons of Jesse had been summoned before Samuel and David's youngest older brother was the seventh in line. David had not been called, no use wasting the prophet's time. Jesse, the father of this brood, was so proud at the sound of the words of God, "I have provided myself a king from among his sons."

Jesse's pride was shaken while his firstborn stood before Samuel. Jesse expected this to be a short-lived process. Eliab was such a fine specimen, no doubt he was the one to rule. Samuel looked at the young man, "Surely the Lord's anointed is before Him." Jesse's heart swelled, as did that of his seventh son. "My older brother, the king! It will be well for me then!" But then Samuel hesitated, cocked his head as if listening to some inner voice, then shook his head. In his heart he heard these words, "Do not look at his appearance or at the height of his stature, because I have refused him. For the Lord does not see as man sees; for man looks at the outward appearance, but the Lord looks on the heart." Can't tell old Jesse all that, Samuel must have thought. He just kept shaking his head.

Jesse called Abinadab and made him pass before Samuel. Son number seven swallowed hard. If God did not want Saul who was so tall and imposing, nor Eliab who was so impressive, what did He want? Abinidab had not been as much of a hero to Jesse's next to the last son. In fact, he had not been good at all. Number seven was thinking that it wouldn't be so good for him if Abinadab was king. But . . . wait a minute! Samuel was shaking his head again. Abinidab was not the one, either. That was close, thought son number seven.

He looked over to his father who was trying desperately to hold on to his pride, his dream of a son as king. One by one the six older brothers stood before Samuel as the old man's eyes penetrated the darkness of each soul. Finally, the time came for the seventh son.

Samuel looked at the young man, unable to hide his disappointment. The young man did not want to stare back but he did. If it was meant for him to be king, he would just have to be king, that's all. God would help . . .

The old man's head shook slowly at first and then faster and more violently. He whirled to confront Jesse. "Are all the young men here?"

Jesse was dazed, confused somehow by the successive surprises. None of the seven brothers would dare speak. "There remains the youngest, and there he is keeping the sheep."

"Send and bring him. For we will not sit down till he comes here."

Seven brothers and their tired old father needed to sit down. But they didn't. What was God looking for? All each young man knew was that it was something inside, something each did not have. When David came, Samuel examined him. Seven brothers had seven variations on the same thought, "Not him! He's little—just a boy!" But Samuel saw a handsome young man with bright eyes, a clear complexion and skin of an outdoorsman. That same voice spoke in Samuel's heart, "Arise, anoint him; for this is the one!" The Lord had chosen David from among the sheep pens to be a king after God's own heart.

Son number seven was secretly relieved that he was not chosen but he joined with the others as they stared at their despised little brother who was soon to rule over them. Cruelties and injustices, which were just the normal sibling strife, loomed large in the memory now as they considered the object of their derision, their little brother, rising to the nation's throne.

God Looks on the Heart.

As Samuel searched the faces of Jesse's sons looking for a king to lead God's people we can only imagine the discomfort each of the brothers must have felt when the judge-prophet looked into his eyes. We can only wonder at the rejection each must have experienced when he proved to be unworthy of God's call. Can we begin to understand their dismay when their youngest brother David was anointed to be King? What was God looking for? It was not something that the eye of man could see. It was something inside.

Much like Samuel, the Father is looking for someone. He looks at each of us but not as man looks. God looks deep inside. Evidence of the object of His search, the True Worshiper, abides beneath the outward trappings; it is a matter of the heart. Worship that pleases God is, always has been, and always will be a matter of the heart. The externals, how we act, look, and sound, are of supreme interest to us but God looks on the heart. As the Father searches throughout the earth for True Worshipers, He is on a heart search, seeking out hearts set on things above. These are the ones who will worship in spirit and in truth, with passion and reason.

As we survey the bewildering landscape of Christian worship today, King David's question comes to mind. "Who shall ascend the hill of the Lord? or who shall stand in His Holy Place?" In other words, "Who are the True Worshipers?" His answer in Psalm 24:3-5 is still true today:

Who may ascend the hill of the Lord? Who may stand in his holy place? He who has clean hands and a pure heart, who does not lift up his soul to an idol or swear by what is false. He will receive blessing from the Lord and vindication from God his Savior.

The Assent of Zion — Psalm 24:3-6

Who may
ascend the hill of the Lord?
Who may stand in his holy place?
He who has clean hands and a pure heart,
who does not lift up his soul to an idol or swear by
what is false. He will receive blessing from the Lord and
vindication from God his Savior. Such is the generation of
those who seek him, who seek your face, O God of Jacob. Selah

---

The blessing of the Lord's manifest presence and the life-changing righteousness every child of God longs for await in the Holy Place at the summit of Mt. Zion, the hill of praise. Who may climb this hill, proclaiming thanksgiving and praise and humbling his heart before God? Who may dwell in that Holy Place, drinking in His love, peace, and holiness? The one whose hands are clean and whose heart is pure, the humble one who does not lift up his soul to the vanity of modern idols, and the one who does not live a lie.

Clean hands. There are two applications of this truth: righteousness in Jesus, and the biblical purity of what we do in our worship. Biblical purity in worship will be the subject of the next chapter. The first is a constant emphasis. Only by His blood can we enter the presence of the Lord. The techniques of worship must never overshadow Jesus himself. He is our righteousness, peace, and joy. Our hands are clean because He has cleansed them in His own blood.

A pure heart. He who has a pure heart will "ascend the hill of the Lord" (praise) and "stand in His Holy Place" (worship). The heart (our soul, our true intentions, our deep motivations) is made pure by the Holy Spirit. Its contents are expressed in our attitudes, passions and actions; if our hearts are pure so will our worship be. If impurities linger in the heart eventually they will spoil our offering to the Lord. We will have more to say about the refiner's fire and the fuller's soap, God's provisions for the cleansing of the heart. For now, let us echo another of King David's prayers. "May the words of my mouth and the meditation of my heart be pleasing in your sight, O Lord, my Rock and my Redeemer" (Psalm 19:14).

Vanity and idols. The worshiper-king also specified that one must not lift up his soul to "vanity." Modern translations say "idols." Strong makes it clear that both these translations are correct. The word King David used as the object of false worship refers to "desolating evil, ruin, guile, idolatry, uselessness, lies, and vanity"—vivid synonyms for the spiritual conditions of modern society. Vanity abounds and idols are everywhere. All of these evils are based in pride, the antithesis of worship. If our passion is spent here, if we lift up our souls at modern pagan altars we cannot expect to be a True Worshiper of the Most High God. We will not find righteousness, peace, and joy but guile, ruin, and vanity. This is only reasonable.

False declarations. To "swear deceitfully" means basic dishonesty, saying one thing when really something else is true. Why does this concern the heart of the True Worshiper? Performance before men can deceive many into thinking we are one thing when we are really something else altogether. But ascending "the hill of the Lord" or standing "in His Holy Place" offers absolutely no opportunity for deceit. God knows what we really are and how we really feel. If we are to be True Worshipers, we must learn to be honest with God. Thus worship becomes a process of self-revelation as the Lord peels back the layers of our self-deceit and shows us the real truth about ourselves. This may sound threatening but remember the tenderness of the Lord in His office place. The same Lord who strips away the rotting rags of our righteousness also pours in a healing balm and with gentle hands wraps our wounded souls in the soothing, white linen of His righteousness. Humility and soul-deep honesty are essential to the heart of the True Worshiper.

So, the True Worshiper has clean hands and a pure heart. He has not lifted up his soul to vanity or idols and what he says is really true. What is his reward? "He will receive blessing from the LORD and vindication from God his Savior" (Psalms 24:5). In other words, the True Worshiper will know the presence and power of the Lord in very personal dimensions. King David continues, "Such is the generation of those who seek him, who seek your face, O God of Jacob. Selah" (Psalm 24:6).

Are we in that generation? Let us set our hearts to seek Him, to seek his face. We can be among those whose passion leads their ascent of the hill of praise to stand in the Holy Place of worship. It is reasonable that these are the ones who receive blessing and the righteousness. It is a matter of the heart.

THE HEART FASHIONED AFTER THE HEART OF GOD

How can we know we are not just assuming our hearts are right before God, hoping our heart's affections are really set above? We turn to the Scriptures to reason this out. They tell an impressive tale of hearts. King David was a man "after" God's own heart. That is what we want to be said of us. To understand the heart that received this commendation, we must trace David's spiritual lineage through Samuel back to Hannah and contrast these godly hearts with that of the tragic King Saul. We will see that King David's heart is a model of the heart of his greater son, King Jesus and that Jesus' heart is the heart of God revealed!

Hannah

She was a desperate woman—barren, and her husband's *other* wife taunted her while producing child after child. Hannah's husband did not understand her desperation. He thought his love should be enough to make up for the lack of a child. The spiritual climate of Israel was barren also, a time of incredible spiritual darkness. Worship at the Tabernacle under Eli, the high priest, had become so corrupt that no one heard from God anymore. Eli's sons made gluttons of themselves on the meat intended as a sacrifice for God and actually brought prostitutes into the outer court to ply their trade. But in the midst of personal, family, and spiritual circumstances as bleak as any we can imagine, something in the heart, some deep passion of this great lady, would not let go of her desire for a child.

Hannah went to God. The apostate religious structure actually opposed her but she pressed through man's religious failure to touch the heart of God. She went to the gate of the Tabernacle and poured out her heart to God. Her prayer became so intense that she made no sound but her heart's cry echoed through heaven. Eli rebuked her thinking she was a drunken prostitute, a more likely prospect in those dark times than a heart seeking God. She protested her innocence and explained that she had been praying. Eli prophesied that her prayer had been heard and would be answered. This satisfied her heart and she rose up, ended her fast, and got ready to have a baby. She had vowed to the Lord that she would give her first child to Him.

Soon Samuel was born and all too quickly weaned. She brought her son back to this tottering, backslidden priest who daily tolerated the desecration of God's house by his own sons. Eli would raise Samuel. What faith and passion! What faithfulness to a vow! What reasonable trust in God! Hannah went on to have more children, their names long forgotten, yet this first son, this child of the desperate heart, is one of the great men of Scripture, the last judge of Israel, one of the great prophets, and the one who would anoint Israel's first two kings.

What can we learn from Hannah's heart?

- Her heart was discontented with the way things were.
- Her heart was misunderstood by others.
- She went her way rejoicing in God's answer.
- She submitted herself to the Lord.
- She was faithful to her vows.

All of these characteristics are instructive to us.

A Holy Discontent. Hanna had a deep conviction that things did not have to be the way they have always been. These are the hearts that change the world through passionate prayer and obedience. She had a vision of how things could be which quickened her heartbeat and became the driving pulse of her life. She got her answer and changed her nation in the process. How about you? Are there barren places in your life with which you have grown complacent? If our hearts accept the unacceptable, we will not see answers to our prayers the way Hannah did.

Submission to the Lord. She had no reasonable options except those found in God. If she was to remain pure before the Lord, her barrenness could only be solved by a sovereign act of God. So, she set her heart on God. How many of us waste our energies on man's solutions or even resort to unrighteousness to solve the problem, when only God can meet our needs. If we follow Hannah's example and pour out our hearts before the Lord, He will hear our prayer and direct us to the answer. That answer may come through the hands of men, but we will know, just as Hannah did, that God has undertaken. Because of her heart's prayer she knew Samuel was from the Lord as well as from her husband.

Misunderstood by others. Eli misjudged her but she did not let the prospect of being thought of as an evil woman detract her from her heart's desire. If seeing an end to the spiritual barrenness of your church life is your heart's prayer, be prepared for the misunderstanding of others. You may even be accused of wickedness. It hurts to have motives questioned. Hannah defended herself but she never attacked Eli. She let the integrity of her heart be her protection. She did not petition to have Eli removed nor did she seek to stir up the people against him. She passionately poured out her heart to God and reasonably let God handle the corrupt leadership.

He is still able to do that today. An important part of the heart of the True Worshiper is the respect for the anointed of God, even when they might be wrong. They belong to God and we must pray for them, leaving their correction to God. Many times passion, a deep desire for spiritual renewal, can be perceived as a threat to entrenched leadership. Like Hannah, we might be misunderstood or even falsely accused. The purity of our hearts and a genuine love for the church and its leadership are our only reasonable defenses.

Rejoicing in God's answer. Hannah's song of rejoicing in I Samuel 2:2 is still sung today:

> *There is none holy as the Lord:*
> *For there is none beside Thee:*
> *Neither is there any rock like our God*

When the answer comes, the heart of the True Worshiper can rejoice in God, knowing full well that God has intervened. Seeing God move into impossible situations causes great rejoicing.

Faithful to her vows. What faith it took for this new mother to take her firstborn and abandon him to the corrupt spiritual leadership in Eli's house! He had already ruined his own sons and the Tabernacle worship in the process. But she had made a vow and it must be fulfilled. She trusted God to watch over the boy. Great answers to prayer always require further obedience on our part. Can God trust us to be faithful to our promises after the crisis is past? The true-hearted worshiper never forgets the promises made in prayer. God can do great things through people whose hearts do not forget what they have promised.

The Heart of Hannah was . . .

**Discontented with the way things were,
Submitted to the Lord,
Rejoicing in God's answer,
Faithful to her vows.**

Samuel

What a powerful time each annual visit with his mother must have been for Samuel! Somehow, her heart for God was reborn in the boy. In a dark age, he found light. In a time when no one heard from God, Jehovah called to Samuel in the night. In a climate of lawlessness, Samuel developed a passion to obey God. When the Levites failed to worship, God raised up an Ephrathite who would seek His face. Here at the beginning of Samuel's long and dramatic ministry are given three secrets of his greatness:

- **He ministered before the Lord.** That is, he lived his life before God and not men. The Bible record contrasts Eli's sons with the young Samuel. "This sin of the young men was very great in the Lord's sight, for they were treating the Lord's offering with contempt. But Samuel was ministering before the Lord—a boy wearing a linen ephod" (1 Samuel 2:17).
- **He ministered to the Lord.** He learned to worship! His service to the nation was the outflow of his service to God. "And the child Samuel ministered unto the Lord before Eli. And the Word of the Lord was precious in those days, there was no open vision" (I Samuel 3:1, AV).

- **The Lord revealed himself to him.** Because Samuel's passion positioned him near the presence of God, Samuel received a revelation of God himself. "The Lord was with Samuel as he grew up, and he let none of his words fall to the ground. And all Israel from Dan to Beersheba recognized that Samuel was attested as a prophet of the Lord. The Lord continued to appear at Shiloh, and there he revealed himself to Samuel through his word" (I Samuel 3:19-21).

With these three secrets hidden in his heart, it is only reasonable that Samuel became a lion for the Lord, unafraid to anoint kings, to rebuke kings, or even to announce the doom of kings. Other characteristics of his heart speak to us today.

His heart was set on ministry to the Lord. In the sin-darkened ritual of the Tabernacle, Samuel must have sensed what was lacking, passionate ministry to the Lord. When our worship—when our lives—take on some lesser purpose than ministry to the Lord, form will replace function, uselessness will supplant utility, and barrenness will blight the vine of our life, marring the beauty of our offering to the Lord. When ministry to man becomes foremost in our worship, some form of prostitution is always the result. Divine love will be cheapened, existing not just for its own sake, but for our lesser purposes and aims.

We are appalled at the actions of Eli's sons but have we not prostituted our worship when we set our hearts to please men, to give them the desires of their heart in the very gate of Temple? Our worship is for God, not men, not *any* men. Public worship is not a church growth tool. It is not a lifeless custom of our culture. It is not entertainment. It is not preliminary to some more important event. Worship is loving God with passion, with all our collective heart and strength, and reasonably with all our soul and mind. Public worship services can never really make sense until we turn them upward, in their proper direction, toward the Lord. Samuel never forgot what he saw early in his life. He set his heart to minister to God no matter whom he might displease in the process. God, give us leaders like that today!

His heart was one that heard from God. This is the outgrowth of his ministry to the Lord. God is always speaking but only those who draw near to Him in the silence of their own souls hear what He is saying. God does not enjoy our ignorance of Him and His plans. The deep desire each of us has to be understood by those we love came from Him. He has the same desire to be known by us. The whole salvation plan speaks of this passion. If we will diligently seek Him (minister to the Lord) He will reward us. If we draw near to Him, He will draw near to us. It has always been so. Samuel found this out. He always knew what God was doing because he was always ministering unto the Lord. God speaks to those who position themselves to hear. This makes sense.

His heart was set on pleasing God. No one, be he king or commoner, intimidated Samuel. Because he sought God, he knew what God wanted. And because he knew what God wanted and obeyed, he pleased God. It is really that simple today. What we lack is the courage Samuel had. In the matter of Israel's becoming a monarchy, Samuel obeyed God even when it went against his own judgment Saul feared Samuel because he could not corrupt him. Jesse honored him because he knew that the real power of Israel was in the prophet's heart. David took Samuel's word to be the word of the Lord. Such is the pure heart set on pleasing God and not man. Hell has no counter-plan for such single-hearted obedience.

His heart was one that hungered for the glory of the Lord. Because Samuel ministered to the Lord, because he heard from God, and because he obeyed God, Samuel sought the glory of the Lord. He heard Him in the Tabernacle as a child and many, many times during his life. Samuel saw the ark taken away and he did not live to see it return in triumph to the heart of the nation. But he lived long enough to see that David had a heart for God. Perhaps he saw a hunger in David's eyes for the glory of the Lord. If so, he knew that was enough to guarantee the glory would return to God's people.

The Heart of Samuel was one that . . .

Ministered before the Lord,
Ministered to the Lord,
Heard from God,
Pleased God,
Sought the Glory of the God.

King Saul

One of the most tragic figures in all the Scriptures, King Saul provides us with the contrast we need to fully understand the heart that pleases God. In Saul we see the results of the natural heart of man unrestrained by the hand of God, untouched by His grace, and un-yielded to His Spirit. His heart was plagued by a lack of self-esteem and devoid of trust. It was filled, instead, with unbridled ambition capable of using supernatural things to satisfy its own ends. He first met Samuel in an effort to use a prophet of God to find some donkeys he had lost. Later on he would lose the kingdom because of his desire to use the sacrificial worship of God to political advantage. Even after Samuel was dead, Saul had no hesitation to consult a witch to try and communicate with the prophet.

Why did God choose such a man to be king? Did God set Saul up just to see him fail? Before we judge Saul too quickly, we must realize that the darkness that lurked in Saul's heart can be found in ours, too. We all have self-esteem problems as we vacillate between over-reaching pride and debilitating self-doubt. Trust is not easy for us, especially after we have been burned a few times by faithless people. Each of us stands in danger of letting ambition take over our hearts. We are quite capable, in the fires of that ambition, of using the supernatural to further our own selfish plans. We must see Saul's heart as the natural heart of man, cold as frozen rock, before the Holy

Spirit ignites the refiner's fire. We must see the tragic hues of Saul's history as the fate of the man who does not receive the cleansing of the fuller's soap, the heart that never shines with the color and brightness of redemption.

But, the Scriptures say something that is essential to our understanding of Saul: God "gave him another heart." God did not set Saul up to fail. On the contrary, he gave Saul exactly what he needed to be a great king—another heart! This heart was one that could hear from God and prophesy the great things he heard in the voice of the Spirit. As physical evidence of this new heart, God sent a roving band of musician-preachers from the "hill of God" Saul's way. When the new king was in their company, his new heart began to stir with revelation knowledge of who God is (surely this is what a king must know). The young man who was known to hide among the baggage, the young man so self-conscious of his imposing height, began to sing, dance, and prophesy. This public passion was such a departure for him that those who knew him developed a proverb to express supreme amazement when events beyond explanation unfolded before them, "Is Saul among the prophets?"

This new heart and these new friends marked the beginning of a new relationship with God, one that would give him wisdom and strength, the passion and reason, required by the demands of leadership. Saul should have appointed these prophets as court musicians and kept them near his throne. Instead, he was embarrassed by them and by his behavior when they were near. Because he failed to develop the heart-building relationships God had given him, his natural heart was never permanently replaced by the spiritual heart God gave him. The anointing of God coupled with an unchanged heart is always a formula for tragedy.

What about us? Are we frightened by the things we see in Saul's heart because we know they are in our hearts also? Do we secretly suspect that God has called us to failure? This is the fearful voice of the unchanged heart. God has called us to success! Yes, He calls us to things far beyond us, but he always has "another heart" planned for us. He always sends people into our lives, like the prophets He sent Saul, who ignite our godly passion and encourage us to the spiritual life. We may not even like the heart-builders God sends us. We may be uncomfortable with their effect on us or how we act around them. He may have sent us to a church whose worship is not what we are used to. But when we are with these people, God speaks in our hearts! We find ourselves worshiping with them and enjoying the presence of the Lord. Reason demands that we recognize the heart-builders God sends into our lives. These are some of the most important relationships we have; our success in the kingdom lies in large measure in their effect upon our heart.

The unchanged heart can ruin the plan of God. The rebellious heart of Saul led him, as it always will, to disobedience. The same prophet who anointed him, announced to all that God would take the kingdom from him for his disobedience. God would seek out another man, a man whose heart would please the Lord. Saul's tragedy can be ours if we do not cultivate the relationships God sends us.

The Heart of Saul was . . .

Natural, Shameful, Untrusting, Ambitious, Pragmatic

King David and King Jesus

King David, the exceptional worshiper-writer-musician-soldier-general-designer-statesman-administrator of the Old Testament, Israel's greatest king, is called the "man after God's own heart" (I Samuel 13:14). That means his heart was fashioned in the likeness of God's heart. If we compare the heart of Jesus with the heart of King David we can see this clearly.

- Both King David and King Jesus had a shepherd's heart.

- They had hearts that hungered for God's presence.
- They each possessed principled hearts, filled with God's Word, and patient hearts, able to wait on God.
- And, each of their hearts was broken by sin.

The shepherd's heart. Whereas Saul is first seen as a donkey driver and this characteristic predominated his reign, David is first seen as a shepherd and this characterized his. His shepherd's heart made him a great leader. Using this analogy for the Lord's care of His people, David gave us perhaps the greatest song in the Bible, Psalm 23. He foreshadowed the Messiah's heart for Jesus who would later identify himself as "the Good Shepherd."

The heart that hungers for God's Presence. As we have seen, David prioritized the presence of the Lord. His many statements in the Psalms concerning his devotional life sound like Jesus could have written them. Compare: "I myself will awake early" (David, Psalm 57:8) with "And in the morning, rising up a great while before day, He went out, and departed into a solitary place, and there prayed" (Jesus, Mark 1:35). This illustrates another meaning to the phrase, "after God's own heart." David passionately *pursued* the heart of God. He was after God's heart; no other pursuit mattered as much to him. When the likeness of God's heart failed to be found in David's heart, the pursuit of God's heart took over. David failed God but he did not wallow in his failures. He got up, dusted himself off, and set about trying again to serve the Lord. Reason demanded it.

When David's heart failed him, repentance could always be found in the king's heart. David was a terrible father and his love for women just about destroyed him, but through all his failures, the greatest fear expressed in his anguished repentance (Psalm 51) is that Jehovah would withdraw His presence from the heart of the king. David never turned to idolatry. His hunger for God's presence marked his heart as one fashioned in the image of God. Jesus' passion for God's presence reveals the heart of God to us—He longs to be with *us!* God's heart hungers for loving fellowship with His beloved creation. When our hearts are fashioned after His heart, and when we are in pursuit of God's heart, we long to be with Him and we will prioritize His presence.

The principled heart, filled with the Word of God. No writer has composed a more moving hymn to the Word of God than King David, Psalm 19. Psalm 119 is not attributed to David, but it is certainly written in the spirit of Psalm 19. In the Word, David found the principles on which he would base his life. Like Samuel, he would not violate a principle even when to do so would serve to advance his own purposes. When Saul was delivered into David's hands, he would not kill him though such was acceptable in his day. Why? Because there was a principle, "Touch not mine anointed." The heart that is after God's heart is one of principle, of reasoned responses.

As a young man David must have found the Word intriguing. When pursued by Saul, it must have been his strength. As king it was his wisdom. His long life proved that the heart of the True Worshiper is one that hungers for the truth of God. Jesus was so steeped in the knowledge of the Word that it flowed forth in His everyday speech. Many times He quoted David and the other psalmists. If we are to be True Worshipers, we must ask God for a heart that hungers for the Word. Worship leaders and musicians cannot afford to be spiritual lightweights, lacking in reasoning skills based on a knowledge of the Word of God.

A patient heart. The heart after God's heart is patient, able to wait on God's timing. Eternity will reveal the damage done to the purposes of God by impatient hearts. As we stated, David was able to wait on God's time to be made king. Several years elapsed between David's anointing by Samuel and the day he finally became king. Jesus waited till age thirty before He began His ministry. Surely, we must see the value to God of a patient heart. When it seems to us nothing is happening, that God's plan for us is languishing, intense preparations may be underway in the spirit realm. Perhaps God is doing a work in our hearts or the hearts of those with whom we will work. We do not know what is happening in unseen worlds while we are waiting on God's time. To accomplish God's will we need to have three things: God's plan, God's method, and God's time. Reason insists that falling short of any one of these three things will guarantee our falling short of all that God has planned. The heart of the True Worshiper has reached this level of trust—it can wait on God's time.

The heart broken by sin. David failed God. His shameful deeds are as faithfully recorded in Scripture as his great successes. But David's sin broke his heart. We find no hint of self-justification, self-defense, or excuse. His broken heart was his pathway back to the presence of God. Jesus' heart was also broken by sin, not His own sin but yours and mine. The Garden of Gethsemane reveals the broken-hearted Savior, the God who mourns for our sin-separation more than we ever will.

The heart of the True Worshiper cannot be comfortable with sin. Secret sins will not be tolerated. Attitudes of the heart others may never see will become the focus of intense prayer, until the refiner's fire burns them away. Sin separates from God, and the True Worshiper has set his heart to seek God. These two things cannot co-exist. A constant vision of how personally God takes our sin will keep the tears of repentance close to the surface. If our worship is meant to please Him, we must see that our sin grieves Him. When sin, petty and private or powerful and public, hurts Him, it should break our hearts.

THE HEART OF DAVID AND JESUS IS . . .

The shepherd's heart,
The heart that hungers for God's Presence
the principled heart, filled with the Word of God,
A patient heart,
A heart broken by sin.
It is the Heart of God Revealed!

THE HEART TRANSFORMED

Imagine yourself the seventh son of Jesse standing in your place, last in line before the prophet Samuel. One by one, your brothers are rejected. You are amazed that your older brothers do not possess what God was looking for. For that matter, you are amazed to hear that King Saul has been rejected, though he was taller, smarter, and stronger than other men. What is God looking for? The other brothers rejected, now it is your turn. The old prophet turns to you and looks deep into your eyes, searching for something, mumbling to himself and listening to the voice of God, no doubt. Your heart stops as the prophet's gaze searches the dark corners of your soul like the very lamp of God.

Like the prophet of old, the Father in Heaven paces the well-ordered ranks of our worship looking from pew to pew, from pulpit to pulpit, for True Worshipers who would worship Him in spirit and in truth, with passion and reason. What is He looking for in us? When He stops in front of us and looks deep into our worship, what does He see? Clean hands? A pure heart? A humble soul free of idols and vanity? An offering in honesty? A heart centered upon Him?

He is looking for transformed hearts, for Saul's turned into godly kings because of God's grace in their lives. Saul was not the only one given a new heart.

- Matthew, the tax collector, became an itinerant evangelist with no thought of earthly gain.
- Peter, the unthinking racist, became an apostle to the Gentiles.
- Paul, the proud religionist, became the humble tentmaker and seeker of men's souls.
- Onesimus, the slave, became the freeman of the Lord and his master, Philemon, became the love slave of Jesus Christ.

Each one was given "another heart" and changed into "another man." We have been, too. This transformation is the key to worship that pleases God.

Maintaining the New Heart

The brand-new heart each new believer in Jesus receives from the Lord is designed to be filled with the Word and Presence of God himself. It functions best when it is centered on God himself. Saul failed because he did not cherish the holy things God put in his life and he did not keep the prophets near. We will maintain our new hearts by attending to these very things, by cherishing the holy things and cultivating the heart-building relationships God gives us. These are the holy things to be cherished:

- the Word of the Lord
- the presence of the Lord (prayer, praise, worship)
- the Lord's body (the Church)
- the Lord's Table (the means of sustaining grace)
- the Lord's day (It is His not ours)
- the Lord's Prayer (the outline of prayer that the Lord is listening for)
- the Lord's tithe
- the Lord's call upon our lives

Who are the "prophets" in your life? Your old friends may make fun of them and you for being with them, but when you are in their company, Jesus grows in you. Cultivate these new relationships! They are precious gifts from the Lord to your new heart. They help you center your life on God. They ignite your passion for God and inform your reason so that you can love God with heart, soul, mind and strength and your neighbor as yourself.

The heart transformed is the heart that is centered on God himself.

- It is the heart of the True Worshiper, like the heart of Hannah: dissatisfied with the status quo, prostrate before the Lord as the only source of help, unhindered by misunderstanding, and rejoicing in God's provision.
- It is like the heart of Samuel: set on ministering to the Lord, hearing from God, and pleasing the Lord; one that sees the glory of the Lord.
- The heart of the True Worshiper is like the heart of God, foreshadowed in David and revealed in Jesus: filled with love for the sheep, hungry for fellowship, brimming with truth, patient, and broken over sin.

Only the depths of worship in spirit and truth can satisfy such a heart. Jesus said in John 4:23,24, "Yet a time is coming and has now come when the True Worshipers will worship the Father in spirit and truth, for they are the kind of worshipers the Father seeks. God is spirit, and his worshipers must worship in spirit and in truth." This True Worship from the transformed heart to the heart of God, performed continually with passion and reason, is the ministry of every believer.

WORSHIP THAT PLEASES GOD IS AND ALWAYS HAS BEEN A MATTER OF THE HEART.

Worship That Pleases God
The Passion and Reason of True Worship

PART TWO

THE KINGDOM OF GOD IS PEACE

The real and overriding result of worship
Is peace with God.

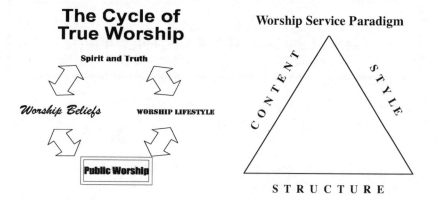

Chapter Six

PURITY IN PUBLIC WORSHIP
Corporate Peace With God

The Woman at the Well

The Master sensed in His Spirit that the Father was finished for now in the regions around Jerusalem and in the city itself. The Pharisees were at it again, stirring up opposition, or trying to, with the disciples of John. It was time to head back to Galilee. The thought of being with His family again pleased Him. Even if He didn't make it to Nazareth, maybe James and the others would bring His mother, Mary, to hear Him preach in the countryside or by the sea.

But there was something more in His Spirit. He needed to go through Samaria. The Father had business for Him there. Someone had an appointment with destiny, with grace. "This will not be good news to the men," he may have thought. It was the hard way to go, mountainous the whole way, an exhausting trip. There was an easier road. A traveler could descend from the hills around Jerusalem to the Jordan and make the northward journey on the easy road by the river. He had warned them, "Foxes have holes, birds have nests, but the Son of Man doesn't have a place to lay His head." They had learned it was more than a saying. So, the hard road it would be; appointments must be kept.

They conquered enough hills and valleys to get as far as Sychar where Jacob's well still supplied the village. Jesus was weary and the day's heat was approaching its fullness. He sent the men into the village for provisions. Twelve men were not really needed for such work, but He had an appointment to keep and only one man was needed for that.

Soon she came, bearing a water pot to the well. She was pretty, or at least she had been at one time. As she squinted against it, the noonday sun brought out the wrinkles around the corners of her eyes. Jesus could see that she was thirsty, too.

He approached her. She saw Him and started to shrink back from the well. He had all the markings of a Jew, one who thought himself above her in every way. Then she dared to look into His eyes. There was no pride there. It was a friendly face. She did not retreat.

"Will you give me a drink?" He asked, indicating her jar.

This startled her. Perhaps the friendly face masked a hostile heart. It could be a trick to get her in trouble with the Jews or her own leaders. Men cannot be trusted. She knew that for a fact.

"You are a Jew," she answered, "and I am a Samaritan woman. How can you ask me for a drink?" She would follow the acceptable lines of behavior. She knew the games men played. She must not be seen with them in public, but at night, they were interested in her company. But this man . . . this man seemed different from all the rest. There was something in His manner that set her at ease . . .

"If you knew the gift of God and who it is that asks you for a drink, you would have asked Him and He would have given you living water."

"Living water," that was a new one. Her thoughts began to race. This one certainly *was* different. "If I knew who it is", what does that mean? A deep instinct told her to leave this one alone. Get him a drink and send him on his way. But a deeper need said stay. Stay and hear what he has to say.

"Sir, you have nothing to draw with and the well is deep. Where can you get this living water?" Now her words raced almost as fast as her thoughts. "Are you greater than our father Jacob, who gave us this well and drank from it himself, as did his sons and his flocks and herds?"

"Everyone," Jesus broke into her stream of questions, "who drinks this water will thirst again, but whoever drinks the water I give him will never thirst." This stopped short her rapid analysis of Jacob's well. She squinted her eyes even more than the noonday sun required as if to better target His face. "Indeed," He went on, " the water I give him will become in him a spring of water, welling up to eternal life."

Silence for a moment. She tried to connect these thoughts: Living water . . . a spring inside . . . never thirst . . . eternal life. A curtain seemed to open slightly in her mind. Perhaps He was talking about her other thirst, not for water but for . . . life. There had always been something in life that escaped her grasp. She had searched for it in the people she had known, in the religion of her fathers but whatever the something was, it had eluded her. Perhaps this man . . .

"Sir . . . give me this water . . ." Perhaps she was too forward. She slowed down. " . . . so that I won't get thirsty and have to . . . keep . . . coming here to draw water." Settle down, she told herself. You just met this man. You don't know anything about . . .

"Go, call your husband and come back."

That stopped her short. My husband, she thought, I don't even know where he is . . . but, maybe he means . . . wait a minute. He doesn't know anything about us, about . . . me. He's just fishing for information. Men, they're all the same.

"I have no husband." Let him think about that.

In the moment of silence that followed, a friendly breeze stirred the dust around the well. I wish you could have the breeze without the dust, the woman thought. But that's the way life is, the good with the bad . . .

"You are right when you say you have no husband. The fact is, you have had five husbands, and the man you now have is not your husband. What you have said is quite true."

The little breeze was suddenly most inadequate. She needed air as if she were in a closed chamber. Her thoughts raced again, even without adequate oxygen. How could he know? . . . five husbands? . . . The village only knows of four.

The first was when I was so young and only someone from my hometown could . . . How did he . . . ? But this one, now—the village thinks we are married, but we never have bothered . . . Who has he been talking too? No one knows what He knows? Maybe He is . . .

"Sir, I can see that you are a prophet." She said it and thought it in the same instance. A prophet, she thought, yes that must be it. But he has struck too close to the mark when he starts counting the men in my life. Let me get him on some other subject . . . "Our fathers . . . worshiped" (yes, that's a good topic!) " . . . on this mountain, but you Jews say that the place we should worship is in Jerusalem." Would he follow her into a safe, discussion about tradition and leave her love life to the village gossips?

"Believe me, woman," He replied. Something in his voice made her think she should do exactly that. "A time is coming when you will worship the Father neither on this mountain nor in Jerusalem. You Samaritans worship what you do not know; we worship what we do know, for salvation is from the Jews. Yet a time is coming and now is when the True Worshipers will worship the Father in spirit and truth, for they are the kind of worshipers the Father seeks. God is spirit, and his worshipers must worship in spirit and truth."

Every word he spoke stirred her heart. He was right. Her people had tried to have it both ways—a little bit heathen and a little bit godly. Perhaps this is what is missing. But, if she understood him correctly, the Jews weren't altogether right either. "Neither in Jerusalem" he had said. Was this just more confusion? If not the Samaritans or the Jews, who was right? What she did not need was more confusion.

"I know that Messiah is coming." She sighed with resignation. "When he comes, He will explain everything to us." The breeze stirred again. The swirling dust assaulted her eyes. The Messiah. Was he real? Or was He just a breeze himself, scattering the dust of their lives with brief moments of hope.

She looked up from her thoughts, not really expecting a reply. Discussions usually ended with references to Messiah.

She saw that the man was staring at her waiting for her to look at him. Reluctantly she lifted her face to his. When he spoke, His words were like water to her thirsting spirit.

"I who speak to you am He."

Twelve men approached from the path to the village. They were shocked to see Him speaking to such a woman. He should be more careful. But none of them had the courage to correct Him. At the sight of other men, the woman quickly withdrew, leaving her water jar behind. She ran into the village telling anyone who would listen, "Come see a man who told me all I ever did. Could this be the Christ?"

The Lord's followers urged Him to eat what they had procured. "I have food to eat that you know nothing about." Had someone else brought Him food? He certainly looked refreshed. Perhaps the woman . . .

"My food," said Jesus, "is to do the will of Him who sent me and finish His work." He went on to talk about the harvest and how to tell when it was about to happen, about reaping and sowing, but not a word about the food they had brought.

Soon, the Lord did partake, and all the food was eaten. He was grateful to the men who had found it for Him. As the meal was just finished, a delegation came to the well from the village. The woman had told them about Him. As He spoke to them, answering their questions, they soon forgot all their errands and duties for a day that was only half spent. They asked if He could stay with them. He did, for two days. Later one of the men was overheard telling the woman, "We no longer believe just because of what you said; now we have heard for ourselves, and we know that this man really is the Savior of the world." It was an appointment with destiny.

THIRST

If all we do is count the men in her life, we may miss her true significance, for the Samaritan woman represents all of mankind. She was thirsty for more than just water from Jacob's well. She was thirsting for life itself. We may not identify with her in knowing so many men, but don't we know people who have tried five or six jobs, weight-loss plans, or even five or six churches? She was looking for something to satisfy her thirst. She was desperate. A Samaritan, she was even willing to defy the rules of society to talk to a Jew. She was willing to try something called "living water" without even talking to man-number-six at home. She looked in the religion of her fathers and tradition failed her. But she found life one day at Jacob's well. She found it in Jesus and He became a well in her, springing up to life everlasting.

We know people just that thirsty. They have thrown over any concern for what society may think. We see those around us ready to try any scheme that promises happiness advertised on late night television, or on the internet, sending their credit card numbers to total strangers. She looked for a relationship in men and didn't find it.

But notice please that the first line of dialogue is spoken by Jesus, "Woman, give me to drink." Just as she represents a thirsting humanity, Jesus represents a thirsting Divinity. It is true that Jesus was tired and thirsty that day because of the rough road He had traveled to get to Sychar; and He is certainly no longer tired and thirsty, seated at the right hand of majesty on high. But He is still thirsty, thirsty for a drink from the well of our thanksgiving. He wants to drink deep from the waters of our adoration. God is thirsty for our worship. It means as much to Him as water to a parched tongue.

As Jesus dealt personally with the woman at the well, He articulated what I believe to be the heart of the whole Bible on the subject of worship. The Father is looking for True Worshipers, those who will worship Him in spirit and in truth. This reveals the passion of the Father and the reasoning behind His plan. It also reveals much about us.

The Father is seeking each of us for the purposes of a relationship. He isn't passively sitting by in some heavenly alcove watching our goings and comings on the earth. He is seeking. By His Spirit, He is pursuing us. In spite of all man has said and done to the contrary, the inner conviction that there is a God persists in the heart of modern and post-modern man. Why?—because God the Father is seeking. His Spirit is striving with man, with each human being.

It begins with a conviction of sin. When salvation comes, the inner prompting becomes the voice of the Shepherd sounding within the hearts of the sheep. He constantly calls us upward into godliness, integrity, love, passion, discipline, and fruitfulness. The engine that runs all these processes in our lives is the Holy Spirit, the life of God. When we worship God in spirit and truth, our spirits connect with His Spirit and all of this quality of life becomes possible. "God is spirit." We must activate the spirit part of us if we are to connect with Him. That can only happen within the arena of truth: total sincerity on our part, and faithfulness to His promises on His part.

We, on the other hand, are not as focused. We are not sure what we are seeking. Vaguely identified impulses move us. Natural tendencies define how we organize our response to the world around us. These tendencies are formed by natural causes:

- genetics,
- environment,
- culture; and by
- spiritual influences: God himself, (through Scripture, godly institutions and traditions), satanic influences (directly or indirectly), and our own human spirit.

The sum total of all these influences means that each of us can be found somewhere on the spirit-and-truth scale.

SPIRIT AND TRUTH SCALE
(Extremes of Human Nature)

SPIRIT——————————TRUTH	
(Passion)	(Reason)
Emotive	Intellectual
Expressive	Reserved
Impulsive	Compulsive
Extreme Mood Swings	Slight Mood Swings
Undisciplined	Disciplined
Empathetic	Sympathetic
Loves New Things	Hates New Things
Hates Routine	Loves Routine

The extreme "spirit" personality is:

emotive	capable of wide emotional swings	loves new things, experiences, methods, and ideas
expressive	undisciplined	hates the routine, etc.
impulsive	empathetic	easily moved toward change

The extreme "spirit" personality is:

intellectual	capable of limited emotional swings	hates new things, experiences, methods, and ideas
reserved	disciplined	loves the routine, etc.
compulsive	sympathetic	difficult to move toward change

Most of us fall somewhere on a line between the two extremes but we lean toward one or the other. Most likely, we have conquered the negative aspects of our natural extreme and adopted enough of the opposite characteristics to get by in the world. Jesus was saying that we cannot worship God within the natural confines of our personalities. True worship will stretch us beyond our comfort zones. As we study the scriptural accounts of those who encountered God, we see that their comfort zones were casualties of such encounters. In the Bible we see God consistently stretching His people into new areas of truth and spirit. He still seeks to do the same for us today. A balance of "spirit" and "truth" characteristics will lead us through an effective life of worship/service to the Lord.

> *True worship will stretch us beyond our comfort zones.*

SPIRIT AND TRUTH SCALE
(Supernatural Balance of Spirit-Controlled Temperament)

SPIRIT	BALANCED	TRUTH
Emotive	Feeling and Thoughtful	Intellectual
Expressive	Expressive	Contemplative, Reserved
Impulsive	Spontaneous, Organized	Compulsive
Extreme Mood Swings	Creative, Consistent	Slight Mood Swings
Undisciplined	Flexible, Dependable	Disciplined
Empathetic	Sensitive, Compassionate	Sympathetic
Loves New Things	Embraces both New and Old	Hates New Things
Hates Routine	Innovative, Structured	Loves Routine

The Lord insists that our worship expression not be limited to what comes naturally or easily to us. The "spirit" personality grows bored easily. He prefers innovation to tradition, new songs to old songs, spontaneity to planning, and emotion to reason. The "truth" personality is comforted by the familiar and discomforted by the new. He prefers the old songs. He is secured by well-planned events. He distrusts emotion and prefers a careful, well-reasoned approach. The "spirit" person will find simple songs useful because he wants to pour out his heart to God. The easy tunes and repeti-tious lyrics give all the framework needed for his heart-song. His is the song of the innovative church, in tune with the times, in touch with what the Spirit is saying to the churches. The "truth" person prefers complicated songs that challenge the mind. He respects the work that has gone into them. He is touched by the many-faceted truths these songs celebrate. He too is pouring out his heart to the Lord, but in a reserved, careful manner. His heart-song is that of the historical church, in tune with what the Spirit has said to the Church. He is joining his voice to the generations of the past who have celebrated these truths and prayed these prayers with these same words and melodies.

If our goal is to please ourselves, we can leave things there. But if our goal is worship that pleases God, passion and rea-son demand that we stretch beyond what comes naturally for us to those things that must come supernaturally. We all have work to do. The "spirit" person must learn to appreciate the truth and spirit of the historic songs of the faith. He must learn that God can lead us to *plan* as well as to *lead* worship; that God values preparation as much as heartfelt spontaneity; and that God may still be moving in traditions that are biblical. The 'truth" person must learn that every song doesn't have to be a treatise. Some songs are simple so that the human spirit can soar on winds of worship. He needs to loosen up and enjoy the presence of the Lord. After all, joy is commanded, too! Emotional expression is a God-ordained part of worship.

With these thoughts in mind let us pursue the purity of expression the Father is looking for—spirit and truth. We must take a truthful look at what is happening when people gather to worship.

Current Worship Practice

Worship services on any Sunday morning in any city, town, or country lane contain an amazing variety of activity and sound. Even if we narrow the field to those who hold to the Scriptures as the supreme authority in faith and practice, the bewildering display of contrasting events and sounds remains. How have so many who claim both a personal relationship with Jesus and the Bible as their source of truth come to so many different conclusions about what worship should involve?

Part of the answer is found in the diversity of society itself. People in particular geographic areas or sections of society like different music and different types of public expression. This is nothing to be alarmed about as long as culture does not overthrow the Word as the guiding influence, the voice of reason.

More powerful than the general cultural influence is the history and tradition of each definable group. Here passion enters the picture. The oft-repeated history of most traditions is this:

- In the first generation men and women seek to restore biblical authority and practice, and the fires of revival burn brightly.
- In the second generation, the methods of the first generation are analyzed and refined into traditions; revival fires began to flicker and dim.
- The third generation either accepts and perpetuates these traditions or rebels and seeks to renew the fervor of the first generation. If not stoked with new fuel, the revival fires go out. Church tradition becomes as important as biblical revelation. What God has said is rehearsed, but what God is saying is ignored. When institutionalized, the vestiges of former revivals can become barriers to the fresh move of the Spirit. Styles of music and orders of worship that once may have flowed with the anointing of the Spirit may now have little or no use in the hands of the Holy Spirit.

How can we know which traditions to let die? How can we recognize the fresh winds of the Spirit so we can open up the windows of our souls in that direction? Again, the Word is the only sword capable of dividing the soulish call of tradition from the spiritual call of God. The Holy Spirit will guide our reasoning as we consult the Word of God. We must ask telling questions:

- Does all this cultural/worship activity result in corporate peace with God?
- Is there peace in our churches?
- Or, is the church riddled with self-interest and strife?
- Are leaders more concerned about careers or power or position?
- Is the church one kingdom led by King Jesus, or is it a loose confederation of little provinces with border wars constantly being waged.

True worship will result in one kingdom—the kingdom of God here on earth as it is in heaven. His kingdom is defined as peace. If peace has not come to a church, there is work to be done on the worship experience of that church.

To do that work, we must pull the camera back from the issues of our own hearts to a much wider view, that of the local church gathered to worship God in spirit and in truth. Just as God the Father is searching the world for True Worshipers, Jesus the Son is seeking throughout the earth to present to himself a spotless Bride, a glorious Church. "Husbands, love your wives, just as Christ loved the church and gave himself up for her . . . to make her holy, cleansing her by the washing with water through the word, . . . and to present her to himself as a radiant church, without stain or wrinkle or any other blemish, but holy and blameless" (Eph. 5:25-27).

The King James Version of this passage is filled with fascinating word meanings. Here are a few definitions from Strong's:

- *"church"* 1) a gathering of citizens called from their homes into some public place; an assembly 2) in a Christian sense a) an assembly of people gathered for worship in a religious meeting b) a company of Christians . . . those anywhere, in a city, village, constitute such a company and are united into one body; the whole body of Christians scattered throughout the earth; the assembly of faithful Christians already dead and received into heaven.

- *"sanctify"* 1) to render or acknowledge to be venerable 2) to separate from profane things and dedicate to God, consecrate 3) to purify
- *"cleanse"* 1) to make clean a) from physical stains and dirt: e.g. utensils b) in a moral sense; to free from defilement of sin and from faults; to purify from wickedness; to free from guilt of sin; to purify; to consecrate, dedicate
- *"present"* 1a) to place beside or near . . . to bring to, bring near; metaph. i.e. to bring into one's fellowship or intimacy 2) to stand beside, stand by or near, to be at hand
- *"glorious"* 1) held in good esteem, of high repute a) illustrious, honorable, esteemed b) notable, glorious c) splendid
- *"spot"* 1) a fault, moral blemish; of base and gluttonous men
- *"without blemish"* 1) free from faultiness, unblameable

Let's reason out the definitions into a paragraph.

Jesus wants to present (to stand near; to have at hand) **to himself a Church** (called out ones) **which is glorious,** (notable, splendid), **spotless and without blemish** (without blame). **To do this He is washing us with the water of His Word, sanctifying us** (setting us apart from profane things, dedicating us to God, consecrating us to himself, making us wholly true, venerable) **and cleansing us** (from physical stains and dirt, from defilement of sin, from faults, from wickedness and from guilt of sin).

Just as Jesus is concerned with us as individuals, He is concerned with us as a group. He has called us out from privacy to public lives of effectual worship, excellent works, and eloquent witness. He wants to wash us with the water of the Word (the point of this whole study) until we are recognizable any place in the world as the people of God. He wants to take us, as one would dirty utensils, and cleanse from us the filth of this world and the defilement of our own hearts. He wants to shine us until we gleam with the reflected light of His excellence and are useful for His purposes. He wants to ignite in us a passion for Him and to light the pathways of our lives with reason.

In this chapter we will pursue those purposes by the examination of our public worship practice. We will search for the "clean hands" we discussed in Chapter Five. This search begins with our motivation for worship.

Purity in Motivation

In Chapter One we dealt with the imposition of culture and personality on the worship experience. This happens without effort on our part. With effort (obedience to Scripture), we can develop a worship practice that pleases God and at the same time reflects the unique characteristics of our culture and personality. The same is true concerning our motivation to worship. Without effort on our part, base motivations, personal needs, and public pressures shape our worship practice. Our passion will be spent on these things. It is natural for us to impose our motivations, good and bad, upon our worship. It is supernatural for us to worship God from a pure heart, free from selfish motivations. It is here, in the area of motivation that we need the Refiner's Fire and the Launderer's Soap. God's peace will never come to a church riddled with self-interest.

The words of God through Malachi speak to this process. "See, I will send my messenger, who will prepare the way before me. Then suddenly the Lord you are seeking will come to his Temple; the messenger of the covenant, whom you desire, will come," says the Lord Almighty.

"But who can endure the day of his coming? Who can stand when he appears? For he will be like a refiner's fire or a launderer's soap. He will sit as a refiner and purifier of silver;

he will purify the Levites and refine them like gold and silver. Then the Lord will have men who will bring offerings in righteousness, and the offerings of Judah and Jerusalem will be acceptable to the Lord, as in days gone by, as in former years" (Malachi 3:1-4).

As the New Testament "Levites", as "Judah", and as the "spiritual" Jerusalem, we can welcome the Lord's ministry as Refiner's Fire and Launderer's soap. What do these terms mean? They are God's plan for preparing us to worship Him in ways that please Him—"offerings . . . acceptable to the Lord." The Refiner's Fire was used to melt the precious metal so base metals could be separated from them. The Launderer's Soap was a strong cleansing agent used to deeply clean cloth before it was dyed. To me, these biblical images illustrate two ways God deals with us. Let's use reason to apply these to our lives.

The Refiner's Fire is at work when the Lord allows heat to be applied to our lives, the heat of circumstance, of pressure, of life itself. As the best part of us melts away under the heat, impurities come to the surface; bad attitudes, impure motivations, all manner of fears, and any number of flaws. When they suddenly appear, we may be shocked by them but the Lord knew they were there all along, hidden by His grace in our lives. It took the Refiner's Fire to reveal these hidden passions. Once revealed, they can be disposed of at the Cross.

In a similar way, the Lord will act upon the deepest fibers of the fabric of our lives with **The Launderer's Soap.** As we obey Him day by day, plunging ourselves into His Word and His Presence, He begins to reveal to us the remnants of worldly thinking deep in our hearts, flawed reasoning, left-over particles of our previous lives that cling to the inner weavings of our human garment. If these things are allowed to remain, the true colors of redemption will not be absorbed in these places. But the Launderer's Soap cleanses them away so that Jesus can go to the deepest part of us. The Launderer's Soap promises a thorough cleansing through an ongoing process of revelation and redemption.

On occasion the Lord has allowed my soul to be heated to the boiling point by the pressure to produce which is inherent to the music ministry. Invariably those times have revealed impurities in my heart. I've been amazed at some of the things I have said under pressure. These remarks and reactions have served to reveal to me the hidden things in my own heart and they created work for me as I have had to seek out those wounded souls who witnessed a staff pastor "lose it." There have been other times when, in the routine of study and prayer and attendance to worship, God has revealed impurities in my spirit. I need both the passion of the Refiner's Fire and the reasoning of the Launderer's Soap.

The Lord promises to act upon us like a purifier of precious metal. He does not change iron to gold, he purifies gold from base ingredients. He further promises to change the basic colors of our soul to match His splendor. In other words, He takes our motivations and purifies them so that our offering to Him (what we say and do in worship) will not be spoiled by hidden impurities. It will be "an offering in righteousness," "pleasing unto the Lord." Our natural motivations will be acted upon by the Holy Spirit; changed, sanctified, and energized. The end result of the Refiner's Fire and Launderer's Soap is peace.

So, we come to face our motivations for worship. What are some of the common impurities for worship, especially worship leading? Since worship often involves music, the impure motivations for making music must be included in the survey of motivations for worship.

- Sometimes **talented people** are problem people. Talent can be a frightening thing, especially when developed into prodigious musical skill. Many times talented people are looking for a stage and an audience, seeking the applause or appreciation of men. To deny this motivation in the musician's heart is to be less than honest. Music is made to be heard. It is incomplete until it is shared with someone else. When music is presented it is an intensely personal thing. A musician's performance or composition is like a child of his soul. If it is accepted and brings joy to someone else the deep satisfaction to the musician can be intoxicating. He can begin to set his heart on pleasing men and this motivation can spoil his offering to God. The worship service becomes a place for talent to shine. This is idolatry.

- **Insecure people** can seek recognition. When people are insecure about themselves or their gifts, many will seek out the church as a little pond where they can be the big duck. It is opposite of what is said of New York City, "If you can make it here, you can make it anywhere." In the church it is, "If you can't make it anywhere else, you can make it here." Because "whosoever will may come" into the fellowship, people with abnormal needs for recognition can find it in singing, or playing an instrument, or leading the singing. Someone must sing, play, and lead but some people are in it for the recognition it brings them, not the service they bring to God.

- **Lonely people** can be looking for acceptance. So much in our world isolates people. People with musical skill are admired but held suspect, sought out but misunderstood, and sometimes, required but resented. Many in church have found the joy of gathering with people like themselves. There is sweet fellowship among the people of God but this is a by-product of worship, not the chief motivation.

- **Manipulators** are always seeking subjects. If there ever was a playground for manipulators it is the church. We are so dependent on volunteers and those who can push and organize and get things done, we are ripe for the manipulator. Many churches suffer because there are too many kingdoms and too many kings ruling over petty little power-patches. This is not the purpose of worship.

- **Driven people** are always looking for results. Many of us are driven to succeed and the church is our means to that success. For the worship leader, pastor, or musician the worship service may become a means to an end and not an

144 / Stephen R. Phifer

end in itself. We have an agenda and the worship service is such an effective way of meeting our goals and those we have for our people. Before I experienced the "Ministry to the Lord" revolution I looked at public worship this way. I wanted my singers, musicians, and actors to attend worship so they would hang in there until the next production when I would need them again. I was driven to succeed, to *produce*, and I needed these people to do what I wanted to do. If they were faithful to worship, they would be available to me when I needed them. I have long ago repented of this but I do not think I am the only music leader, or the only pastor, to have this base motivation.

- **Anointed people** can be looking for satisfaction. Many people are called to sing, play or lead. This is a heavy responsibility, creating deep needs. These needs can only be satisfied by ministry. If ministry is not available there is an almost unbearable restlessness. The temptation is to force ministry just to meet our own needs. This satisfaction, too, is a by-product of public worship, not the main point.

Now, let us take the same list, after the Refiner's Fire and Launderer's Soap have done their work.

- **Talented and skillful people** are now empowered by the Holy Spirit. They look for places to serve not shine.
- **Insecure musicians** now secure in the revelation of the Holy-Royal Priesthood are content and secure in a relationship with Jesus.
- The **lonely ones** now lost in the crowd at Mt. Zion and citizens of the kingdom stand confidently among the throngs of the redeemed.
- **The manipulator** now humbled under the mighty hand of God is under God's control, seeking colleagues not subjects.
- **Driven people** now relaxed and resting in the call of God, seek His pleasure and discover the joy of obeying God and watching Him do the work.

- **Anointed ones** now satisfied with His touch, patiently wait for the open door and never envy the doors God opens for others. The Refiner's Fire and Fuller's Soap have cleansed the impurities from the heart. The talented are still talented; the anointed are still anointed but corrosive motives have been cleansed from their lives. Talented people can live and work together in the peace of God only when these conditions are met. Otherwise there will be constant skirmishes if not all out war.

What are the proper motivations for worship? Really, there are only two: He is worthy, and He commanded it. The worship service should be focused on God not on us. Unless this is in view, biblical principles and directives will not make sense. We must take our hands off worship and turn it back to Him. Leaders must not use worship to their own ends. We gather together simply because He is worthy and He has commanded it. Our agenda must be set aside and His agenda sought. If our needs are the focus, we will most likely carry them out the door with us when the service is ended. If His desires are the focus, He will indwell our ministry to Him and ease the burdens off our shoulders. We can exit the sanctuary free of them. It is not our service, not one minute of it. It is His, beginning to end. Why? Because He is worthy, and He has commanded it.

Purity in Method

Now, for the clean hands—biblical methods of worship. Remember this is for Him, not us. What pleases Him, what He has called for in Scripture, is what matters. If something God desires offends us, *we* must be the one to adjust our values. *He* will not change to match our sensitivities. Perhaps this is the place to ask the three questions presented in Chapter One:

- **Will I worship to please myself?** Will my worship goal be to function within my comfort zone of cultural and personal preferences? Is the point of the service to worship until I feel better, to the point when I am refreshed?

- **Will I worship to please others?** Will I constantly bear in mind the preferences of a power group within the church, or the standards of a previous generation? Will tradition, and not the Word of God, be the source of my standards of content and intent?
- **Will I worship to please God?** Will God's expressed preferences be my goals? Will I pour out my appreciation and love for Him obediently, as led by the Holy Spirit, regardless of man's assessment? Will I praise and worship God according to the glory due unto His name, or the decorum due unto my name?

If we are to be the end of the Father's search, a True Worshiper, and, if we are to be a part of the "glorious Church" that Jesus is seeking, there is only one answer—"I will worship to please God!" This is the only answer that leads to peace; the others will end only in strife.

Principles and Directives

As we apply reason to the biblical study of worship, we must realize that there are two types of biblical truth on worship, principles and directives. Biblical directives are specific instructions for specific instances. The principles are higher, more general, guiding truths. Principles are always true. Directives are true only as the Holy Spirit leads. This is one of the many applications of the spirit and truth revelation. The principles and the directives form the body of truth about worship and are used as the Spirit leads. The directives are tools for the expression of our passion in worship. The principles are the guidelines for our reasoning as we plan our organizations and services.

Biblical Directives for Worship. Directives are found in several forms in the Bible, direct commands, testimonies of True Worshipers, and historical records of worshipers who pleased God. There are three types:

- inward expression,
- vocal expression, and
- physical expression.

Since worship must be an outward expression flowing from the heart let us begin with the directives toward inward expression.

Inward Expression

DIRECTIVE	PSALM REFERENCE*
Behold the Lord	27:4
Commune with the Lord	4:4
Consider the Lord (His works or one's heart)	8:3
Contemplate Him	119:15
Delight in Him	37:4
Desire Him (His ways or house)	27:4
Hope in the Lord	31:24
Inquire of the Lord	27:4
Know the Lord	100:3
Long for God	63:1
Meditate on His law, or deeds	1:2
Rest in Him	36:7
"See" Him	97:6
Seek Him	22:26
"Taste" that He is good	34:8
Trust in Him(most frequent directive)	118:8,9

*References from the book of Psalms are most frequent and will be cited only as chapter and verse. Is this an imposition of Old Testament worship on New Testament believers? On the contrary, the New Testament commands us to use the Psalms—three times (Colossians 3:16, Ephesians 5:19, James 5:13). New Testament worshipers used the Book of Psalms. It remains our textbook for worship that pleases God today. Is it not remarkable that there are so few references to animal sacrifices in the Psalms and so many, many references to spiritual sacrifices? This has been God's desire from the beginning.

Authentic inward expression is essential to True Worship. Jesus said that the passions of the heart will come pouring out of the mouth. "You brood of vipers, how can you who are evil say anything good? For out of the overflow of the heart the mouth speaks" (Matthew 12:34). These immeasurable directives will become obvious in our worship.

Worship, and especially worship leading, reveals the contents of the heart. When people get upset about worship, or when a worship leader gets frustrated, it is important to listen carefully to what they say. What are the real issues, musical things or spiritual things? What attitude is presented, a humble, Christ-like spirit or prideful, critical spirit? Proper inward expressions and attitudes of worship will lead to the proper vocal expressions of worship. Lack of these internals will weaken and destroy the worship experience.

Vocal Expression

DIRECTIVE	PSALM or OTHER REFERENCE*
Be silent	Habakkuk 2:20
Bless the Lord	103:1
Call upon God	17:6
Corporate praise	22:22
Corporate prayer	Acts 4:31
Corporate worship	95:6
Cry unto the Lord	3:4
Declare His name, glory, deeds	118:17
Exalt His name, deeds	34:3
Extol His virtue	30:1
Give thanks	18:49
Glorify Him	22:23
Magnify the Lord	34:3
Play musical instruments	150
Praise the Lord	150
Pray with understanding and with Spirit	I Corinthians 14:15
Proclaim His Glory, deeds, name	96:2
Rejoice in the Lord	2:11
Shout unto the Lord	5:11
Sing with understanding and with spirit	I Corinthians 14:15

Some of these modes of expression run afoul of western sensibilities. That should not be surprising since the Bible is not a western book. People in or from different cultures express themselves in decidedly different ways. Culture defines how people express emotion publicly. Northern European cultures are generally reserved and do not esteem the public display of emotion. Mediterranean, Latin, or African cultures express emotion very freely in public. Sincere worshipers whose sensitivities have been forged in the fires of a reserved culture are going to have difficulty with public praying, crying out to God, shouting, rejoicing and so forth. At the same time sincere worshipers from warmer climates will take to these public expressions readily.

While all of this is interesting and important to note, none of it changes what the Bible has to say. All of these methods of expression are biblical whether we are comfortable with them or not. That does not mean that there are no controls or mechanisms to regulate when such expressions are proper. We will reason them out in relation to the principles. Keeping these sensibility problems in mind helps us approach the next category of directives.

The Scriptures do not overlook our physical activity while these inward expressions abide within us and while we vocalize our praise.

Physical Expression

DIRECTIVE	PSALM or OTHER REFERENCE
Bow before Him	22:29
Clap our hands	47:1
Come before Him	65:2
Dance before Him	150
Enter His gates	100:4
Fall prostrate before Him	72:11
Fast unto God	Isaiah 58
Kneel before Him	95
Lift our hands unto Him	8:2
Lift up our heads	24:7,9

Look up to Him	5:3
Offer unto Him	119:108
Process before Him	68:24-25
Rest in Him	16:9
Sacrifice unto Him	107:22
Stand before Him	134:1
Tremble before Him	96:9

This list is not exhaustive, but it is amazing. Each of us, and certainly each denomination or tradition, is tempted to add footnotes and explanations.

- "We do not stand very long."
- "We don't dance in our church."
- "We don't lift our hands."
- "We don't like banners."
- "We don't believe people should fall down."
- "We don't do processions."
- "We will never clap our hands in this church."

There is great potential for confusion in these contradictory commands. Let us look carefully at this clash of traditions remembering the woman at the well. She presented the Lord with a clash of traditions. Surely the answer is still the same—get things on a spiritual level, find out what the Father wants, and put His desires first.

How do we know when to be silent and when to shout? Or how can we know when to be still and when to process, or when to stand and when to bow? How do we know when to consider the Lord's goodness or when to inquire in His Temple? How do we avoid worshiping in the ways that feel natural to us at the expense of things we would rather not do? Is this a biblical menu where we choose the things we like to do and leave the rest alone? Have we elevated our feelings and traditions to the level of biblical authority? It is evident we need more than biblical directives to guide us in our worship.

The biblical principles of worship guide us in knowing what to do and when. There is no way I can overemphasize the importance of the difference between the directives and the principles. If we take only the directives, our worship will be divisive and exclusive, engendering strife, but when we understand the principles behind the directives we know how to let the Holy Spirit lead in worship that pleases God. Our worship will be unifying and inclusive, passionate and reasonable, bringing in His peace.

The Biblical Directives for Worship:

INWARD — How to Worship with My Mind and Heart
OUTWARD — How to Worship with My Voice
PHYSICAL— How to Worship with My Body

Spirit and Truth. The highest truth about worship in all the Scriptures is found in Jesus' words to the woman at the well—"God is spirit, and his worshipers must worship in spirit and in truth" (John 4:24). From the wellspring of this revelation come the principles of worship. True worship will exalt the Lord. True worship will be appropriate, edifying the Body. True worship will flow decently and in order. How do these principles flow from this verse? Again, Strong's definitions help us:

- *"worship"* -to kiss . . . ; to fawn or crouch to, to prostrate oneself in homage (do reverence, to adore)
- *"spirit"* -a current of air, i.e., breath (blast) or a breeze; by anal. or fig. a spirit, i.e. (human) the rational soul, vital principle or superhuman) an angel . . . or God.
- *"truth"* -verity; is not concealing.

What does it mean to worship in spirit and truth? From these definitions we can see that to worship God in spirit involves two things and to worship God in truth involves two things. What spirit can the worshiper bring to the process and what spirit does God bring?

- To worship in spirit is to adore God from our deepest selves, our spirit, and
- to do so at the direction of and in the power of His Spirit.
- I worship in spirit when I worship from my spirit at the direction of His Spirit.

I worship in spirit when I worship from my spirit at the direction of His Spirit.

It is possible to sing on automatic pilot. We know the songs so well, the words don't engage our consciousness. This is not worship in spirit. To engage the spirit, it is necessary to fully engage our soul and body. We can engage body without engaging the mind. A hundred menial tasks are done this way each day. We can engage the soul without engaging the spirit. We have all seen music carry people away emotionally when nothing spiritual was going on at all. But to engage the spirit is to involve the whole person, mind, soul, and spirit. *True worship engages the whole person*. It cannot be half-hearted. It must be wholehearted, hot-hearted, whole-minded, and whole-spirited. It is no light thing to enter the realm of the spirit. To worship in spirit also means to worship at the direction of the Holy Spirit. He can direct us as we plan worship and as we worship using the plan. He can lead us to be spontaneous or He can lead us in structured ways.

What truth does the worshiper bring and what truth does God bring?

- To worship in truth is to worship Him in total sincerity with no hidden purposes and

- to worship the God of the Bible according to the teachings of Scripture.

The skill of knowing God's ways is essential to the free flow of worship in Spirit. To worship in truth is to worship in ways spelled out in Scripture. It also means to worship the God who is revealed in Scripture.

I worship in truth when I worship in total sincerity according to the truth of Scripture.

It is also possible to try to use worship to some other ends. If this is attempted it is not worship in truth. There can be only one motive, to give unto the Lord the glory due His name. I have heard pastors say, "I'm ready to get our church into worship. We tried busing." Worship is not a church growth tool. It must not be used to some other purpose no matter how high-minded or noble. "Praise the Lord, O my soul; all my inmost being, praise his holy name" says the Psalmist David. It is a complete command. Nothing else need be said. But the great worship leader goes on in Psalm 103:1-5:

> *Praise the Lord, O my soul, and forget not all his benefits who forgives all your sins and heals all your diseases, who redeems your life from the pit and crowns you with love and compassion, who satisfies your desires with good things so that your youth is renewed like the eagle's.*

We get the benefits confused with the command. The command to worship is based on God's worthiness not the benefits that we might receive. If we keep our motivation clear and bless Him with all our heart, soul, mind, and strength, He will shower us with benefits. But if we worship only to get the benefits, this is known to Him Who knows all. I have had some very troubled times in my life as a worship leader, but when it came time to lead in worship, I have had to lay all my troubles at the door and worship from a single heart, dedicated to the glory due unto His name. Only this single-hearted, carefully reasoned passion can be called worship in truth.

Worship in Spirit and Truth:

I worship in spirit when I worship from my spirit at the direction of His Spirit.
I worship in truth when I worship in total sincerity according to the truth of Scripture.

Biblical Principles of Worship

In the truth about the Holy Spirit we see the principles of worship. True worship will exalt the Lord. The purposes of the Holy Spirit in the world have to also be His purposes in public worship. The night of the last supper Jesus told the disciples what the Holy Spirit's purposes were.

> *And I will ask the Father, and he will give you another Counselor to be with you forever—the Spirit of truth. The world cannot accept him, because it neither sees him nor knows him. But you know him, for he lives with you and will be in you. But the Counselor, the Holy Spirit, whom the Father will send in my name, will teach you all things and will remind you of everything I have said to you.*
> *When the Counselor comes, whom I will send to you from the Father, the Spirit of truth who goes out from the Father, he will testify about me"* (John 14:16 ,17, 26).

> *But I tell you the truth: It is for your good that I am going away. Unless I go away, the Counselor will not come to you; but if I go, I will send him to you. When he comes, he will convict the world of guilt in regard to sin and righteous-*

ness and judgment: But when he, the Spirit of truth, comes, he will guide you into all truth. He will not speak on his own; he will speak only what he hears, and he will tell you what is yet to come. He will bring glory to me by taking from what is mine and making it known to you" (John 16:7,8 13,14).

If a worship service is led of the Holy Spirit, Jesus will be the absolute center of it for the Spirit has come into the world to reveal Jesus to us. His peace will be our portion. If worshipers are caught up in how they are worshiping rather than who they are worshiping, it is the work of man and not of God. Strife will result. This is why the worship service must be centered upon God and not man. If we allow the Holy Spirit to invest our worship with truth about Jesus and to crown each service with the presence of Jesus, the Church will be edified and the world will receive a powerful witness. Why? Because Jesus has been exalted in that service by the power of the Holy Spirit. Jesus edifies the church. Jesus convicts the lost. We are the earthen vessels. Jesus is the treasure in us.

True worship will be appropriate, edifying the whole body. In First Corinthians we see this principle. If worship is led of the Spirit, it will be "in order." Our public passion will be poured into appropriate, Christ-honoring expressions. In the same passage Paul gives us a guiding principle for what is and what is not appropriate for public worship. "Let all things be done unto edifying" (I Corinthians 14:26 AV)

In some cultures some directives may be appropriate for private worship but inappropriate for public worship. The Lord wants to lead us in appropriate worship. The Holy Spirit is never at a loss for what to do. He always knows just the right song or just the proper thoughts to speak to make each part of the service appropriate. When the moment and music do not match, or when remarks make sudden turns, man is at work and not God.

True worship will honor the presentation of the Word. Some try to establish a conflict between worship and preaching. Such a thing is not in the heart of God. In the Last Supper teaching about the Holy Spirit, Jesus repeatedly calls Him, the "Spirit of Truth." When a worship service is in the hands of the Holy Spirit, people will always be allowed to worship, and the Word will always be presented in one form or another. Worship leaders who try to take over the service and speakers who are threatened by dynamic worship reveal either an un-founded fear or their own insecurity about who they are in God. These attitudes are rooted in the same error: claiming the Holy Spirit's work as ours.

Worship does not belong to the worship leader and preaching is not the property of the speaker. If we claim them, then we must guard them against those who would take "our time" away from us. This strife is not of God. If worship lead-ers and speakers are sensitive to the leadership of the Holy Spirit, a balance of spirit and truth will result. Jesus will be honored in worship and preaching. The church will be edified in worship and preaching. The lost will be convicted by the worship and the preaching. This is precisely the balance of Spirit and truth for which the Father is looking. This is worship that pleases God, full of reason set on fire by passion and passion focused like a beam of light on the Lord Jesus. This is His kingdom come in peace.

This mutual submission to the leadership of The Holy Spirit requires a mature and unassailable bond of trust be-tween the speaker and the worship leader. If there is no trust in this relationship, everything that happens on the platform will be weakened and hindered if not completely destroyed. Preachers and worship leaders must learn to trust and to be trustworthy. The harm done to the kingdom of God by those who seek to turn their platform ministry into a power base is incalculable.

True worship is not concerned with emotional peaks. These are human measures of the soulish response of the peo-ple. True worship is concerned with touching God. When both the worship and the preaching are led and empowered by the Holy Spirit, there is no need to worry about wearing out the saints. Spirit-led worship does not wear out the saints or "peak" too often. Human-powered music can wear people down as well as endless displays of oratory. Since there is no conflict in God's heart between worship and preaching, His leadership will renew the worshipers through both the worship and the preaching. The Holy Spirit wants both to happen in mutually complimentary ways.

True worship will flow decently and in order. If worship is led of the Holy Spirit, the experience will reflect the nature of the Holy Spirit's other creations. The service will flow together in an amazing synthesis of beauty and function. Paul concludes his classic passage on the public worship service this way: "But everything should be done in a fitting and orderly way" (1 Corinthians 14:40). Works of God are like that, "decently and in order," (to use the King James Version language) making sense, going somewhere by a discernible route. Worship services that are disjointed and wandering are the works of man, not the Holy Spirit.

"Fitting and orderly" explains many things that are otherwise puzzling. Why can a great song fall flat in a service? One possible reason is that as great as a song might be, it must be in the right place in the service. I have often described music ministry as having the right song for the right moment. It isn't enough just to have the "truth", we must place it where the Spirit says it should go. God wants to lead us to the right materials and then He wants to help us put them in the right order.

BIBLICAL PRINCIPLES OF WORSHIP:

True Worship Will Honor the Lord.
True Worship Will Edify the Church.
True Worship Is Fitting and Orderly.

Whatsoever

The astounding list of "spirit" directives (stand, bow, be silent, shout, seek, rest, be still, dance) must be approached in the truth of the biblical principles (Christ-centered, appropriate and edifying to the body, Word-honoring, flowing) and in sensitivity to the Spirit of God. In this context of spirit and truth, we can employ the "whatsoever" clauses of the New Testament.

> Let the peace of Christ rule in your hearts, since as members of one body you were called to peace. And be thankful. Let the word of Christ dwell in you richly as you teach and admonish one another with all wisdom, and as you sing psalms, hymns and spiritual songs with gratitude in your hearts to God. And whatever you do, whether in word or deed, do it all in the name of the Lord Jesus, giving thanks to God the Father through him. Whatever you do, work at it with all your heart, as working for the Lord, not for men. (Colossians 3:15-17, 23)

The passage found in verses 15-17 is squarely in the context of the public worship service: "called in one body," "teaching . . . one another . . . singing . . . giving thanks." Verse 23 is given in the context of serving God daily. In other words, those who try to limit worship activity to those things specifically mentioned in Scripture are placing an unnecessary limitation on worship. If we follow the leadership of the Holy Spirit, knowing He will always be consistent with His purposes (the principles) and the Bible (the directives), we can effectively seize the "whatsoever" life presents us and use it to the glory of God. This holds true inside and outside the worship hall. It means the auto mechanic can repair cars as praise to the Lord as my father did. The hospital dietitian can prepare food to the glory of God as my mother did. It also means the modern church can use electric lights, electronic instruments, computers, or any other modern devices in worship.

As long as we are led of the Spirit and are consistent with the Word, we can do "whatsoever" in the name of the Lord, giving thanks, heartily, as unto the Lord and not unto men.

Worship in spirit and truth is the interaction of the principles and the directives. It is as if the Holy Spirit were a painter whose goal it is to paint a portrait of Jesus in each service. He wants to paint a portrait that honors Jesus, blesses the church, and makes sense to each one who sees it. We, the worshipers, from the preacher to the worship leader to the singers and players to the congregation, are the brush in the painter's right hand. In His left hand is a palette full of amazing colors. These are the directives, the biblical methods of praise and worship. Sometimes He draws from vibrant colors and paints a portrait of a rejoicing Jesus taking joy over His people, a returning prodigal, or a lost one found. At other times, the painter may dip into darker hues to paint a portrait of a Jesus who weeps over the city or the wounded multitude, or who is broken-hearted over the apathy of His people. Most portraits will be somewhere between these extremes but each can be a presentation of the Lord because the Holy Spirit is leading and we are following.

> **Worship in Spirit and Truth is the Interaction of the Principles and the Directives.**

Purity in Music

Music is as important to public worship as water is to life. Just as water is the carrier of life's essentials, music is the carrier of our offerings of praise and worship to the Lord. Music occupies a special place among the arts. We know that music pre-dates creation of man because before this world was formed the Morning Stars, the angels, sang together (Job 38:7).

We also know that music is an important part of Heaven (Revelation 5, 14, 15). In fact, when Jesus cleansed the Temple he quoted Isaiah 56:7 where a word meaning "hymn" is used for the prayers that belong in the house of God. The Lord 's declaration was, based on Isaiah's word, that the Father's house must be called a house of singing prayer. Is it any wonder then that musicians are such a target of hell? The enemy knows how important music is to God, so, he singles out those gifted in music and tries his best to confuse their passions and distract them from using their gifts to honor God. Can we really be surprised then that music is such a volatile subject, dividing denominations, generations, and even musicians themselves? This is all Satan's work.

God's work is exactly the opposite. He wants to use music to *unify* worshipers. With a song, thousands can pray the same prayer, praise the same praise, and express the same adoration and worship at the same time. There is tremendous power in this corporate agreement. Through music we can collectively "come away" from the cares of this life and ascend the hill of the Lord and stand in the Holy Place, entering into His peace.

The Role of Musical Excellence

"Out of Zion, the perfection of beauty, God hath shined." (Psalm 50:2, AV). Music is not only important to us, it is important to God. He invented it. He knows when it is right and He likes it to be right. While it is true that He hears the music of the heart, He also has compassion on those who must listen to the music in the air. Just as an inventor cares for the way his invention is used, God is concerned with the quality of our music.

The story of Mary of Bethany (Matthew 26, dramatized at the beginning of this book) illustrates the proper attitude behind the offering (whether musical or otherwise) that pleases God. Jesus was visiting the home of Lazarus, Martha, and Mary. The occasion was a dinner party in honor of Lazarus who had just been raised from the dead. It was the last time Jesus had such a relaxed evening with friends. While He was still eating Mary took an alabaster box of fragrant oil worth a year's wages of a common laborer, broke it and poured it over Jesus' head and feet. The disciples rebuked her for what they considered a wasteful act. Jesus rebuked them. He commended what she did with these words, "She has wrought a good work on me." Modern translations say it something like this, "She has done a beautiful thing to me."

Every Christian musician should strive with passion and reason to do "a beautiful thing" to the Lord. As a musician, this is my opportunity every time I pick up my clarinet to play, or raise my baton to conduct, or lift my voice to sing, or sit down to compose or arrange. I can minister to Him. I can bring joy to His heart. I can do something beautiful to my Savior. The thought that He would listen to my instrument, my choir and orchestra, my voice, my song or my arrangement and declare it to be of eternal value is almost overwhelming. But this is the personal level of musical offerings that please God.

We can learn three vital things about the proper attitude of the musicians' heart from this story. Mary's offering was valuable by objective standards, not subjective ones. It was willingly poured out to the Lord and it was her very best.

Mary's worship had objective standards of excellence. Mary's gift was not a possession with only personal, family, or sentimental value. It was worth a year's wages on the open market. In the church we are sometimes so absorbed in our own closed systems that we value our offerings by personal standards that only apply within the church. "Church" becomes a qualifying adjective for lower standards of excellence. "Church" choirs are not expected to be as good as other volunteer choirs. "Church" productions are not expected to be on par with other volunteer productions in the community. This is an affront to the Lord Jesus. Things done for Him should be excellent by the objective standards of each particular discipline. To have lesser standards for church expressions is delusion of a tragic order. When we fall prey to this attitude, the world laughs at us for the shoddy nature of what we do. On the other hand, a great opportunity is before us. When we are excellent *and* anointed, the world will listen to us and be touched by the truth and power of our artistic expressions. This is something to be passionate about.

Musical standards (good pitch, tone quality, precision, balance, performance quality, subtlety of arrangement, harmonization, orchestration, key relationships and continuity) are objective quantities. We are either in tune or we are not. The trumpets are too loud, too soft, or balanced. The sopranos either sing a good unison or they do not. The vowels sung by the choir are either pure or mixed. The arrangements are predictable and boring or well thought out and effective. The harmony is either the same all the time or appropriate for the text and mood. On and on we could go. Musicianship is musicianship, even in the church. Church music of a deliberately inferior quality is a wall of noise that the unbeliever must scale to get within earshot of our message. It is time for church music leaders to be knowledgeable of musical excellence so musical offerings in the name of the Lord Jesus can be worthy of Him. Reason demands no less.

Mary willingly poured her offering out to the Lord. No one begged Mary to break the alabaster jar. She was so in love with her Lord she had to find her most prized possession to lavish on Him. The church needs singers and instrumentalists who have this heart, the passion, so in love with the Lord they *must* sing and play for Him. A musician that must be begged or handled with care so as not to hurt his feelings or trip his temper is more in love with himself than his Lord. Exodus records that the Tabernacle of Moses was built by skillful people with willing hearts. The same is true of our praise today. The minimal standards that have grown up in the church are closely related to minimal commitments. Churches who become excellent for the Lord are the ones who are willing to train until the skills are developed, to rehearse until the music is ready, and to persevere until excellence in musicianship is routine. Even this process is endued with the peace of God.

Striving for excellence is a cornerstone of music and musical instruction systems. Serious musicians never strive to be mediocre. A professional musician friend of mine said, "We get paid not to make mistakes. Is it any wonder we are perfectionists?" But, excellence to what end? To promote our career or reputation? For the sake of the music itself? The Christian musician has the best reason of all to be excellent—for Jesus! Mary's gift was poured out *to the Lord.* This willing heart is the outflow of a passion for the Lord. Our music can appear outwardly to be focused on God but inwardly be wrapped up in us. People may be fooled for a while but God is not. This type of music will not gain His recognition. Our music should be an offering to the Lord as personal and costly as Mary's precious ointment. If it is for Him, it must be excellent, as excellent as we can make it.

Mary's gift was her personal best. God knows what we are capable of and when we are doing our best. Wherever we may be on the objective scale of musical excellence from beginner to professional, we all have equal opportunity to do our best *for Him.* The Lord certainly appreciates the local standards and cultural conditions that shape how excellent we can be in a given place. After all, He has the heavenly choir and orchestra at His feet—how excellent their music must be! Who are we to think that we are going to be so excellent Jesus will signal the angelic conductor to stop the music so He can hear us? If in itself our excellence will not gain the attention of the One who sits on the throne, how may we please Him?

There is a song not found in the angelic folio, "The Song of the Redeemed!" When we, out of a profound passion for our Savior, begin to pour this song out of our hearts, giving it our best effort, something touches God's heart and the angels must fall silent. We can please the heart of Jesus with music in the mode of Mary of Bethany's gift:

- if our music is of integral worth,
- if it is willingly poured out to the Lord, and
- if it is our very best.

In return, He grants us His presence and His peace.

In Colossians Paul instructs us to teach and admonish each other "in all wisdom" as we use psalms and hymns and spiritual songs. Wisdom is one of the pressing needs of the hour. Unwise music and worship leading can polarize a congregation rather than unify it. Thoughtful leadership is essential when handling something as powerful as music. It is like a delicate high explosive. If the leader is not careful he can blow himself away, and those around him, in an instant. Carefully reasoned wisdom in this area of leadership will be discussed in the appendix in the section on worship leading.

Psalms, Hymns, and Spiritual Songs

Now it is time to discuss the content of our music. Just as the music must be pure, so must the message of our songs. In two passages, in Colossians with relation to the Word of Christ (truth) and in Ephesians with reference to the Holy Spirit (spirit), Paul instructs us that the content of our songs must be "psalms, and hymns, spiritual songs". The explanations of what these terms mean have been many and varied. Again we turn to a standard reference source, Vine's dictionary:

- *"psalms"* . . . a sacred song . . . to musical accompaniment
- "hymns" denotes a song of praise addressed to God
- *"spiritual songs"* "ode"(song)is always used in the New Testament. in praise . . . ,
- *"pneumatikos"* always connotes the ideas of invisibility and power . . . it is an after-Pentecost word— things which have their origin in God, and which, therefore, are in harmony with His character . . . the purpose of God revealed in the gospel by the Holy Spirit. Spiritual songs are songs of which the burden is the things revealed by the Spirit.

Psalms

Psalms are sacred songs, that is, songs set apart to God. They are to be accompanied by instruments. This includes psalms from throughout the Scripture. Singing Scripture must please the Lord—the Bible commands it. Sacred songs with instrumental accompaniment are still being written today. How can we recognize them? If they are set apart to God, they will glorify Him and will encourage others to glorify Him. Note the emphasis, by definition, on instrumental music. The repeated command of Scripture is that we sing *and make music* in our hearts to God.

> *Then my head will be exalted above the enemies who surround me; at his Tabernacle will I sacrifice with shouts of joy;* **I will sing and make music** *to the LORD.* (Psalm 27:6)
>
> *My heart is steadfast, O God, my heart is steadfast;* **I will sing and make music.** (Psalm 57:7)
>
> *My heart is steadfast, O God;* **I will sing and make music with all my soul.** (Psalm 108:1)
>
> *Speak to one another with psalms, hymns and spiritual songs.* **Sing and make music in your heart to the Lord.** (Ephesians 5:19

When the instrumentalist is esteemed as highly as the vocalist, we are on our way to biblical music. Spiritual leaders must be aware of technologies that take away the ministry of those who make music. Living instrumentalists are more work than soundtracks or midi connections but they are worth it. Modern musical technology is a blessing but it must not take the place of people. Manufacturers know this. Some of the leaders in music technology are also leaders in music education. They realize we have to keep training people to make music whether it is with traditional or modern instruments. We leaders must develop a greater passion for musicians than for music. It is part of the biblical plan of God for man.

Hymns

Perhaps no other musical word is as misunderstood as the biblical term "hymn." This word is most often used in a cultural sense than a biblical one. Biblically, when a song of praise is directed to the Lord himself it becomes a hymn or a song of prayer. We tend to think of hymns as old songs printed in books but Paul had no such reference in mind. What he is saying to us is this, "Sing songs of prayer!" He is echoing King David's oft-spoken exhortation, "Sing *to God!*" Psalms can be directed on a horizontal plane as we sing our testimonies and words of encouragement to each other *about* God. But hymns are vertical in direction, speaking *to the Lord.*

It is essential to the Lord's purposes in the Church that we *all* sing prayers of dedication, adoration, and commitment. These may be from Scripture, from the songwriters of the past, or from contemporary writers. This is the vital link between the great worship songs of the historic church and the exciting new music of today—so many of the great songs are songs directed to God himself, songs of prayer. This is the music of the Throne Room of God where God's presence and sovereignty dwell.

Spiritual Songs

Spiritual Songs are songs of invisible power, the power of the Holy Spirit. We call these anointed songs. They are born in the heart of God and throb with His power. Our psalms and hymns may be touched by the Holy Spirit in this way. Also, spiritual songs are those supernatural songs born within the worship service itself, extemporaneously, as the Holy Spirit leads. "Singing in the Spirit" is referred to in the New Testament (I Corinthians 14:15) and has been recorded in revival movements throughout Church history.

Why is there such worship? For one of many reasons, I believe it has to do with the Lord's command that we become as little children to enter the kingdom. With children, singing is spontaneous but soon society squeezes out the impromptu song, leaving it to the accomplished improvisational musician.

I remember our oldest daughter, Nicole, singing in the child's seat on her mom's bicycle when the family was out for a ride. With the wind in her face, she was totally without self-consciousness in her song-making. She was just a toddler with no words to her song, just pure music from the happy heart. In our worship, our hearts can become so full of love for the Lord, that He renews the childlike song-maker in each of us. We can sing these extemporaneous songs with the fresh breeze of the Holy Spirit in our faces, in full knowledge of the Lord's pleasure and in the fullness of His peace.

It is time for church musicians to seek out psalms, hymns, and spiritual songs. We cannot just follow the hits of today or great music of the past and think we have material that pleases God. We must be critical of the lyric content of our songs. God is listening to what we are saying. He wants us to sing Scripture. He wants us to sing prayerful songs and songs of invisible power. There is little room for sentiment and none for shallow "me-oriented" lyrics, or incomprehensible museum music.

Style, Content and Other Biblical Songs

Much of the energy expended in music ministry is spent on issues of style not content; as if God's preferences matched our own. If His character is revealed in His creation, God loves variety. Witness the extravagant display of fish, fowl, and floral beauty. All creation is telling us of a Creator who loves variety. It is inconsistent with His revealed character to conceive of Him as having one favorite style of music. I believe God loves more styles of music than any of us. Our styles, however excellent, will never interrupt the pattern of the heavenly conductor, but our content will, when ministered with excellence of heart and hand.

There are other types of biblical song and other biblical ways to make music. The Bible makes it clear. God wants us to sing joyful songs, new songs, and all types of songs that express praise and worship. He wants us to sing and make music:

- joyfully,
- willingly,
- focused on Him,
- with instruments,
- with the spirit and the understanding,
- to Him as well as to each other and
- he wants us to do it skillfully.

OTHER TYPES OF BIBLICAL SONG

Types of Song	# References*
Joyful Songs (songs of joy, jubilant song)	11
New Songs	9
Songs of Praise(psalms)(with instruments)	6
Songs of Thanksgiving	4
Song of Testimony witness)	3
Songs in the night	3
Hymns (songs of prayer)	3
Celebration songs	2
Spiritual Songs (empowered by the Holy Spirit	2
Songs of the Lord(His song)	2
Song of teaching(song of the Law)	2
Songs of deliverance	1
Songs of Zion	1
Sacred Songs	1
Love Songs	1

*NIV

WAYS TO SING AND MAKE MUSIC

	# References*
Joyfully	25
Willingly (I will sing)	24
To the Lord	22
With instruments (make music)	15
With the spirit	1
With the understanding	1
To one another	1
Skillfully	1
	*NIV

With purity of motivation, method, and music we can please the Lord with our passionate and reasonable worship. We can center our lives on God himself. He will inhabit our praise, be enthroned upon our obedient worship, and use our services of worship as His Office -Place. The River of Life will flow from His Throne in our services and peace will come to our hearts. This True Worship is the ministry of each believer.

Chapter Seven

MINISTERING TO THE LORD
The Path of Peace

Martha of Bethany

From her position near the fire with the lamb turning slowly and the cakes baking in the oven, Martha could just see the corner of Mary's robe. That was all she needed to see. She knew the rest from memory. Jesus was seated in a corner of the largest room in her house. Followers were scattered all over the room in a variety of positions, all with one thing in common—they had to see him and they had to hear him. Mary's position was set. No one dared challenge her place at his feet.

Martha did not need to see that angelic face that men seemed to love so much, staring up into Jesus' eyes . . . not while sweat ran from her own hairline and streaked across her face, a face no less attractive, except for an extra helping of worry lines here and there. With a fire and no cool breezes, how can she look her best and do all the cooking? Martha would love nothing more than to join them, to somehow relax and enjoy His presence. It was like taking a journey to a far away land without any effort. Instead of a vacation without the agony of travel, Martha was stuck in the kitchen while everyone else enjoyed the trip.

But it was worth it, she told herself, to have Jesus in her home. He really seemed to love it here. She, Mary, and Lazarus did everything they could to make him welcome. He was quite simply the most delightful guest she had ever served. He appreciated everything she did for Him and always seemed so surprised that they would honor Him as anyone special. How can one man be so great and so humble at the same time? The one man of all the ones she had seen who could rightfully have demanded so much, demanded, instead, so little.

She wished she could hear what He was saying. Often a burst of laughter would attempt to break through the wall of heat around her but seldom with any success. She knew that if she were in the room with Him she would detect other reactions, too—sudden silences, fleeting glances, and much nervous squirming. As funny as He could be with His stories and observations about life, He could be just as . . . disturbing. Sometimes people stomped away, angry as so many hornets. Sometimes she saw others slink away like guilty little animals of the night.

But many stayed—many! He always seemed to travel with a crowd. Of course there were always the twelve with Him. Why couldn't He do his work with just five or six? Those Galileans could eat! She loved Jesus but she wasn't so fond of some of His men. She wondered many times what He saw in them. And the women they seemed to dredge up! Not polite company at all, the women or the men: prostitutes, adulterers, lepers (now healed, of course), tax collectors. But if He accepted them, she must accept them. And she must feed them. As she stooped to look at the cakes she was baking, the fire suddenly flared up as fat from the lamb dripped onto the burning logs. She needed at least two more hands. She needed . . . Mary!

Her gentle reverie boiled into a rage against her lazy sister, and though she would never admit to it, against Him. She was just Mary, but he, HE was a prophet. He was supposed to know things. Why wasn't He aware of her and her needs? Why would He be so moved by the plight of the multitude or the fate of His disciples during a storm at sea (they were fisherman, for goodness sake!) and care nothing for her with all the work she had to do? Why shouldn't He care as much for her? Why didn't He send some of the others in here to help her? Surely one or two of those . . . women could cook!

She took the cakes out before they burned and stirred the fire so that it was no longer dangerous. But her inner fire was just getting stoked. She paused just long enough to wipe the sweat from her face, remove her apron, and smooth her hair. She burst into the room where Jesus was at just one of those moments of silence.

She didn't know if He was just about to say something incredible or He had just said it, but she didn't care. She had something to say and the Messiah (as well as the others) needed to hear it. She succeeded in destroying the moment and fastening every eye on her. Jesus gave her a knowing smile.

"Lord, don't you care that my sister has left me to do the work by myself?"

Jesus didn't answer.

Martha settled down some and added, more quietly, "Tell her to help me."

The aroma of the nearly-prepared meal drifted through the room. Many realized that they were about to enjoy the fruits of Martha's labors. Maybe they should help some, too. Mary began to stir.

"Martha, Martha," the Lord answered, "you are worried and upset about many things, but only one thing is needed. Mary has chosen what is better, and it will not be taken away from her." The knowing smile never left His face.

All movement stopped. Eyes throughout the room jumped from Martha, to Jesus, to Mary, and back again. Mary mumbled something and, with Lazarus' help, guided Martha back into the kitchen. A pair of women, whose backgrounds one dared not inquire about, moved to help them. Soon the meal was served and a festive mood slowly returned, but everyone seemed to sense that an important moment had passed before them. The meal would be soon forgotten but the words Jesus spoke would stay with them forever, challenging them to remember to spend time at the feet of Jesus, no matter how much work there was to be done.

The Threefold Mission of The Church

And there *is* much work to be done. We are here for a reason. We have a world to win for Jesus. There is a church to build, a kingdom to extend to the ends of the earth. This story, more than any other, illustrates the essential role that worship plays in the church. Why *are* we here? What function does the Church have in the world today? What function will the Church have in heaven? Why do we have all these buildings, instruments, choirs, songbooks, and leaders? If we are to understand worship that pleases God, we must understand the mission of the Church. This truth is the gateway to peace with God.

If our worship services are to be pleasing to God, they must conform to a biblical vision of the mission of the Church. My fellowship, the Assemblies of God, has expressed the mission of the Church in a most challenging way. The mission of the Church is threefold and in this priority:

- **Ministry to the Lord** (worship/word-obedience),
- **Ministry to the Church** (discipleship/fellowship)
- **Ministry to the World** (intercession/evangelism).

What do these terms mean?

- **Ministry to the Lord** is *loving God* as we give Him thanks, as we praise and worship Him, and as we obey Him from the heart.
- **Ministry to the Church** is *loving the Church* with our commitment, fellowship, discipleship, and service, bearing the easy yoke and the light burden. In other words, it is finding our place in the body and doing the "whatsoever" God gives us as unto the Lord and in His name.
- **Ministering to the world** is *loving the lost.* This is done by living holy lives before them, interceding for them in the Holy Place, and communicating to them the truth of the gospel.

How can an evangelical body seemingly place evangelism as the third priority of mission? The answer is this simple. There is only **ONE MISSION** but it is carried out in three dimensions. Worship is the first dimension because we must touch God before we can touch man, either our brothers and sisters in the body of Christ, or a lost humanity. Unless we harbor in our own hands the ability to build great congregations, or in our minds the power of utterance required to speak to the world around us, we had better touch God early and often in each ministry effort. As we have demonstrated from the Scriptures thus far, we touch God with our passionate adoration, our worship and obedience. We can then undertake each endeavor with hearts brimming with His peace, knowing that He is with us.

But, can the priority of worship be the teaching of Scripture? What about the Great Commission? Is not the chief purpose of the Church to reach the lost? This is the ministry of the church in the world *today*. In *eternity*, when all the souls have been saved and all the churches have been built, the church will have only one purpose, the first one, to minister to the Lord.

If we take any one of the four accounts of our Lord's ascension, we will miss an important emphasis, one that be-comes clear when everything Jesus said that day is put together.

MATTHEW'S ACCOUNT (Matthew 28:18-20):

Then Jesus came to them and said, "All authority in heaven and on earth has been given to me. Therefore go and make disciples of all nations, baptizing them in the name of the Father and of the Son and of the Holy Spirit, and teaching them to obey everything I have commanded you. And surely I am with you always, to the very end of the age."

MARK'S ACCOUNT (Mark 16:15-18):

He said to them, "Go into all the world and preach the good news to all creation. Whoever believes and is baptized will be saved, but whoever does not believe will be condemned. And these signs will accompany those who believe: In my name they will drive out demons; they will speak in new tongues; they will pick up snakes with their hands; and when they drink deadly poison, it will not hurt them at all; they will place their hands on sick people, and they will get well."

LUKE'S GOSPEL ACCOUNT (Luke 24:44-49):

He said to them, "This is what I told you while I was still with you: Everything must be fulfilled that is written about me in the Law of Moses, the Prophets and the Psalms." Then he opened their minds so they could understand the Scriptures. He told them, "This is what is written: The Christ will suffer and rise from the dead on the third day, and repentance and forgiveness of sins will be preached in his name to all nations, beginning at Jerusalem. You are witnesses of these things. I am going to send you what my Father has promised; but stay in the city until you have been clothed with power from on high."

LUKE'S ACTS ACCOUNT (Acts 1:4-9): (John does not record the ascension or the Great Commission.)

On one occasion, while he was eating with them, he gave them this command: "Do not leave Jerusalem, but wait for the gift my Father promised, which you have heard me speak about. For John baptized with water, but in a few days you will be baptized with the Holy Spirit." So when they met together, they asked him, "Lord, are you at this time going to restore the kingdom to Israel?" He said to them: "It is not for you to know the times or dates the Father has set by his own authority. But you will receive power when the Holy Spirit comes on you; and you will be my witnesses in Jerusalem, and in all Judea and Samaria, and to the ends of the earth." After he said this, he was taken up before their very eyes, and a cloud hid him from their sight.

Taking the whole of what Jesus said that day, especially if we take John 14-17 as Jesus' last words to His disciples in that book, two great truths emerge: We are to preach the gospel to the world, and we need God's power in our lives to do this.

- In the Matthew account, He calls us to preach and then promises to be with us personally.
- In Mark, He is quite detailed in describing the power of the supernatural life to which He is calling us.
- In Luke, He instructs the believers not to try and fulfill the commission until they have received the power from on high.
- In the Acts account, Luke is even more specific in recording the Lord's command to stay in Jerusalem until the power came to communicate with the world.

The story of every great revival is the coming together of these two parts of the Great Commission: seeking God until His power is received, and touching the world with that supernatural power. The story of every great decline from revival to institutionalism is the separation of these two things. Programs and plans are perpetuated without seeking God's plan, and the power of the work is natural, seated in the power of man not God. History makes the degenerative pattern clear: the inertia of organization seems sufficient to carry on the work; there is no need to touch God; the work becomes man's work, done in his power, without the touch of heaven. As we begin the twenty-first century, many Christian groups are following this pattern. One of the first losses in this pattern is corporate peace with God.

The threefold mission of the Church is a call to revolution. It upends our philosophies and programs. If this is really what the Bible teaches, many, many things in our churches and organizations need to change. This is a call to renewal, to revival, and to the most eloquent and powerful witness the world has ever seen. When the people of God learn to prioritize the ministry to the Lord, the Church of Jesus Christ will arise with newfound power, beauty, and integrity. But, questions remain. Is this the path of peace? of True Worship? Is this the way to receive the power to witness? Does the Bible teach the priority of worship? I believe it does.

The priority of worship is consistent throughout Scripture. Consider these facts:

- Before the work of creation began, the Spirit of God moved (Genesis 1:2). Even God delayed the work of creation until after the move of the Holy Spirit. (When will we learn this?)
- The first four of the ten commandments deal with worship (Ex 20:1-11).
- Jesus said that the first duty of life was to seek God and His kingdom. (Matthew 6:33).
- He also said the first and greatest commandment was to love God. (Matthew 22:37-40).
- On the Day of Pentecost before the great sermon was preached, the one hundred twenty sought God in one mind and one accord and their worship was dynamic. (Acts 2)
- The writer to the Hebrews twice exalts worship to the pinnacle of the New Covenant (12:22-24, 13: 15,16).
- Both Paul (Ephesians 1:1-6) and Peter (I Peter 2:9) declare praise to be the purpose of the Church.
- Jesus rebukes the church at Ephesus because service had supplanted the *"first love"* which He identified as the love for God (Revelation 2:1-7).

The most succinct statement of the threefold mission is found in Hebrews 13:15,16.

MINISTRY TO THE LORD: "Through Jesus, therefore, let us continually offer to God a sacrifice of praise— the fruit of lips that confess his name."

MINISTRY TO THE CHURCH: "And do not forget to do good."

MINISTRY TO THE WORLD: "And to share with others, for with such sacrifices God is pleased."

The Mission of the Church
Hebrews 13:15, 16

One Mission in Three Dimensions:

To Minister to the Lord in Worship and Obedience,
To Minister to the Church in Fellowship
and Discipleship,
To Minister to the World in Evangelism,
Holy Living, and Intercession.

This is the only priority that works. " . . . and to share with others, for with such sacrifices God is pleased" means not some other priority, but this one. The placing of priorities does not state that one aspect of the mission is more important than the others. It states instead that one must precede the others. It is not that worship is more important than fellowship-discipleship or evangelism. Some evangelicals are more comfortable saying that worship is central to the mission of the church. Whether we state it as a priority or a centrality, the truth is the same. Our ministry to man *must flow* from our relationship with God—our worship-life.

Why must worship be the source of all other ministry? Let's reason this out:

- If we can live holy lives by the force of our will,
- if we can intercede for the lost in our own power; or
- if we can effectively communicate the gospel through our own eloquence, **there is no need to worship before we witness.**

Further:

- If we can learn about Jesus with the power of our intellect,
- If we can lead the church by the skill of our own hands and the force of our own personalities,

- If we can fellowship with God's people and love them all because of the loveliness of our nature,
- If we can maintain our commitments to the church by the strength of our intentions, **then there is no need to worship *together* and crown Jesus King among us.**

But, if the power *to do* is only found in Jesus by the Holy Spirit, it must be preceded by the power *to be*—to be *"witnesses"* (Acts 1:8) and to be *"sons of God"* (John 1:12). Clearly the true message of the gospel is that we *become* before we *do*. The overwhelming weight of Scripture speaks to us of first things first; we must love God (worship) before we can love man (serve). Our service to man must be the overflow of our love for God. This is the only peaceful flow of power.

This is a practical priority. If ministry to the Church is the first priority in our mission, the Church turns inward and becomes the "Church of the First Families." The Lord will have little opportunity to rule among these people and they will have little impact on their world. If evangelism is the highest priority of the Church, the body will grow in numbers, but there will be little opportunity for new believers to make the Savior their Sovereign. Leaders and their followers will have shallow relationships with God, factions are inevitable, and church trouble is on the way. If worship is the first priority but evangelism is the second priority, numbers and programs will be more important than people. Christians will be regularly used up and thrown away. This certainly does not please God and will not bring in the rule of His peace.

How does True Worship lead to fellowship-discipleship and evangelism? Let us look to Isaiah's life-changing experience. Isaiah was a prophet whose ministry was centered in the two seats of power in Israel, the Temple and the palace. As a young man, his hero was King Uzziah, a good king whose early accomplishments were so impressive that Isaiah was writing his life's story. But, in later years, when Uzziah became important in his own eyes, he lost his throne. He went into the Holy Place and offered incense to the Lord, something only priests could do. He was stricken with leprosy, ending his life in isolation and defeat.

In the year that King Uzziah died, Isaiah received a vision of the Lord, high and lifted up and a commission to speak for the Lord, *"the King,"* as he called Him. Isaiah's life was changed by this tremendous spiritual vision of God. For us as well, this vision of God is primarily a result of worship. The vision is needed so we can hear His call upon our lives and respond. Service at impulse of God's commission is always of a higher quality than service done at the impulse of man. Every service should be structured so that it can be an "Isaiah 6" experience. Praise leads to revelation which leads to worship and commitment which leads to commission which leads to service.

I have let my imagination take me back into Bible times often in this book. Now, let me imagine the future, a time when the church will really be the church. If True Worship were the norm (and I hope someday it will be) the effect upon the lives of the people in the church would be life transforming. I'll look at the church from three complimentary perspectives: corporate worship, corporate life, personal worship. Here is an ideal scenario from the perspective of the total church experience.

CORPORATE WORSHIP EXPERIENCE

As believers express thanksgiving to God and begin
   to verbalize—
His character and deeds with their praise,
His healing presence is visited upon them.
Just like Isaiah, they receive a vision, by the Holy Spirit,
   of the majesty of King Jesus.
The only response to a such a revelation is worship.

CORPORATE LIFE EXPERIENCE

Believers relate to each other in an environment of
genuine love, truth, and peace.
They mature because the church where Jesus reigns is
a good place to grow.
The love of God and the love of brothers and sisters
promote Christian maturity.

PERSONAL EXPERIENCE

At some point, like Isaiah, worshipers break out of
the past.
Seeing the Lord for who He is, they also hear
Him calling them to ministry.
They go out and minister to the world having been
cleansed, empowered, and sent by God himself,
all in the atmosphere of worship in spirit and truth.

The Consequences of Misplaced Priorities

Misplaced priorities are the curse of the modern church.
The social gospel is a case in point for in it ministry to man
supplants ministry to God. Expressive worship is not allowed.
The only way one can express love for God is through acts of
kindness to a hurting humanity. The result is a form of godliness devoid of power.

Evangelical (Pentecostal or not) and fundamentalist
churches are not immune for the ministry to man is also
evangelism out of balance. Events and activities that please
God but do not yield a stack of commitment cards are considered of lesser value than those producing prodigious
"results." For some events the bottom line *is* "souls." For
others an equally valid bottom line is simply the glory of the
Lord. No one was saved when Mary poured her adoration on

Jesus but the glory of the Lord was revealed in her actions. Her service of worship has lead to the salvation of a multitude whose ranks are still growing.

Up-reach must precede outreach. Nothing should rank higher in our philosophy and programs than the worship of God. Idolatry is so subtle. Our service to God can become an idol, as can our preaching, our churches, our homes, or anything else that captures our affections. In many of our churches, "worship" services have become "preaching" services; music programs have become entertainment events; and education and evangelism programs have become Christian trivia meets and high-pressure sales courses in selling the gospel.

Against the backdrop of the darkest hours of Israel's history, the exile to Babylon, a drama is played out that defines the choices that face us today. The priests, singers, instrumentalists, and craftsmen of Israel were uprooted and taken to Babylon. Family after family passed before the priests in exile. Some of these priests elevated the ministry to these dispossessed people above the rituals of worship, joining them in idolatry. Ezekiel pronounces the terrible sentence of God's judgment on those who put the ministry to man above the ministry to God. Other priests had been faithful to the worship of Jehovah with great blessings promised to them

It is not difficult for me to see that the judgments placed by God on unfaithful leaders in Ezekiel's day have also been visited upon the modern Church. As different denominations have strayed from the truth of Scripture or have elevated their traditions to the level of biblical authority, these same results can be seen.

The first loss is the assurance of salvation ("must bear the consequences of their sin"). Many "mainline" churches are filled with people who don't know if they are saved and they don't know how to get saved because salvation is never preached. Instead, a gospel that emphasizes social good is preached. And, just like the Old Testament leaders, they are limited to the ministry to man ("for the people and stand

---

GOD'S JUDGMENTS AGAINST PRIESTS AND LEVITES WHO FAILED TO KEEP WORSHIP PURE (Ezekiel 44)

THEY BEAR THEIR OWN INIQUITY:
The Levites who went far from me when Israel went astray and who wandered from me after their idols must bear the consequences of their sin. (44:10)

THEY ARE LIMITED TO THE MINISTRY TO MAN:
They may serve in my sanctuary, having charge of the gates of the Temple and serving in it; they may slaughter the burnt offerings and sacrifices for the people and stand before the people and serve them. (44:11)

THEY ARE BANISHED FROM THE PRESENCE OF THE LORD:
They are not to come near to serve me as priests or come near any of my holy things or my most holy offerings; they must bear the shame of their detestable practices. (44:13)

---

before the people and serve them"). The ultimate loss is the presence of the Lord. Because worship is not emphasized in the fullness of Spirit and truth, the Lord's presence is not visited upon their services. All that is left is a boring, predictable routine that never connects the heart of God with the heart of man.

Just as God announced judgments on the unfaithful leaders, he made great promises to those who kept their lives centered on God himself. These promises are the opposite of the judgments—God's presence, His work, His strength, His truth, His very life.

These blessings can be seen in the post-modern church that restores True Worship, involving passion and reason and centering all of church life on God himself. They know the healing presence of the Lord. They do the work of the Lord at His direction and His power. They are restored, not depleted as they work for the Lord—burnout is unknown among them. They teach eternal truths to the next generation and the Lord

GOD'S PROMISES TO THE PRIESTS AND LEVITES WHO KEPT THEIR WORSHIP PURE (Ezekiel 44)

THEY ARE PROMISED HIS PRESENCE:

Yet I will put them in charge of the duties of the Temple and all the work that is to be done in it. (44:15)

THEY WILL DO HIS WORK:

But the priests, who are Levites and descendants of Zadok and who faithfully carried out the duties of my sanctuary when the Israelites went astray from me, are to come near to minister before me; they are to stand before me to offer sacrifices of fat and blood, declares the Sovereign LORD. (44:16)

THEY WILL KNOW THE SUPERNATURAL RESTORATION WITHIN THEIR WORK:

When they enter the gates of the inner court, they are to wear linen clothes; they must not wear any woolen garment while ministering at the gates of the inner court or inside the Temple. They are to wear linen turbans on their heads and linen undergarments around their waists. They must not wear anything that makes them perspire. (44:17, 18b)

THEY WILL TEACH THE PEOPLE:

They are to teach my people the difference between the holy and the common and show them how to distinguish between the unclean and the clean. (44:23)

THE LORD WILL BE THEIR INHERITANCE:

I am to be the only inheritance the priests have. You are to give them no possession in Israel; I will be their possession. (44:28)

is their inheritance. The irony of all this is that the priests who prioritized the ministry to the Lord were the ones who were truly able to minister to the people. The choice facing us today is one of omnipotence or impotence. If our first priority is worship, we can minister to people with God's omnipotence. But, if we place ministry to man on a higher priority than worship, this misplaced passion means we can only approach man in our impotence.

A suffering humanity is waiting for the Church to put God first. The lost have had enough of man's plans masquerading as God's work, man's abilities passed off as God's power, and man's fleeting affections offered as the love of God. It is time for us to touch God with our passionate worship. It is time for a new vision of His majesty. It is time to cast all our crowns at His feet so that He can rule in the Church in truth. When worship, (the establishment of His kingdom in our hearts, our homes, our churches, and our services of worship) becomes the first order of business in each meeting and the central ministry around which all other ministries revolve, a new vision will break upon the hearts of the rank and file of the Church. Like Isaiah, we will see the Lord high and lifted up and we will be changed. This is only reasonable!

"Where there is no revelation, the people cast off restraint" (Proverbs 29:18). Through the generations, some church leaders have tried to apply the restraints of Christian living to believers who have not had a revelation of the majesty of their King. It has not worked and will not work. Only revelation justifies restraint. "Where there is no vision, the people perish." The same verse in the AV speaks of a larger tragedy when there is no "Isaiah 6" vision of Jesus. Because the Church falters, millions of souls perish. It takes both a vision of the lost *and* of our wondrous King to make a believer into an evangelist. When the Church lacks this vision, the world suffers, hell enlarges, and the enemy is unchecked. The apostles turned their world upside down because of these things:

- They had a vision of a resurrected Lord,
- They had a relationship with their Lord, through this relationship,
- They had His power flowing in their lives by the Holy Spirit, and,
- They had a vision of a lost humanity.

We cannot inspire others to reach the world by only imparting to them a vision of the lost. A vision of the lost is discouraging and depressing without a vision of the Savior who can reach them through us. If we learn anything from the full account of the ascension, we must see that Jesus never intended for us to try to win the world in our own power. This being the case, then worship, both private and public, must have the highest priority.

A Personal Search

As a third-generation Pentecostal, I have sought the secret of my grandfather's generation. What did they have that we have lost? Years ago I discovered that it was not the outward trappings of "holiness" such as the length of sleeves or hair, the list of things one did not do, or the places one did not go. I believe it was this: My grandfather's generation worshiped God! Huge sections of each service were devoted to corporate praise and worship. Rank and file Pentecostals had vibrant personal relationships with Jesus, relationships maintained in the fires of personal devotion each day and renewed in public worship each time they met together. Subsequent generations have focused on various external expressions trying to legislate them into practice. But without a heart-filling relationship with Jesus, the externals were only that—externals. God is calling us back to the internals, to an overriding vision of HIM and to hearts overflowing with passion for God and love for man. Only this can bring peace and power to the Church.

Obedient Praise

This vision and love will come from the Holy Spirit as we praise God obediently. All of us, whether Pentecostal or non-Pentecostal have taken a position on obedient praise.

- Some Evangelicals sing songs about shouting but would never dare shout in their services.

- Some classic Pentecostals have the freedom to *respond* in worship but are fearful of raising hands or voices before they receive the unction of the Spirit.
- The place we all need to come is this—obedient praise.

Traditions cannot be placed on equal footing with the commands of Scripture. Personal taste cannot be the final court of opinion on what pleases God. Personal feelings cannot be allowed to inhibit our offerings of love to the Lord. If we will praise Him out of obedience, regardless of how we feel and over the objections of our culture and personal preference, then we are really offering the sacrifice of praise and Jesus will inhabit it and be enthroned upon it as we center our lives on Him. All we really need is a vision of His worthiness and a knowledge of His command.

So, the world awaits the believer's ministry. And the Lord himself waits for us. When we put Him first in everything, when loving Him with heart, soul, mind, and strength becomes the Priority One Ministry, when worship becomes central in the mission of the church, we will know the peace of His presence and power of His reign.

OBEDIENT PRAISE

I will praise God because He is Worthy.
I will praise God because He has commanded it.
I will praise God regardless of how I feel.
I will praise God beyond my personal
tastes and traditions.
I will praise God obediently, from my heart.
This is obedient praise.

Chapter Eight

THE PRIORITY OF WORSHIP:
A PREACEFUL REVOLUTION

An Expert Lawyer

He was the silent type, unusual for a lawyer. Not that he couldn't speak—indeed, he was eloquent when it came time to speak—but he was also an expert listener. He had long ago observed that there were many lawyers who were more than willing to speak. He could always count on them to ask the stupid questions or say the wrong things. He determined to do more listening than talking, and this policy had served him well.

For the last few minutes he had been listening to his lawyer friends debate issues of their religion with this one called Jesus. With so many details of the Law of God there were endless trails to run as opinions pursued opinions. It was amusing to watch, especially those who took things so seriously. This observant lawyer was more detached, keeping a safe distance between his opinions and those who might pursue them. He was more of a spectator at these endless races.

By now his colleagues were mentally out of breath, intellectually panting for air. Jesus had beat them. There was no trail they could run that He couldn't outrun them. Our lawyer friend had never seen anyone who knew the Law so well. As he mused over these things, something stirred within him, something that challenged his determination to keep his distance. As long as he could remember he had wondered if there was a heart to it all, some single strand of law that bound all the rest together, that made them all make sense, a single ray of light that illumined all the rest. At times he thought he had seen it only to see the light diffused by the refracting lenses of all those traditions and opinions. Now those lenses were broken and scattered before him and his lawyer friends. Maybe this Teacher from Galilee had discovered what was missing. He had certainly put his time in studying, perhaps . . .

Risking the safety of his detachment, he broke the silence, "Of all the commandments," he asked, and suddenly the attention was focused on him. He squirmed. His colleagues leaned forward; he was the brightest among them and they knew it. It was about time he spoke up. Jesus turned to look at him, and their eyes met. That stirring within him excited an expectation that overcame his discomfort. "Which is the most important?"

The crowd seemed to draw one gigantic breath. Faces jumped back to Jesus. For some it seemed a great trap. How could any answer be right? Every answer had to be wrong. Who has the power to declare one law more important than any other? Who would dare? They had him now.

"The most important one," Jesus answered with almost no hesitation, keeping his gaze fixed on the questioner, "is this: 'Hear O, Israel, the Lord our God, the Lord is one. Love the Lord your God with all your heart and with all your soul and with all your strength.' The second is this: 'Love your neighbor as your self.' There is no commandment greater than these."

All the lawyers except one dropped their glances to the ground. He got away again. That one exceptional lawyer kept his eyes on Jesus. He let the Teacher's eyes search deep into his soul. This was no momentary opinion pursuit, this was the single beam of light he had been looking for that made all the rest make sense. "Well said, . . . Teacher," the man replied, his mind racing faster than he could possibly speak. He thought of the religious systems and how he and the other leaders used all the rules and regulations to control people's lives. He had heard Jesus speak strong words against them. This was why—it was not about rules and regulations, not about control, it was about a relationship with God and, most amazing of all, He with us. Only through this relationship could we really love and help each other . . . "You are right in saying that God is one and there is no other but him. To love him with all your heart, with all your understanding and with all your strength and to love your neighbor as yourself . . . (he turned to his colleagues) is more important than all burnt offerings and sacrifices."

Protests erupted from the other leaders. "How can you say that anything is more important than our sacrifices? Can just anyone approach God without leaders? This will destroy the structure of our nation!" Jesus waved them silent and looked again at the brave one.

"You are not far from the kingdom of God." The questions ended there. We are not told what happened to the lawyer. But we can be sure that if he set about to love God with heart, soul, mind, and strength, that he ended up following Jesus. Surely he made it all the way to the kingdom of God.

Peace

How far is the Church—your church, my church—how far are we from the kingdom of God? Are we lost in rituals and rites or rules and regulations? Do we seek to control people or release them? When we see strife in our organizations from the local level to the highest levels, can we say that the kingdom has come? The kingdom of God is not strife. "The kingdom of God is peace," so our text says and it must be God's will for us. Peace is the legacy of Jesus.

"Peace I leave with you, my peace I give unto you: not as the world giveth, give I unto you. Let not your heart be troubled, neither let it be afraid" (John 14:27 KJV). But, where is this peace? Believers take as many antacids and sleeping remedies as those who do not know Jesus. At minister's conventions, workshops on stress are always heavily attended. Many young ministers are disillusioned within their first few

192 / Stephen R. Phifer

years of ministry while too many veteran ministers burn out just when experience should be taking them into the prime of their ministries. Where is the peace that Jesus left us? Perhaps the better question is, "Where have we left the peace that Jesus left us?" The peace of Christ comes with His sovereignty, when we let Him rule in our hearts. He left His peace for us in His Throne Room. If we have forsaken worship in spirit and in truth, we have forsaken His Throne Room. Only there, beneath the canopy of sovereignty, will we find peace again. "Let the peace of God rule in your hearts" (Colossians 3:15 KJV). If *His* kingdom is peace then *ours* must be stress and strife, hurry and hassle. It must be that His kingdom has not come and His will has not been done but ours has.

We are in need of a revolution of peace, one that returns the Church to its rightful ruler, the Prince of Peace. Changing the music or even the order of our services is not revolution enough. We must change our thinking about who we are, why we are here, and what we are to do. If we root out the crumbling stones of man's fallen philosophies and replace them with the bedrock of the Word of God, Jesus will build His throne on that foundation and begin to reign. If we take the priority of our threefold mission seriously, everything will be altered and the peaceful revolution will begin. Like that of the individual, the ministry of the Church must be the overflow of our corporate worship relationship with God. God's way is this:

- Doing is the result of being,
- Works are the outflow of worship.

A Biblical Balance in Church Philosophy and Programs—A Revolution

We have a model, a measuring stick—the threefold mission of the Church: Ministry to the Lord, Ministry to the Church, and Ministry to the world. These points of mission become qualifying questions for our philosophies.

- Are these priorities reflected in our stated goals?
- Are they reflected in the budget?
- Are they taught to our children?
- Do the leaders agree?

The threefold mission is the acid test of each program.

- Are we ministering to God with this program?
- Does this event build up the body?
- Is the purpose of this activity evangelism?

If a program or activity cannot be said to fulfill at least one of the three points of ministry, it should be dropped from the schedule.

- Is the *order* of priority of the mission reflected in our thoughts, our plans, and our actions?

IMPORTANT QUESTIONS

PHILOSOPHIES

Is the Threefold of ministry reflected in our stated goals?
Are these points reflected in our budgets?
Are they taught to our children?

PROGRAMS

Does this program minister to the Lord, the church, or the world?
Does this program take time and energy away from our primary mission?

If we desire a revolution of peace, we must let the truth of the Scriptures sink as deep as our thoughts can go. The public worship service will not please God until the private philosophy, planning, and practice please God.

Perhaps the best way to describe the revolution this must bring is to imagine a church where this philosophy is the engine running every program. This description will be idealistic

THE IDEAL CHURCH EXPERIENCE

The children and the youth lift their hands and voices in praise to the Lord Jesus *because they have been trained to worship God* in every Sunday school class, auxiliary group, and age-oriented service. Their talents are recognized, encouraged, and channeled toward the glory of the Lord.

Every skill the people possess is valued and employed in the work of the church. No one is working outside of **his area of anointing** because all the places are filled by those whose divine calling puts them there.

Leaders are content and humble before the people of God. The people are **joyful and productive** in their work, respectful of their leaders. **No energy is wasted in internal strife,** plot and counter-plot, insurrections or preemptive strikes. **Recognition** is given to those who do well but all the glory goes to the Lord. There are **no stars** on the music or dramatic stage. All are supporting players, never upstaging the King in whose court our little stage shines. **Craftsmanship and creativity** are encouraged as people are always coming up with better ways of doing things and better things to do. **Public worship** services are jewels of praise with exquisite music from those whose gift it is to sing and play, eloquent declarations of truth from those who are gifted to speak, and electrifying worship from everyone for each sees himself as God's Holy-Royal Priest, ministering unto the Lord his personal Sacrifice of Praise. **The Lord reigns** in hearts, homes, and in services of worship. There is righteousness, peace, and joy in the Holy Spirit. **From His Throne flows the River of the Spirit to the healing of the nations.**

but we are imagining the rule of King Jesus over His Church, so perfection in Mt. Zion is what we must see.

Yes, this vision is idealistic, but the Lord has only one kingdom rule. Wherever and whenever He is allowed to rule by His Spirit and to the extent He is given reign, His kingdom will be the same—righteousness, peace, and joy in the Holy Spirit. That is why worship, the establishment of His kingdom, must precede all other points of mission.

For the practical outworking of this philosophy of ministry priority I must give personal testimony. Trained as a school band director and with a call of God on my life to preach the Word, I began my ministry as a staff music pastor in 1975, after several years of teaching school while preaching and singing on weekends. My training in music education and my pastor-teacher calling made ministry to the saints my favorite part of the ministry. I functioned this way for the first five years of my pastoral ministry. Early on, I took a youth choir on tour with a musical entitled *Come Together* by Jimmy and Carol Owens. One of the phrases in the narration was "This is our ministry to the Lord." This phrase did not make any sense to me but every time I heard it something would respond in my spirit, an assurance that it was true and someday I would understand it.

An inadequate concept of ministry blocked my thinking. I had the idea that the strong always ministered to the weak. If one *needed* ministry one was in deep trouble. God was never weak or in need, so how could I ever minister to Him? In those early years of my ministry, I *knew* that the most important thing we were supposed to do as a church was win the lost. But what I really enjoyed was teaching God's Word and music to God's people, seeing them develop and grow. Worship was not very important to me. I knew all my little projects (my singers and players) would do much better if they were faithful to God's house. Getting and keeping people saved was the purpose of public worship. My vision was horizontal, man-centered.

Then a teacher came to our church—Roxanne Brant, who had such a deep and peaceful walk with the Lord. One of her books was a little volume called *Ministering Unto the Lord, A Vision, A Search, A Discovery.* There was that haunting phrase again; someone had written a book about it. I consumed Roxanne's book. She tests by the Scriptures the hypothesis of the priority of worship much more thoroughly than I have done in this volume. (I consider her volume a modern classic and made it mandatory reading for all those in my ministry.) With this book my personal revolution began. My guilt over enjoying the development of God's people subsided when I realized it was one of the things the church was supposed to do.

During those first five years of vocational ministry a hunger for worship grew in my heart. In 1980, we moved to a new position in a new state where for the first time leading the congregation in worship was assigned to me. The church I served (Bethel Assembly of God, Wichita, Kansas) was far ahead of me in their ministry to the Lord. My pastor, John Gifford, helped me understand what I was doing when I led worship. Above all, I began to see worship as the heart of all music ministry—it was all meant to be ministry to the Lord. This simplified things so much.

- The Lord was both the object of our singing and the subject of our song;
- Pleasing Him was the goal.
- Worship was no longer *preliminary*—it was *primary*! It was not just a warm-up for the Word; it was the first order of business! We would not dare do anything else until we had done our best to give unto the Lord the glory due His name.

Psalm 29:1,2 KJV became the job description for my life:

Give unto the Lord, O ye mighty,
Give unto the Lord glory and strength.
Give unto the Lord the glory due unto His name;
Worship the Lord in the beauty of holiness.

We started an arts organization called Bethel Arts Ministries with this philosophy as bedrock. Everyone—singers, instrumentalists, actors, writers, technicians—everyone, was to center his or her talent on the Lord Jesus. Each rehearsal and

performance, whether musical or dramatic, was to be presented to the Lord primarily and to man secondarily. Selection of
music became simple and exciting. No longer would I try to
appease all the musical factions in the congregation. (Former-
ly, this was a source of pride in my own musicianship.)
Instead, I would find music that my choir and orchestra could
use to minister to the Lord. He became the subject of our song.
Long before I knew about "psalms and hymns and spiritual
songs," I used them because I set out to find Scripture songs,
prayer songs, praise songs, and worship songs. I discovered
that He indeed would inhabit our music if it was ministered to
Him and that, through His presence in our praise, He would
minister to everyone in the house who wanted ministry. After
all those years of working on the earthen vessel, I finally let
the beauty of the treasure in the vessel pour out.

For more than twenty-five years we have seen the results
of this philosophy. Our music ministries have been peaceful,
productive places. Conflicts have been the exception, not the
rule. While it certainly has not been the millennial reign, we
have done everything we can to ensure that Jesus is the center
of everything. Singers, instrumentalists, actors, and technicians have gathered together. Those who use their talents to
glorify themselves either change or leave. They just do not fit
in. Self-glory seekers are most uncomfortable around those
who seek only His glory.

A meaningful moment illustrates this. When it came time
to leave the church at Winston-Salem after almost nine years
of fruitful ministry, I resigned first to the choir and orchestra
after a Wednesday night rehearsal. In two weeks we would be
gone. Peggy Bost, a dear lady of the church, told me something that ranks at the top of my list of compliments paid to
our ministry. "Pastor Phifer, in all these years you have never
made me feel insignificant." She was not a soloist, just a faithful, anonymous alto who was there almost all the time. In the
eyes of man, she was no star. But in the eyes of God she was
extremely important. Our leadership had somehow communi-
cated her importance to her. She was a valuable to me as those

who get the microphone, the solo, the feature role, the spot-
light. God helped me succeed with Peggy Bost!

Music departments do not have to be "war departments."
Arts ministries do not have to be entertainment centers with
"stars." These problems stem from two things: too many kingdoms and man-centered performance. If each artist of whatever discipline is centered upon pleasing the Lord and
ministering to Him, a unity emerges among all the arts.

- Musicians can support actors.
- Technicians can support musicians.
- Writers, directors, and conductors can serve them all.
- The alto on the back row is just as important as the top
  soprano soloist.
- There are no "bit parts."
- All have equal opportunity to please God. The indi-
  vidual level of skill is important only as far as the
  assignment made to that individual.
- All are committed to one kingdom and one King.

My little prayer song says it this way:

> Let there be but one kingdom in our hearts, O Lord.
> Let there be but one King, one Throne.
> Casting all our crowns before Your Majesty,
> Let all glory fade but Your own.
> Let all glory fade but Your own.

"One kingdom" Copyright 1993 by Gospel Publishing House

When there are too many kings and kingdoms within the
church, too much energy is wasted in building, maintaining,
and defending the walls between the provinces. The Lord
receives no glory from strife. As Paul told Timothy, "And the
servant of the Lord must not strive; but be gentle unto all men,
apt to teach, patient (II Timothy 2:24 KJV). As long as our
ministries are man-centered, they will reflect man's nature—
the strife of kingdom against kingdom, king against king.

When they become God-centered, they will reflect His nature: peace, order, beauty, and function. Our ministries can be marked by passion and reason. When we re-think our philosophy of church ministry we are faced with two choices: the Mary-Martha choice, and the Mary-Judas choice.

Philosophical Choices

The Mary-Martha choice. Lazarus' two sisters, Mary and Martha, illustrate a choice facing each of us today. We first see them in Luke 10 where Martha welcomed Jesus into her house in Bethany. Mary sat at Jesus' feet drinking in His every word and the peace of His presence. But, there was much to be done and Martha was trying to do it all while Mary just sat there, as if all a woman had to do was be with Jesus. Martha rebuked her and asked Jesus to send her to the kitchen where she belonged. Jesus rebuked her. "'Martha, Martha,' the Lord answered, 'you are worried and upset about many things, but only one thing is needed. Mary has chosen what is better, and it will not be taken away from her'" (Luke 10:41,42).

This is another of those times when Jesus took what seems to the natural mind an indefensible position. It does not make sense! If there was to be a dinner, someone was going to have to do the work! After dinner, after the dishes are done and the kitchen put back in order, then if there is time sit at Jesus feet, if your exhaustion allows you to stay awake. We all have our kitchens and dinners to prepare, and all for the Lord. We find ourselves "careful and troubled about many things" while Jesus sits in our parlor ignored.

Amazingly, Jesus rebukes the worker and praises the worshiper. Jesus wanted something other than the dinner Martha wanted so desperately to prepare; He wanted her! There was room at His feet for both Mary and Martha. Instead of being worn out by the cares and troubles of serving, Martha could have been refreshed by her guest. There are more Martha's than Mary's in the ministry today. Churches rush to service man's needs before they have given Jesus what He wants. He wants *us* more than He wants what *we can do* for Him. No doubt Mary did help serve at a later moment, *after* she had spent time loving her Lord. It is easy to imagine that she glided through her kitchen duties with the glow of His nearness on her face, her heart brimming with His words. She was neither full of care nor troubled. How could she be? Jesus was in her house and she had spent quality time with Him.

This Mary-Martha choice faces each church musician, each artist of whatever discipline, and each worshiper. Each church leader faces it as well.

- Will I serve God in the energy of my own flesh, or
- Will I serve man as a result of my ministry to the Lord?
- Will I sit at His feet and take in His every word, or
- Will I rush to my kitchen laden with cares and troubles?
- Will I surrender my ambitions, my drivenness, and my dreams to His presence and plans, or
- Will I charge into the future, using my gifts to build my dreams regardless of His approval?
- Will I structure the ministry of God's people around the work that needs to be done or the work each of them is called to do?

The choice is ours: His presence, His Word, His plan, His approval, or our hot kitchen with its cares and troubles.

The Mary-Martha choice faces us each time we gather to worship.

- How many times, in public worship, do we take the time to sit at His feet?
- Is it more common for us to watch the clock, rushing through our worship routine so that we get to the real business at hand, the preaching of the Word and the saving of souls?
- Do we keep Jesus waiting for us to worship Him?
- When we speak to Him is it only to vent our frustration at all the work others are not doing?

- Have we viewed time spent in worship, or even money spent just to glorify the Lord, as wasted time and money?

We are not the first to feel this way.

The Mary-Judas choice. At another dinner in Bethany in honor of Simon the leper, Mary again is commended for her worship. As we discussed earlier, she took her most prized possession, a flask of perfumed oil worth a year's wages for the common man, and poured it on Jesus' head and feet. This time the disciples, led by Judas, rebuked her, claiming that this was a waste of funds. The oil should have been sold and the money given to the poor. The story is told in three of the Gospels. Let us look at Jesus' response in Matthew 26:10-13:

> *Aware of this, Jesus said to them, "Why are you bothering this woman? She has done a beautiful thing to me The poor you will always have with you, but you will not always have me. When she poured this perfume on my body, she did it to prepare me for burial. I tell you the truth, wherever this gospel is preached throughout the world, what she has done will also be told, in memory of her."* (Matthew 26:10-13)

> *She did what she could.* (Mark 14:8)

Today, when worshipers set their hearts to do what they can, to do beautiful things for the Lord, others are still quick to cry "wasteful spending." Many times the protesters have control over the money, just as in the Bible story. Their protest songs have many lyrics:

- "We cannot afford to put a new sound system in the sanctuary."
- "The old piano is good enough."
- "Why must we tune the piano four or five times a year?"

- "We should not spend money on new music for the choir and orchestra. Use the old music again."
- "We had better not rent lights for this Christmas production. Can't you put some flood lights in some tin cans?"
- "We don't need to sing all these songs. Let's cut back on the preliminaries and get to the preaching."
- "We don't need to buy all these new songs, and this projector and screen. Let's sing the songs we already know."
- "New hymnals? Let's tape up the old ones."
- "What do we need with timpani?"
- "Why does the orchestra need music?"
- "What's with all these lights? We're building a church here, not a theatre!" "What do we need with a full-time worship leader? All he would do is work on music."

On and on go the endless songs of those who see beautiful worship as a waste of time and money.

This is not to imply that musicians and other artists do not get crazy ideas from time to time that need to be reigned in by more level-headed leadership or that all those who control the finances are akin to Judas. It only means that many times it is not viewed as "practical" to spend money, time, or effort on something as "non-productive" as worship. Practicality was on Judas' side but Jesus was not. Jesus knew that if the poor were ever to receive life-changing ministry, the disciples would have to learn to minister to Him the way Mary had. So He made an absolutely amazing promise. Wherever the Gospel would be preached (the Greek word implies "declared in full power and authority") what Mary had done would be mentioned. Has that happened? It has indeed. Every revival has followed a time of passion, of intense seeking of God's face. Revival passion dies out when the emphasis shifts away from seeking God's face. Mary's example must be rediscovered in every generation if that generation is to hear the gospel preached in the power of the Spirit. The Mary-Judas choice is ours each time we gather to worship.

A Biblical Balance In Public Worship

How can we know that we have achieved a biblically balanced corporate worship experience? The principles of worship become our tests: the spirit and truth test, the honor-the-Lord test, edify-the-body / honor-the-word test, and the flow-of-worship test.

The spirit and truth test. Each Lord's Day the Father searches our pews and pulpits for True Worshipers. What does He find? It is time to evaluate what goes on in each service of worship. The spirit and truth principle must be the key to understanding how to balance a public worship service. Look at each event in the service and ask,

- "Is this a `spirit' activity?
- Or is it a `truth' activity?"

If it cannot be called either one, it should be dropped from the agenda. When parishioners object, the reasoning can be explained to them, along with the plans to cover that event in some non-worship setting. It takes courage to reduce a service to only *"spirit and truth"* events.

In the middle 1980's because of tremendous growth in our congregation, my pastor, Ron McManus, and I had to figure out how to add an additional morning service (there were already two) without adding to the total time spent on a Sunday morning. There were concurrent Sunday schools with each service. We applied the *"spirit and truth"* test and eliminated some things: baby dedications would be in evening services, awards would be at night, the special music would be the offertory, almost all announcements would be made in the bulletin, no spoken introductions to songs, no teaching about worship while leading in worship, and no one rambling away aimlessly in the pulpit. That left us these service times:

8:30-9:40 a.m.

9:50-11:05 a.m. and

11:15 a.m. -12:30 p.m.

The services were simple with 1 hour and 10 to 15 minutes per service.

Three Morning Services

PRINCIPLE	EVENT	ELAPSED TIME
SPIRIT:	Call to Worship (opening chorus) Prayer	8:30
	Praise and worship	8:35
	Prayer for needs	8:50
	Choir and orchestra anthem Offering/Offertory	
TRUTH:	Message	9:00
BOTH:	Invitation	9:35

(Times scheduled to each event were flexible and each worship leader was encouraged to follow the direction of the Holy Spirit. Additional time was taken from breaks between services.) *Note the equal balance of spirit and truth activities.*

The effect was wonderful (though tiring)! We discovered how to keep a service moving without hurrying, how to avoid detours and stay on course. After our new sanctuary was built and we had only one morning service with all the time we needed, we kept all the restrictions we had placed on the short services. We expanded the amount of time given to corporate worship, musical expressions, preaching, and altar services.

The Honor-the-Lord test We need to ask these questions:

- Do events center on the majesty and grace of the Savior?
- Is each participant set on the glory of the Lord and not his own glory?
- Do all the worship activities center the attention of the people on the Lord himself and not the modes of praise and worship themselves?
- Was the Lord's name lifted high above every other name whether principle, personality, or particular denomination?

The Edify-the-body test / Honor-the-Word test Here are important questions:

- Do the services edify the church?
- Can the people reflect back on the service and feel that God has spoken to them in some way?
- Have they learned something about Jesus?
- Have they been refreshed and challenged by His presence?
- Was truth about Jesus the sum total of the information transmitted during the service?
- Did we come face to face with the Living Word in our worship and the Written Word in our study?
- Was adequate prayer time given to the people to respond to the declared Word of God?

The Flow-of-worship test Test the flow of worship with these questions:

- Does the worship service flow together decently and in order?
- Does it make sense?
- When it is all over can worshipers look back on the experience and recognize the mind of God in each event?
- Worship services led of the Spirit start someplace and go someplace. They are not "slice of life" non-happenings. Each one is an encounter with the King of kings!

This biblical balance of worship: spirit and truth worship; honor-the-Lord worship; flowing worship; edify-the-body worship; honor-the-Word; passionate and reasoned worship, is hard to find and difficult to maintain. Why? The reasons are varied but fall into three categories: control, fear, and provincialism.

Control There is an element of power in controlling the worship experience of others. Those who control the service control the public interaction between God and man. This is something that must be done carefully. If the congregation begins to worship God in spirit and truth (according to the definitions in Chapter 6) control of the service must be yielded to the Holy Spirit. In other words, we will not be able to plan every event in advance. Things may happen that are not in the bulletin! Spontaneity is essential to passionate and reasoned *congregational* worship, to worship in spirit and truth. The leadership must be brave enough to yield control of the service to the Holy Spirit as He moves the hearts of the people.

The people must be taught what the "due order" of worship is. Much of what goes on in "free worship" situations is the cultural remains of previous generations, not a fresh move of God. Why? Because many people in classic Pentecostal churches and other free worship traditions have had the freedom to worship but have not been taught biblical truth on worship. At the same time, many worshipers from other traditions have been told every move to make. The control of both services, from extreme liturgical worship to unbridled free worship is at issue. It is possible that both are in the hands of previous generations, not the Holy Spirit.

Fear Another emotion which keeps us from a biblical balance in public worship is fear. If the leadership does not call the shots, someone else will and it might not be the Holy Spirit. It may be old Brother What's-his-name, or old Sister So-and-so. The Charismatics will take over the church. The crazy people will take advantage of the freedom and our services will be a mess. Visitors will think we are nuts, or worse, holy rollers! We will lose all decorum and dignity. Fears can go on and on and rightly so. These fears are very real. What is the answer?

As with all adventures of faith, risks are involved. As with all fears, the antidote is love. The Lord loves us and wants to break through the barriers of our traditions and routines to commune with us. Love is also knowledge and communication. These solutions suggest themselves: Let the pastor share his burden for the revelation of the glory of the Lord. Let him teach the people biblical methods of worship. (This means they can discern between the cultural, the personal, and the spiritual.) The pastor must commit himself to minister unto the Lord.

To illustrate this point, an experience Pastor McManus had comes to mind. He visited a dynamic church in Singapore where the congregation was totally involved in worship. He asked the pastor how he got the people to worship that way. His answer, "They sat there and watched me worship for three years".

If people can be taught the Word of God, they can be taught to worship God biblically. When they are armed with the truth, especially concerning motives, they will *want* to worship God and they *will* worship God. Divisive individuals will be unable to rally people to an insurrection against the leadership because the people have learned to treasure unity as essential to worship and how to respect the Lord's anointed. When the truth about worship has been taught to everyone, error has little opportunity. If the leadership will share the vision of ministering unto the Lord, of giving Him the glory due unto His name, those who have a heart to do this will follow. Those who do not may fight, but they will fight against God and lose. *We cannot allow fear of what might happen keep us from worshiping God.* If we fail to *try* to establish worship in spirit and truth, when we stand before Jesus and give an account, our cowardice will be indefensible.

Provincialism This may be the biggest roadblock in the highway of the Lord. If the worship service has become the province of the people, the preacher, the organist, the minister of music, or the ruling board, then returning it to the Holy Spirit will be difficult indeed. Blessed are those leaders who hold their authority with a gentle grip. We may say our work is in the Lord's hands, but the truth is revealed in times of testing. Are we willing to examine our worship traditions in the unyielding light of the revealed Word of God? If they are found lacking in biblical authority, are we bold enough to let them go? To be biblical in our worship practice and philosophy requires that we return the worship service and *the whole church* to the Lord's ownership. We can no longer afford to have "Pentecostal" or "Presbyterian" or "Baptist" or "traditional" or "charismatic" worship. All of these names denote provinces. When our worship is biblical, then it will be God's. Likewise, leaders must not see the church as "theirs." It must be "His."

CONCLUSION

How much of this peaceful revolution do we need? We need the whole thing!

- The threefold mission needs to be part of every curriculum from Sunday school to seminary.
- The priority of worship needs to be encouraged among the people and insisted upon from the leadership.
- Privately and publicly we need to touch God before we attempt to touch men.
- What will be the revolutionary result?

According to I Corinthians 14, these things: a visitation of the Spirit of God as we have never seen, and a powerful manifestation of His power and presence wherein sinners must turn to God! Paul speaks of public worship that is alive with spirit activity, none of which he condemns. His only warning is that *"all be done unto edifying"* and *"decently and in order."* In this chapter we see:

- the balance of spirit and truth (v.15),
- everyone involved in worship (v.24),
- everyone prepared for worship (v.21),
- strengthening of the whole body the goal (v.26),
- all worshipers under self-control (v.32), and all things done decently and in order (v.40).

What is the effect of this worship? Verses 24 and 25 remove forever the fears that soul-winners may have of worship.

> *But if an unbeliever or someone who does not understand comes in while everybody is prophesying,* he will be convinced by all that he is a sinner and will be judged by all, and the secrets of his heart will be laid bare. So he will fall down and worship God, exclaiming, "God is really among you!"* (1 Corinthians 14:24-25)

Is this the testimony of those who visit our services? *"God is really among you!"* How often do we have unbelieving visitors falling on their faces under heavy conviction? The fact that we do not is an indictment against our worship. Can there be any doubt that we need this revolution of peace? Can we see that all of mankind needs the carefully reasoned ministry of the believer? It is time for us to passionately center our lives, church programs, and worship services on the Lord Jesus. A dying world awaits the visitation of Almighty God upon our worship and His indwelling sovereignty in our lives.

* If this means that they all prophesied at once, the only way I can see that everybody can prophecy and still be comprehensible to the unbeliever is to engage in prophetic worship; worship that proclaims the Word of God, most likely in corporate singing.

Chapter Nine

ANOINTED WORSHIP:

Peace Like a River

Aaron

On the night when his staff, the symbol of his authority, waited with those of the other tribal leaders in the Tent of Meeting, Aaron tried to rest his eyes. He thought of all the things his tired old eyes had seen: a brother transformed by a vision in the desert; his same walking stick turned to a snake and back again before Pharoah and his magicians; wholesale destruction and death in Egypt; a sea dividing before them and closing after them trapping Pharoah's army and sealing off any escape back to Egypt; smoke and thunder on the mountain and the disappearance of his brother into the storm; the shameful worship of the golden calf he had made at the insistence of the people; Moses' terrible rage; the giving of the law; the building of the Tabernacle; and now Korah's rebellion. "Oh," thought Aaron, "when will morning come?"

The whole nightmare began when Korah, a Levite, and a few other men from the Tribe of Reuben became insolent. They appealed to the vanity of a people just rising from slavery. It was a power grab. The issue was this: Who were the chosen ones? With 250 well-known community leaders, members of the council, they came as a group to oppose Moses. "You have gone too far! The whole community is holy, every one of them, and the Lord is with them. Why do you set yourselves above the Lord's assembly?" Aaron saw this break Moses' heart. His brother fell face down to the earth. God must have spoken to him there on the ground. He got up with a plan, a test. He instructed each of the 250 rebels to get censers. Tomorrow they would all burn holy incense before the Lord and let God choose who was holy.

"The man he chooses he will cause to come near him," Moses told them. "You Levites have gone too far! Isn't it enough for you that the God of Israel has separated you from the rest of the Israelite community and brought you near himself to do the work at the Lord's Tabernacle and to stand before the community and minister to them? He has brought you and all your fellow Levites near himself, but now you are trying to get the priesthood, too."

If Moses had learned anything from Egypt it was that there was never enough power, if power was what you were after. Now the sickness, the wicked lust for power, for *control*, was taking root in the hearts of these who were slaves just a short time ago. It was a plague that must be stopped. It was also beyond any leader's ability to stop. The more a true-hearted leader shrinks from power, the greater opportunity the power grabbers have to grasp more and more. Moses had shared the leadership with the council and now they were doing their best to make him regret it. No, there was nothing Moses could do to stop them.

But there was plenty that God could do. Thus far in their leadership, Moses and Aaron had seen God work the supernatural many times when that was the only thing that could work. Now would be no different. God had chosen, and He would prove His choice.

"It is against the Lord that you and all your followers have banded together. Who is Aaron that you should grumble against him?" Aaron's throat went immediately dry and resisted his every attempt to swallow. "Thanks, Moses, for putting me in the middle of this!" Aaron managed to think between gasps. But he was already in the middle of it; he knew that. The men were arguing with Moses, refusing to come near him, accusing him of cheating them. Then Moses became angry. Aaron always hated to see that.

"Do not accept their offering," Moses said to the Lord. "I have not taken so much as a donkey from them, nor have I wronged any of them." Then to Korah and his followers, "You and all your followers are to appear before the Lord tomorrow—you and they and . . . Aaron." Aaron's throat has just recovered when it seemed he had swallowed another mouthful of sand.

The next day 250 men gathered with censors at the entrance of the Tent of Meeting. Korah led them and met Aaron there, each with a censor. Each censor was aflame, the multiplied scent of so many fires seemed to rob the atmosphere of oxygen. Tension seemed to seep into the vacuum the retreating oxygen left behind. How would God respond to so many flames offered by those who were not authorized to do so? It didn't take long to find out.

The glory of the Lord came over the entire assembly just as it had the day the Tabernacle was dedicated. It was Korah's turn to struggle for air. Could it be that God would accept his offering? Could it be that a greater share of the power was now his? His co-conspirators, Dathan and Abiram, came with their families to the doors of their tents.

Against the backdrop of a sky blazing with the glory of God, Moses seemed to be listening to a voice deep in his spirit. Aaron had seen this before. God was speaking. Moses seemed oblivious to the crowd, the contest, the cloud of glory. Then he began to speak. The crowd quickly quieted to hear his words.

"Move back from the tents of these wicked men! Do not touch anything belonging to them, or you will be swept away because of all their sins."

They did not hesitate. Soon the leaders, their families and their newfound power were alone, deserted by the nation. Then, as now, those who seek to consolidate power, succeed in cutting themselves off from those around them.

"This is how you will know that the Lord has sent me to do all these things and that it was not my idea: If these men die a natural death . . . then the Lord has not sent me. But if the Lord brings about something totally new, and the earth opens its mouth and swallows them, with everything that belongs to them, and they go down alive into the grave, then you will know that these men have treated the Lord with contempt."

With Moses' last word, the ground began to shake. Under the tents of the offenders the ground opened. Amid the screams of their innocent children, Korah, Dathan, Abiram, along with their families and all they owned disappeared into the chasms. While a nation watched in horror the ground closed over them, stifling their cries and removing all trace of their existence. In the silence that ensued, a realization ran through the camp like a shudder. Suddenly the people pan-icked and ran—some in blind panic but others because they knew that they were as guilty as the leaders. As the 250 men with censors ran, trying to lose themselves in the crowd, a fire came out from the Lord, sought out each man, and consumed him. Their power grab had destroyed them. It always does, eventually. Aaron and his sons stood by the Tent of Meeting, their censors still sending up ribbons of smoke in honor of the Lord. The glory of the Lord lifted from the Tabernacle.

Moses had more to do. He instructed that the censors the rebels had brought be retrieved from the charred corpses of their previous owners. Moses had Eleazar, Aaron's son, melt the brass implements down as a sign that only those whom God has called can come near Him. Aaron hoped that would end it.

It didn't. The next day the people came back to Moses with more accusations. Before Moses could respond, the glory re-turned to the Tabernacle. The people shrank back as Moses and Aaron went toward the Tent. Moses heard the Lord say, "Get away from this assembly so I can put an end to them at once." Moses and his brother fell face down. As they lay there, Moses said to Aaron, "Take your censor and put incense in it, along with fire from the altar, and hurry to the assembly to make atonement for them. Wrath has come out from the Lord; the plague has started."

Aaron did as he was told. People were dying everywhere. Aaron moved through them and wherever he went the dying stopped. He created a line between the living and the dead. Almost 15,000 people died. Such is the harvest of those who sow to the fleshly need for power.

The Lord still wasn't through. Moses did as he was instructed, asking each of the tribal leaders to bring his staff, his walking stick, to the Tent of Meeting. It was a test to determine whom God had chosen. What did that mean? How would God answer? What would He do with all those walking sticks? Like with a shepherd, each staff was a symbol of the power of the man who carried it.

The long night was finally over. Aaron's night of rehearsing their history left him exhausted. Moses looked refreshed. How did he do that? Hearing God's voice must be comforting in time of crisis. Moses entered the Tent, brought out the staffs, and handed one to each of the leaders. Each stick looked just as it had the night before, all except Aaron's. Moses handed it to his brother. Aaron didn't recognize it. It had budded, blossomed and produced almonds. Aaron looked at it in won-der. Slowly he reached for it. He handled it gently. A few almonds fell to the ground. Aaron knew there was nothing here that he had done—this was God's work. Moses took the staff and put it into the Tent as a sign to the rebellious. The rebellion was over at last. God's power had proven God's choice.

The Anointing

One of the most interesting terms in the Christian vocabulary is "the anointing." Growing up in Pentecost, I heard the term often, but I never heard it defined. Respected teachers and pastors would speak of it as a mystery, "Well, I don't know what it is, but I know when it isn't!" When the worship revolution began to take root in my heart, I sensed a need to understand the anointing and prayed that God would open this truth to me. Early one morning I was hand-copying parts for our church orchestra. The television, specifically, the Today Show kept me company. Gene Shallit was reviewing a movie about Russian ballet dancers. The story concerned an audition where only 100 of several hundred dancers would be selected for the next level of competition. In his commentary, he called the dancers who made the second audition "these anointed ones." My pencil stopped and I stared straight ahead into the early morning shadows as if they hid the vision I needed to see. Why was Gene Shallit using "our" word to describe Russian ballet dancers?

Then I saw—it was because they were chosen! The anointing was God's choice! If I had an anointing to lead worship it was because God had chosen me to do this! Thrilled to the core of my being that God would chose me, I glowed with the light of this revelation many days. I called my brother, the senior pastor and theologian in the family, and excitedly shared my discovery with him, "James, I know what the anointing is. It is God's choice!" He said I was right but that was not all. The anointing was also God's power. The weight of his words hit me at once. Of course! God's power must attend God's choice! God would be cruel to choose us and leave us to our own powers to fulfill His plan. In this chapter we will see the confirmation I found in the Word as I tested these definitions. When we understand the anointing, we understand how God moves through us as we worship, how His peace is established in our corporate praise.

Understanding the Anointing

The anointing is God's choice. In the Old Testament when someone or something was chosen by the Lord, a special oil was poured over that person or thing. The oil was made with a special formula and use of it for any other purpose was forbidden. The Hebrew word for the anointing is "mashach" meaning "to draw the hand over, to paint, to consecrate . . . the action is by the Lord."(Novak). We read of worship objects, places, priests, and kings being anointed by the Lord. In the New Testament, the Greek word is "chrisma," meaning, "renders them holy, separating them to God." (Vine) God chooses people and things to be set apart unto Him to fulfill His purposes. God's choice is a powerful thing. Because it is an action of His will, God's choice carries with it aspects of His character.

God's choice is immutable—unchangeable. When God has chosen something or someone, that choice is as eternal as the mind that conceived it and the will that decided it. The Scriptures say "the gifts and calling of God are without repentance" (Romans 11:29). In other words, when God calls (chooses) He never needs to rethink His position. When some-one fails God in his calling, he is still judged against the stan-dards of that calling. This explains why preachers who are living in sin can still be used of the Lord. Even in their sin they are still chosen of God to preach the Word and God honors His Word. Let no one assume they will get away with un-forgiven sin. We can all be sure that our sins will find us out. In fact, fallen leaders eventually lose the power of God but they will forever be responsible for the call of God on their lives.

God's choice is beyond the bounds of time and space. Have you ever wondered how an audio tape can record the anointing? Any hour of day or night the tape is played the anointing is still there. No matter how many times the tape is duplicated, the anointing never loses one generation of quali-ty. Have you thought about how the anointing can be broadcast or even sent to satellites and back to the earth? The answer is this: the anointing of God, because it is His choice, exists without the limitations of time and space. There is no hour of day or night when God cannot give His full attention to His choice. When a recording is made of the image and/or voice of an anointed person, no amount of processing or broadcasting or even a round trip through space can inhibit God from tending His choice each time the recording is played.

God's choice leaves no room for personal boast. This point is so important. How quick we are to take credit for God's work in our lives. When we understand the anointing, we know that our success is really God at work through us. All we do is obey the Lord in what He has chosen us to do, yielding our skills into His hands. He does the work. The writers of Scripture certainly knew this. One of the most eloquent statements is by Paul, "But we have this treasure in earthen vessels, that the excellency of the power may be of God, and not of us" (II Corinthians 4:7 KJV). Those who understand their anointing are never boastful. They are grateful and humble knowing the treasure is more valuable than the earthen vessel that houses it.

God's choice for others is not to be compared with ours and certainly not to be envied. It is sad to see someone whose life is wasted because he feels that what God has chosen him to do is not the right thing. We all have seen people with music degrees who fail as music leaders in the local church. Why? It may not be because they do not have musical skills, or even people skills. It may be because God has not chosen them to be music leaders in the church. Those in church music leadership should not be just qualified musically but they should be anointed by God. We see the same thing in the pulpit ministry. Could it be that some pastors who struggle year after year are really anointed to be staff pastors and not senior pastors? It is the duty of each of us to come to peace with what God has called us to do. This anointing is the chief organizational point of one's life, the secret of happy and productive living. When we set envious eyes on the anointing of others we waste our energies on pursuits that God may not bless, perhaps missing *the one thing* we should do for the Lord. Aspiration within our anointing is perfectly right. We should work to be the very best we can be at what God has called us to do. Aspiring to something God has not called us to do is wrong and only leads to heartache and wasted time.

God has chosen the Church to worship Him. We are now the Holy-Royal Priesthood, set apart from all of mankind to show forth the praises of Him. We are the anointed of God.

Now He which stablisheth us with you in Christ, and hath anointed us, is God; Who hath also sealed us, and given us the earnest of the Spirit in our hearts. (II Corinthians 1:21,22 KJV)

When we gave our hearts to the Lord, it was not only for our salvation but also that we might declare His glory to all mankind. Our hands are anointed to be lifted to Him. Our voices are the chosen voices to sing and speak His praise. Our lives, as expressed by our priorities, personal values and schedules, are His personal choice to reflect His eternal truths.

The Anointing
The Anointing is . . . GOD'S CHOICE.

The anointing is God's power. It makes sense that God's choice would bring with it God's power. It is possible to do the thing that God has chosen you to do and fail. If we undertake heaven's work in earth's power, we will eventually run down and wear out. The Bible tells a powerful story that illustrates the fact that God's power attends God's choice.

In Numbers 16 and 17 we learn of the rebellion of Korah. The test the Lord chose to establish that Aaron was the chosen high priest was this: the head of each tribe was to place his rod in the Tabernacle with His name inscribed on it and leave it overnight. The rod that budded would indicate God's choice. The next day eleven of the rods looked exactly as they had the day before but Aaron's rod had budded, blossomed and produced almonds.

There was no natural power in the dead stick to spring to life and produce fruit. But because the rod belonged to the man God had chosen, God's power touched it and the dead came to life. This is what happens when we obey the Lord in our anointing—the supernatural. There was no way any of the other eleven leaders could make their walking sticks come to life. There was no way Aaron could take the credit for what happened to his. God chose Aaron and sent His power to prove it.

The test of our anointing is the power of God. When we look over our efforts to serve God and see some turn out great most of the time and others just seem never to have much effect, we have indications of what God has called us to do. We may have many interests and skills, but the things we are anointed to do bring results far beyond our skills.

There are general anointings on all God's people. I call them the three "W's": to *worship* (including prayer), to understand the *Word*, and to *witness* for the Lord. We are also called to love one another, to live at peace with on another, to honor our leadership and other such evidences of Christian maturity. When we do these things we are not operating in our power only. We can expect supernatural results. There are also specific anointings God gives to individuals: to preach, to lead worship, to sing or play an instrument, to teach, to administrate, and so on. If God has selected us to do one of these things, we can expect supernatural results when we obey Him in that anointing.

Another way of looking at our anointing is to consider that God has chosen us *to be* a certain person. As that person we then *do* certain chosen things. This vantage point on the anointing helps avoid an over emphasis on doing at the expense of being. Many of us come to see the things we do as something separate from the person we are called to be. Actually, the things we are anointed to do flow from the person we are called to be. The center of my life is not just the things I am called to do but the person God has called me to be. For instance, because God has called me to be a music maker, making music is essential to my spiritual well-being and is part of my personal worship. When this distinction is clearly seen, conflicts between our "ministry" (what we do for the church and the Lord) and our "personal lives" (what we do for our families, ourselves and for our world) are possible to resolve. Our ministry to the church should be a direct reflection of the person God has anointed us to be. Service rendered outside of our anointing will not renew us; it will deplete us. We cannot continue to "do" what we are called to "do" if we are not growing and becoming the person God has called us to "be."

The Anointing
The Anointing is . . . *GOD'S CHOICE.*
The Anointing is . . . *GOD'S POWER.*

The anointing is the partner of skill. In some corners of Christianity, skill is a quality held suspect. If one is skillful, the old non-reasoning goes, he is surely operating in human skill and not spiritual anointing. It is expressed several ways: "They're not anointed. They're trained." "He plays that piano and he never had a lesson!" (as if there were a premium on never having had instruction). "If we hire a music director, he will just be too professional. He might even want to get the people who can't sing out of the choir!" It is as if one can either be good or anointed but not both. Of course, this is a cultural attitude that falls easily before the truth of Scripture.

"Sing unto the Lord a new song; play skillfully with a shout of joy" (Psalm 33:3 NKJ). Chenaniah was chosen to lead the musicians at David's Tabernacle because he was "master of the song" (I Chronicles 15:27). Generations later in the time of good King Josiah, the Levites were still "skillful with instruments of music" (II Chronicles 34:12 NKJ). Clearly the Scriptures entertain no conflict between skill and anointing. In fact, I believe that skill is the partner of the anointing.

Some basic truths of the nature of man help us here. Man is a trinity: body, soul, and spirit. "May God himself, the God of peace, sanctify you through and through. May your whole spirit, soul and body be kept blameless at the coming of our Lord Jesus Christ" (I Thessalonians 5:23). The body is the physical life, our sense-consciousness. The soul is the mental/

222 / Stephen R. Phifer

emotional life, our self-consciousness. The spirit is the worship/Word life, our God-consciousness. Skills reside in the body and soul. The anointing rests upon the spirit. The flow of skill brings natural results. The flow of the anointing brings supernatural results. Skills can be developed from innate talents. The anointing is a gift given by the Lord; we can never achieve it for no one deserves it. He keeps His own counsel about who, what, and when He anoints. Skills are the earthen vessel; the anointing is the treasure within—the power of God!

Talent, the ability to learn to do something, is God's gift to us. Skill, the ability to do something, is our gift to God. When we develop our talents into skills, they can release the anointing within our spirits.

For instance, I heard of a church pianist who could only play in the keys of C and F. Needless to say this person's lack of skill limited the anointing to accompany worship. God can certainly bless music in C and F, but why should we limit Him to two keys? If you can play in one key, you have the talent to learn to play in several keys. At this point it becomes an issue of attitude, not talent. On the other hand, my wife, Freeda , is a most skillful pianist. She can play anything, in any key or style I need as a worship leader. Consequently, her skill releases her anointing as an accompanist, my anointing as a worship leader and the whole congregation's anointing to worship God in spirit and truth. Talent, developed into skill, releases anointing. Underdeveloped skill inhibits anointing.

There is no doubt that every church is anointed to worship God. The sad truth is that anointing is often held hostage by those who refuse to develop their talents into skills required for True Worship. This is not to say that God is weakened by man's limitations. He is infinite in power and no failing of ours limits Him in any way. But He has chosen to work through people. Therefore His power is shaped by the human vessel through which it flows. My point is that we have a wonderful opportunity here. We can take the talent God has given us and develop it into skills He can use. Like the little boy in the crowd when Jesus fed the five thousand, we can see

God take our limited natural gifts and touch them with His power, multiplying them many times over as He meets the needs of people around us. We must not be discouraged by the size of what we offer him. We must keep in mind that it is enough when we place it, all of it, in the Master's hands.

The same is true of the anointing to preach. God anoints the preacher to preach but the preacher must learn to use the English language and master the disciplines of public speaking. The great preachers are skillful communicators whose spirits are touched by the Spirit of God—skillful *and* anointed!

The Anointing
The Anointing is . . . *GOD'S CHOICE.*
The Anointing is . . . *GOD'S POWER.*
The Anointing is . . . *THE PARTNER OF SKILL.*

The anointing is precious—handle with care. David's flight from King Saul illustrates the proper attitude toward the Lord's anointed—hands off! Twice the wicked King was delivered into David's hands but the young man refused to make himself king. David's rule was this: "Touch not mine anointed, and do my prophets no harm" (I Chronicles 16:22, Psalm 105:12 KJV). A revival of this rule would do as much to advance the kingdom of God as any other single truth. We are so quick to strike out at the Lord's anointed. But this truth is a two-way street. Moses pronounces all of God's people are the Lord's chosen, His anointed.

> For you are a people holy to the LORD your God. The LORD your God has chosen you out of all the peoples on the face of the earth to be his people, his treasured possession. (Deuteronomy 7:6)

Let's examine David's rule in the light of this truth: "Touch not mine anointed"—Do not misuse, abuse, or take for granted

224 / Stephen R. Phifer

the people of God; they are the Lord's anointed! "And do my prophets no harm."—Do not misuse, abuse, or take for granted the leaders of God's people; they are the Lord's anointed! David would not harm Saul even when the king was as backslidden as a leader can get. These Old Testament accounts illustrate the New Testament atmosphere of mutual love and respect between leadership and laity that is a true work of the Holy Spirit. This is one of the results of True Worship. We cannot say we love God and demonstrate contempt for God's people, leaders or followers.

The Anointing
The Anointing is . . . GOD'S CHOICE.
The Anointing is . . . GOD'S POWER.
The Anointing is . . . THE PARTNER OF SKILL.
The Anointing is . . . PRECIOUS, HANDLE WITH CARE.

The anointing is your teacher. One of the most enriching and exciting aspects of the anointing is the inner quickening that comes from the Lord in the area of our anointing. John states it this way:

> As for you, the anointing you received from him remains in you, and you do not need anyone to teach you. But as his anointing teaches you about all things and as that anointing is real, not counterfeit— just as it has taught you, remain in him. (I John 2:27)

This is certainly not a teaching against teaching; pastor-teachers are gifts from the Lord to the Church. What is John saying, then? Only this, in the area of your anointing, part of the working of God in your life will be supernatural insight into what He has called you to do. I can remember many years ago in college sitting in an elementary music education class and sensing the prompting of the Holy Spirit in my heart about music ministry. Others were hearing a lecture on teaching music in schools while I was learning about music ministry in the Church because God had anointed me, even then, to it. Those who are anointed to do a certain ministry will always know things about that ministry no man has taught them because an intuition is at work in them. This inner teaching is necessary to the completion of their divine assignment. The inner teacher is the Holy Spirit.

The Anointing
The Anointing is . . . *GOD'S CHOICE.*
The Anointing is . . . *GOD'S POWER.*
The Anointing is . . . *THE PARTNER OF SKILL.*
The Anointing is . . . *PRECIOUS, HANDLE WITH CARE.*
The Anointing is . . . *YOUR TEACHER.*

Our Lives: The Highway of the Lord

Isaiah 40:1-6 challenges us to prepare our lives for the flow of the anointing we have from the Messiah. He wishes to travel through our lives to reveal himself to the world.

> *A voice of one calling: "In the desert prepare the way for the LORD; make straight in the wilderness a highway for our God. Every valley shall be raised up, every mountain and hill made low; the rough ground shall become level, the rugged places a plain. And the glory of the LORD will be revealed, and all mankind together will see it. For the mouth of the LORD has spoken." (Isaiah 40:3-5)*

Valleys. The Lord has chosen our lives as the wilderness His highway must pass through. There is no doubt that His power and glory can flow through us as He, himself, makes His way through our lives. The doubt that remains concerns itself with all the obstructions in His way. There may be valleys where our talents have not been developed into skills: the keys we cannot play in; the music notation we have never learned to read; the mysteries of the orchestra we have not explored; the choral sound we haven't learned how to teach; the conducting we have never really learned to do; the administrative skills we have never developed; the people skills we have never acquired; the public speaking we have never studied; the writing talent we have never drilled; the plan of study we have never completed; the native tongue we have never mastered. The list could go on and on.

Mountains and Hills. And what of the mountains and hills in the Lord's chosen path? When I lived in North Carolina, I observed that it took forever to build a road. Hills and mountains had to be reshaped to make way for the new route. In Kansas road building was easier for builders because there were no mountains to bring down. We human beings are a mountainous lot! We have mind-sets in us that are hindering mountains in the Lord's eyes: patterns of disobedience to which we are devoted, secret sins to which we are addicted, stubborn attitudes with which we have grown comfortable, ungodly alliances that sap our time and energy, or habits that drain our lives in a slow suicide. The road the Lord wants to travel leads straight through these mountains. If we are to see the fullness of His glory, these mountains must come down.

Crooked Paths and rough places. And the "crooked places that must be made straight." What of them? Is God waiting for us to come back into line so He can flow straight through us? No doubt He is. We have attained a comfortable, bendable morality that He will never share. The rough places hinder Him as well. None of us likes to travel on rough highways. Our vehicles are built for speed on smooth roads. Broken pavement unnerves us. Yet our lives are full of dangerous hazards. There are sudden, unmarked turns where we do not travel the path of truth and there are boulders strewn here and there where we have permitted pieces of old mountains to litter the road. There are also holes that threaten to wreck us, some shallow, some dangerously deep, where we have filled nothing in or where the material we have used (books, music, TV, films, friends) has no substance to it. None of us would like to travel such a road. Yet, with sloppy lives lived before the Lord, we ask Him to traverse some truly hazardous routes.

Isaiah's words challenge us—"Prepare ye the way of the Lord." John the Baptist preached the same sermon to the generation that saw Jesus' earthly ministry. Those who built up the valleys, brought down the mountains, straightened the crooked places, and smoothed the rough places in John's day saw the glory of the Lord revealed in the face of Jesus. Those who held on to their hindrances did not see the glory, yet, they were all chosen to live in a special generation. We have been chosen in the same way. They saw Messiah come the first time; we may see Him now in our worship and we may be the ones to see Him return the second time. He has chosen to travel through us.

The anointing demands discipline, elevating the daily disciplines of life to a plane of praise and worship. Each day is a day of function and *preparation* for the next day. The professional musician knows practice is as important as performance so he spends more time in preparation than in actual performance. The athlete trains. The writer writes. The Christian *lives!* Our daily living, as we bow ever more deeply to the Sovereign of our lives, becomes both function and preparation: function as He travels through us on the highway we have given Him and preparation for the incredible journey He plans to make through us in the days ahead. He has chosen to course through us in a blaze of never-fading glory as we prepare Him a way.

BUILD UP THE HIGHWAY!
Isaiah 40:3-5; 62:10

Build up the valleys of insufficiencies.
Bring down the mountains of hindering traditions.
Straighten out the crooked places of non-biblical practice.
Smooth out the rough places of carelessness.

AND THE GLORY OF THE LORD WILL BE REVEALED!

Understanding the Flow of the Anointing in Public Worship—The River of Life

We will shift now to another biblical illustration of how God's Spirit moves through our lives, The River of Life. If the anointing is the flow of God's power through His chosen vessels, then we must understand how His Spirit flows. Let us review the basics of this biblical model of worship.

- The psalmists saw the River: Psalm 1 pictures fruitfulness; Psalm 36, pleasure and life; and, Psalm 46, gladness for the city of God.
- Ezekiel 47 pictures the River flowing from the Temple wherein the Throne of God was established. He saw an increasing flow which I believe to be representative of the four depths of praise and worship: thanksgiving (ankle deep), exaltation (knee deep), adoration (waist deep), and communion (over the head). This progression is the "reasonable service of worship" referred to in Romans 12:1. Ezekiel saw fruit-bearing trees by the river and waters that brought healing and life.

- Jesus revealed that the River of Life is the flow of the Holy Spirit (John 7:37-39) from the Throne of God established in the Temple of our hearts. The River of Life always flows toward human need.

The Church is anointed to worship God! We have been chosen as the channel for this flow of divine life into human need. Because He has chosen us as the channel, and worship as the river of His life, when we obey Him in our anointing, when we worship God in Spirit and truth with all our soul, body, mind, and strength, *supernatural things will happen.*

One of the most joyful things about being a worship leader is listening as people try to describe what corporate worship means to them. They all seem somewhat baffled by it. It is greater than they can find words to express although I love hearing their attempts. How can we categorize the supernatural flow of God's very life through our lives? We use terms like, peaceful, inspiring, powerful, and real—all terribly inadequate words but the best we have. Just as sure as Aaron's rod budded, our dead and dry churches will spring to life when the deep waters of worship flow there. As worshipers and worship leaders, we must permit the waters of life to flow. In the next section we will explore the *flow* of the anointing through the lifestyle aspects of worship.

Before we do, permit one final point that I owe to my great friend Larry Hartley, a worship leader and pastor with a most effective ministry. We don't have to make the river flow. It flows constantly from the Throne of God. All we have to do is dig a channel to it with our passion and *let* it flow through us. As we obey the call to worship God, as we center our lives on Him, we dig a channel from our hearts to the throne of God. Then He flows through us, as a River of Life, a river of peace. As we worship with others, it is reasonable and powerful to realize that each worshiper increases the depth and flow of the River of Life. Is there any wonder that worship is the ministry of every believer? *Let the river flow!*

Worship That Pleases God
The Passion and Reason of True Worship

PART THREE

THE KINGDOM OF GOD IS JOY
IN THE HOLY SPIRIT

The True Worshiper's daily life should be joyfully creative, productive, and victorious in the power of the Holy Spirit.

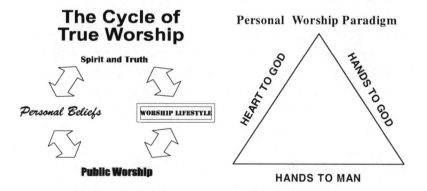

Chapter Ten

CRAFTSMANSHIP, CREATIVITY, AND THE JOY OF THE LORD

Bezalel

As his skillful hands worked with the hammer and the gold, Bezalel thought back to Egypt. He had learned the goldsmithing trade and he was good at it. But it was more than that. Even as he worked on the jewelry and household items for his masters in Egypt, objects that would never be his or make him rich, he was enriched somehow by the process itself. There was joy in it. He loved to look at the things he had made. They were not his things, nor was the gold he made them from. He was a slave in Egypt, a skillful artisan, but a slave.

In spite of slavery, Bezalel enjoyed his work. It satisfied something deep in him. Also within him, though he never spoke of it, there was a voice he could not explain. Every craftsman knows about the voice. It tells him things about his work. Things are just known somehow. It is part of the mystery of creativity and part of the joy of craftsmanship. "All those things I made," Bezalel thought, his mind still back in Egypt, "and nothing to show for it." Then, another, more accurate thought, "Nothing but skill." He stopped work and looked at his hands. What about them was special? What made them know what to do, where to stop, how much pressure to exert on the hammer or chisel? Perhaps the inner voice that gave him insight spoke directly to his hands as well.

He looked at the gold he was preparing, and then, to the Ark. It was carved and ready to be covered in gold. Moses said the plan for it was directly from God. Bezalel believed it. He had never seen anything so perfect. And the voice within had never been so loud and clear. He could not wait to start his part of the creation of the Ark. He was alive with ideas, with insights as to how it should be done and what the end result would be. Before starting back to work, he ran his fingers along the face of his best hammer. It was much like the one Aaron had used. Suddenly he was back to the terrible day at the foot of the mountain. Moses was in the mountain, up there with the smoke and lightning. He had been gone so long. The people were restless, practically leaderless with Aaron in charge. There was no restraint on them. Bezelel could see that they would soon have what they wanted—an idol. Some of his goldsmith friends had been contacted shortly after Moses disappeared. They wanted a golden calf, something familiar from Egypt.

Bezalel wanted nothing to do with it. The voice inside of him would not permit it. The thought of making another idol, here in the wilderness, repulsed him. He had made too many household idols in Egypt. There was no joy in such work and no voice inside to help. The voice deserted him when he had to make an idol. He knew the ancient traditions of his people spoke against such things. He was a son of Abraham, the man who had met the one true God, and spoken with him. He was creator of all things and could be fully represented by no single image. Most of the artisans felt the same way. They carried many rich materials with them from Egypt and were anxious to get to work, but not to make any more idols.

The demand of the people soon became public. Aaron himself did the smithing work. Bezalel watched in sadness as the tools of his trade were used by one of his leaders to make an idol. It made him ashamed, even though he had nothing to do with it, ashamed of Aaron, of his people, of his craft. He wanted to leave and he did. He didn't see the orgy, or Moses' wrath. He was glad to have missed both.

But now, he had work to do. Moses said God would come and live in this vessel. For ages to come God's business with man would be conducted before this ark. Craftsman of ages to come would only hear of this work, for this beautiful thing intended for the Most Holy Place, shut away from men's eyes. This work was for the Lord. The voice began to speak details of how the work should be done. Bezalel's hands began to obey. Egypt was forgotten.

Craftsmanship

Many times we think of God creating the universe but think of Jesus, sweating in a carpenter's shop, carefully crafting the work called for in each contract that came to His business. There is no biblical record of what He manufactured in His shop but we can be confident of His craftsmanship, the skill of His handiwork. Imagine for a moment that you had in your possession a wooden chair Jesus made in his carpenter shop. Try to imagine the quality of workmanship of the Master Craftsman. I'm sure that the detail work of the chair would be exquisite. The parts would fit together perfectly. The chair would sit well, perfectly crafted by the hands of the Master Craftsman.

Today, those wood-worn hands are scarred by nails. But they are gentle in their craftsmanship of the soul for we are His handiwork, His current contracts. With skillful hands He is patiently crafting us into His likeness. We were made in His image, craftsmen also with eternity's work to do. Along the way He wants us to enjoy our work. Like the peace He left us in His Throne Room, He has left us His joy in the work-place. "These things I have spoken to you," Jesus told His disciples on the night of their last supper together, "that My joy may remain in you and that your joy may be full "(John 15:11 NKJ).

"These things" included His teaching about fruitfulness in the power of God. As the Spirit of Truth and as Holy Comforter (Helper), the Holy Spirit would make Jesus real to them. Their lives would be fruitful because God's life would flow

234 / Stephen R. Phifer

through them. They would be like branches in Him, the True Vine. This relationship, this fruitfulness, would keep His joy in them and make their joy full.

Something has happened to our joy. This joyful manifestation of the Lord's inward presence seems to have slipped away from us and in its place is a dull discipline or perhaps a painful disobedience. The last section of this study will deal with this joy in three ways: as craftsmanship, the skills and productivity of our daily lives; as creativity, that spark of the Divine that shines in the work of our hands; and as confrontation with those who oppose us in the spirit realm, for we cannot be joyful if we live in defeat.

The Joy of the Branch in the Vine

What is the nature of the joy of Jesus, this joy of the branch in the vine? The Christian's joy is *the joy of productivity, of making things.* We are made to make things for we are created in the image of the One who made us. He is our Maker; we are makers, too. Just as He chose not to deal with an empty universe, but instead chose to speak worlds beyond imagination into existence, we deplore the vacuums in our lives. We spend our lives making things to fill them. Put a child in the floor with almost any type of material and without prompting from anyone, the child will start organizing the material into something. He may be the only one who can see it, but he has made something out of what was given him. This is what we do with life; we make something out of what is given us. The proper use of this urge is a key to joyful living.

- The salesman makes a sale.
- The homemaker makes a house into an oasis.
- The teacher makes a scholar and the student makes a grade.
- The repairman makes a repair.
- The executive makes a smooth running organization.
- The pastor has been told specifically to make disciples.

Most of life's pursuits can be described in terms of making something. But, if making is the joy of life and we are completely engaged in making, where is the joy Jesus left us?

Our goals have been polluted by the values of society around us. Instead of joy in producing, our culture has taught us to joy only in profiting. There is no joy in writing a song; one must write a hit song. There is no joy in pastoring a church; one must pastor a large church. There is no joy in making a home; one must have a better one than someone else. Our joy has been based in our bank account and not in the work of our hands, profit instead of productivity. At one time American craftsmen took joy in their work and made this country the greatest manufacturing nation on the globe. Now our joy is in our weekends not our weeks, our vacations not our vocations, and other nations are out producing us.

As God's people, we must lead the way back to productivity by taking joy in the craftsmanship of our daily lives. "And whatever you do, do it heartily, as to the Lord and not to men, knowing that from the Lord you will receive the reward of the inheritance; for you serve the Lord Christ" (Colossians 3:23,24 KJV). The word translated "heartily" has to do with the breath of life, "the vital force which animates the body" (Strong's). In other words, our attitude toward our daily craftsmanship is the key to the joy of living. Certainly this joy is part of the "inheritance" promised in Paul's words to the Colossians. When our work is done heartily unto the Lord, we know that He is our source and not the company that pays us. Our joy and confidence are recession-proof for they are based in One who is well beyond market fluctuations. He is the same yesterday, today, and forever.

Are there streams of biblical witness that support this view of life? For me, the story of the tension between two cities, Jerusalem and Babylon, illustrates the tension in our lives between productivity and profit, between devoting our craftsmanship as praise and worship to the Lord and devoting our life's efforts to selfish ends or even to the purposes of the enemies of God.

Jerusalem's Story: The City of God

We first know Jerusalem as Salem, which meant "peace." Melchizedek, a type of the Messiah to whom Abraham paid a tithe, was its king. When the nation of Israel came back from Egyptian captivity, the residents of the city made an alliance with Israel. Called Jebusites (the city was then called Jebus), the people became servants of the Jews and were gradually absorbed into the nation. By the time of King David only a Philistine garrison remained of the city's pagan past. David conquered the fort with its impressive high ground, which he called Zion and made Jerusalem his capital. Because David was a man after God's own heart and the Lord's anointed king, Jerusalem became the capital of the kingdom of God on earth.

Reading through the books of I and II Kings and I and II Chronicles we see that Jerusalem became the city of apostasy and idolatry. Good kings brought good times when their worship (including their daily living) was pleasing to God. Evil kings brought evil times when they corrupted their lives with idolatry. God raised up prophets and sent them to Jerusalem to call the kings, the priests, and the people back to the worship of the One True God. Finally, the cup of iniquity was full. The Lord lifted His protecting hand and Babylon conquered Israel, took the priests, the Levites, the musicians, and the craftsmen captive and destroyed Solomon's magnificent Temple.

A generation later in the time of Zerubabbel, Ezra and Nehemiah, Jerusalem became a city of restoration. The walls and Temple were rebuilt and True Worship re-established. For the next four centuries, whoever conquered the world conquered Jerusalem, but they did not destroy it. Its citizens learned to adapt to the Persians, the Greeks and finally the Romans. Throughout these centuries, Temple-centered worship and ceremony continued.

This was the Jerusalem to which Jesus came. Here He cleansed the Temple, performed miracles, taught God's truth, and wept over the city's rejection of His visitation. He also predicted its complete destruction. Inside Jerusalem's walls He was tried and beaten. Outside the city walls He was crucified, buried and rose to new life. This was the birthplace of the Church. Jerusalem's streets were witness to Pentecost's praise, the preaching of the disciples, and the miracles wrought by God's hand in the name of Jesus. But the city continued to reject the Spirit's work. In AD 70, less than forty years after the Resurrection, Jerusalem was sacked. The Temple was completely destroyed and so it remains to this day.

In Galatians 4 and Hebrews 12, Jerusalem is the name given to the spiritual city of God—the Church! In Revelation 12, Israel is seen as the sun-clothed woman who gives birth to the Messiah. Finally, in Revelation 21 and 22, we see the heavenly Jerusalem. There will be a new heaven and earth with a New Jerusalem as its capital. Here we see the kingdom of God in its final and eternal fullness.

Jerusalem is more than just a historical city. Politically it remains the focus of world attention. Spiritually, Jerusalem is the City of God, the Church, the dwelling place of those who are citizens of the kingdom of God. It is a city of peace, for Jesus rules there.

Babylon's Story: The City of Satan

The story of Babylon also begins in Genesis with the story of the Tower of Babel. Babel meant "confusion" and so it has always been with the Lord's enemy: truth and clarity of thought and purpose are always under attack. Satan deals in counterfeiting, substituting his rotten imitation for God's glorious original. So, in Babylon was found counterfeit worship and craftsmanship. Satan envies the creativity and craftsmanship of God's people so he takes good things and corrupts them with his hellish imitations. Just as he seeks to spoil the earth for it is God's creation, and us, for we also are God's handiwork, Satan seeks to take the good things in life and re-shape them into sins as one would kneed a lump of clay. Love becomes lust. Self-esteem becomes pride. Truths are twisted into lies. This is the work of Babel, later to become Babylon: copy, counterfeit, confuse, and corrupt the work of God so Satan can steal the glory that belongs to God.

During the conquest of Canaan, the time of the Judges, and the establishment of the great monarchies in Israel, Satan's city stood just beyond the horizon developing its counterfeit religions, art, commerce, philosophies, and craftsmanship. During the generations of the struggling kings, the iniquity of Jerusalem mounted until God withdrew His protective hand. Of all cities, Babylon conquered Jerusalem. The captives they took were priests, Levites, (singers and instrumentalists) and *craftsmen*. The wonders of Babylon were not enough for the conquerors, they had to have the craftsmen of Israel. Their pagan songs were the finest the fallen heart of man could produce, but the Babylonians demanded the songs of Zion. When Babylon rules, the worship of the One True God, whether in the Temple or in the marketplace, must be captured, counterfeited, and controlled until it ceases to exist at all.

When Cyrus of Persia conquered Babylon, it was the craftsmen who returned to rebuild Jerusalem, its walls, and its Temple. The priests and Levites returned to re-institute True Worship. The story of Ezra and Nehemiah, the story of worshiping and working in perfect balance, has become an allegory for every generation of men and women who want to rebuild what Babylon has captured.

But the story of Babylon does not end in the Old Testament. Revelation identifies two Babylons: Mystery Babylon, a worldwide religion with many faces and a physical city which will become the habitation of demons. Whether spiritual or physical, Babylon is the devil's capital, the counterfeit of Jerusalem. Modern-day Iraq contains the site of ancient Babylon. In the war between Iraq and United Nations forces in 1991, it was interesting to note the hostility of Iraq toward Israel; Babylon is always at war with Jerusalem.

In Revelation 17, the beast destroys Mystery Babylon. The worldwide religion is destroyed by the Anti-Christ. Satan does not mind masquerading in man's religions. At the moment of Revelation 17, all facades of false religion will be dropped and the world will see these religions for what they really are— Satan worship.

In Revelation 18 when the angel of the Lord is about to strike at the physical Babylon to utterly destroy the kingdom of Satan, he declares that certain things will no longer be the province of the powers of darkness. They will be reclaimed for the forces of light.

> *Rejoice over her, O heaven! Rejoice, saints and apostles and prophets! God has judged her for the way she treated you.'"* *Then a mighty angel picked up a boulder the size of a large millstone and threw it into the sea, and said:* "With such violence the great city of Babylon will be thrown down, never to be found again. The **music** of harpists and musicians, flute players and trumpeters, will never be heard in you again. No **workman of any trade** will ever be found in you again. The sound of **a millstone** will never be heard in you again. **The light of a lamp** will never shine in you again. **The voice of bridegroom and bride** will never be heard in you again. Your merchants were the world's great men. By your magic spell all the nations were led astray. In her was found the blood of prophets and of the saints, and of all who have been killed on the earth."* (Revelation 18:20-24)

Just as Satan's city is destroyed, before the devil is bound and cast into the pit for a thousand years, the angel of the Lord pronounces that the joyful things of life will no longer be the province of Babylon.

- Music (the sound of instruments and voices),
- craftsmanship (of *"whatsoever craft"*),
- industry (the sound of the millstone),
- learning (the candle light), and
- family life (the voices of the bridegroom and the bride) will be found in Babylon no longer.

Until these events unfold and the angel destroys Babylon wresting these precious things from the enemy's hands, while we await the rapture of the church, it is up to us to rescue them every day from the "Babylon" all around us. This is a good description of daily Christian living—taking back what the enemy has stolen from the people of God. This is one of the ways we spiritually extend the kingdom of God. This spiritual kingdom is a foretaste of the material kingdom Jesus will establish during the millennial reign, after the rapture of the church and the destruction of the Anti-Christ's forces.

There is one ultimate result of the capture of the joyful elements of life by the forces of the enemy—death. Verse 24 states that the death of the prophets (those who proclaim the Word of God), of the saints (those who live the Word of God), and of all who were slain upon the earth is attributed to Babylon; the blood of countless millions is found in her. Why? Because Satan knows that to corrupt things God meant for joy is to slowly suffocate the heart. Without music made unto the Lord (and all the arts), without craftsmanship unto the King (the joy of making), without the satisfaction of productive united efforts with fellow believers (industry, symbolized by the sound of the millstone), without the joy of learning changeless truth (the candle light) and without the security of the haven of a godly home (the voice of the bride and bridegroom), there is little in life to bring us joy. Satan has stolen these things, corrupted them into sins and filled Babylon with the noise of their pollution. The blood of all those slain on the earth is on the enemy's hands. Jesus has won the joyful things back for us. He has come that we might enjoy our creativity, our craftsmanship, our industry, our curiosity, and our families and that He might fill our lives with their music so we can *live* in His joy!

The Craftsman's Story

Why does the Bible make such prominent mention of craftsmen? They are specifically mentioned as builders of the

Tabernacle and the Temple, as captives of the Babylonians, as re-builders of Jerusalem, and as hostages of Babylon in Revelation 18. I believe that God desires His people to be noted as craftsmen—skillful makers. In this way we are created in His image. Jesus himself spent His youth and young adulthood as a craftsman. Craftsmanship, the desire to make, discover, design, build, arrange, accomplish, administrate, communicate, teach, repair, deliver and so on, is a characteristic of the child of God. For further evidence of this, let us examine the Scripture. Beginning from Exodus 31 we can understand the nature of craftsmanship.

> *And the Lord spake unto Moses, saying, See, I have called by name . . . Bezalel the son of Uri, the son of Hur, of the tribe of Judah:* **And I have filled him with the Spirit of God,** *in wisdom and understanding, and in knowledge, and in all manner of workmanship, to devise cunning works, to work in gold, and in silver, and in brass, and in cutting of stones, to set them, and in carving of timber, to work all manner of workmanship.*
> *And I, behold, I have given him Aholiab, the son of Ahisamach, of the tribe of Dan: and* **in the hearts of all that are wise hearted I have put wisdom that they may make all that I have commanded thee."** (Exodus 31:1-6 KJV)

> *And they came, every one whose heart stirred him up, and every one whom his spirit made willing, and they brought to the work of the Tabernacle of the congregation, and for all His service, and the holy garments. The children of Israel brought a willing offering unto the Lord, every man and woman, whose heart made them willing to bring for all manner of work, which the Lord commanded to be made by the hand of Moses. . . . See, the Lord has called by name Bezalel . . . and* **hath filled him with wisdom, in understanding, and in all manner of workmanship: and to devise curious works,** *to work in gold, and in*

*silver and in brass, . . . **and He hath put in his heart
that he may teach . . .** (35:21,29,30, 34 KJV)*

***Then wrought Bezalel and Aholiab, and every
wise hearted man, in whom the Lord put wisdom and
understanding to know how to work all manner of
work for the service of the sanctuary, according to all
the Lord had commanded.*** *(36:1 KJV)*

The children of Israel had gone into captivity a collection
of nomadic tribes but they emerged a nation of craftsmen.
They did the work in Egypt. This is why the Egyptians held on
to them so tightly; these descendants of herdsmen were now
the craftsmen of a great civilization. These passages are filled
with insights into the way God feels about the work of our
minds and hands. What do they teach us?

Our work is not a separate thing from our worship. If we
can do something, it is because God has put that wisdom and
understanding in us. Since our ability came from Him, our
greatest joy will come when we give it back to Him. In this
way, our worship and our works serve the same function, to
glorify the One who is the source of it all.

The source of our craftsmanship is God himself. Let no
one say that the desire within us to work is a result of man's
fall, a by-product of sin. Our heart for craftsmanship is a direct
reflection of the heart of the Designer-Creator of the universe.

Craftsmanship is neutral. Bezaleel used his gold-smithing
skills to cover the Ark of the Covenant. Aaron used those same
skills to build the golden calf. This is precisely the choice each
of us has:

- We can use our life-skills to build the habitation of God
  by His Spirit, a spiritual house of praise and worship;
- Or we can use our skills to build an idol to our ambitions.

**God uses the craftsmanship of man to accomplish His
plans.** Amazingly God has chosen to work through our hands.

In current generations we have allowed a dichotomy to replace this concept, thinking that some of what we do is "spiritual" (witnessing, giving, praying, preaching, etc.) and some is secular, (making a living, going to school, etc.). God sees no such distinction. He desires the work of our hands to be praise and worship unto Him. This, too, is the Living Sacrifice of Praise, the ministry of the Holy-Royal Priesthood, *the passion and reason of life.*

Christian Craftsmanship—
God's people do good work.

I am so appreciative of this truth because of my home life as a child. My dad was not a pastor, doing a "spiritual" work. For more than 25 years he was an automobile mechanic. To make ends meet, he sometimes held a second job. Over the years he was a city bus driver, a Dr. Pepper truck driver, and a door-to-door vacuum cleaner salesman, all while working as a full-time mechanic. My mom was a factory worker who became a nurse and then a dietitian in our hometown hospital. From my earliest childhood, these two craftsmen stood for Jesus in our small town. That is more than forty years of consistent, daily craftsmanship unto the Lord, mostly repairing cars and preparing hospital food for the glory of God. In their retirement, they stood tall in that town, known everywhere for their integrity, wisdom, compassion, and skill.

A teacher of mine, who was not a believer in Jesus, said of Dad. "Your Father's Jesus is the fountainhead of his life." She meant that Jesus was the source of Dad's life, like the headwaters of a river. Mom and Dad's retirement accounts may not have compared with most, but they were rich in heaven's currency and their accounts in the bank of eternity are still bearing interest. Yes, they had their "spiritual" ministries at the church. They both taught Sunday school (I was saved in my mother's class). They both made music for the King and my Dad was a deacon. But their lessons, songs and leadership were validated by the eloquence of their daily living. I remember Dad's hands, creased with dirt so deep it couldn't be washed away, the way only a mechanic's hands can be.

I remember the sounds mother made getting up early each day, reading her Bible, praying, and leaving for the hospital while all of us were still in bed. Now I realize that those hands did God's work and that early morning ritual was as powerful as any service of worship I conduct today. It was the work of the kingdom—craftsmanship unto the King!

The thief, lord of Babylon, has come to steal these joys from us—to make our daily living drudgery and not joyful praise. He wants to steal our talents and our dreams. He plans to kill our opportunities and our effectiveness. He intends to destroy our creativity, our productivity, our lives. "The thief cometh not, but for to steal, and to kill, and to destroy." (John 10:10 KJV). How does Satan do this?—by taking something good and corrupting it. Stephen reveals the end result of the process of corruption in his defense, recorded in Acts. "And they made a calf in those days, and offered sacrifices unto the idol, **and rejoiced in the work of their own hands"** (Acts 7:41 KJV).

Here is the process: First, we make something with our hands; next, we rejoice in it; then we idolize it, that is, we worship it. When we worship the work of our hands, it becomes an idol, the habitation of demons, like Babylon itself. Satan is enthroned upon our counterfeit, corrupted worship. Paul indicates that little household idols actually hosted devils (I Corinthians 10:20). Our household idols are no different. The things that we have made or earned can become Satan's opportunity in our lives when they become our idols, our objects of devotion. Satan has come to corrupt the results of our craftsmanship into idols. But Jesus went on to say, "I am come that they might have life, and that they may have it more abundantly"(John 10:10 KJV). By dedicating the work of our hands to the Lord, it becomes HIS habitation and our joy.

Jerusalem and Babylon today—"*COME OUT OF HER!*"
The warning from the angel in the Revelation concerning
Babylon is, "Come out of her, my people, that ye be not partakers of her sins, and that ye receive not of her plagues"
(Revelation 18:4 KJV). Babylon is Satan's kingdom, man's
value system. Jerusalem is God's kingdom, eternal truth. We
must learn to recognize God's image in the people around us
and in our own hearts. Craftsmanship is part of the image of
God in man. Likewise we must recognize the image of the
dark kingdom in ourselves and others. Laziness, self-centered-
ness, disrespect, deceit, pride, and greed have Satan's image
on them. "Come out of her!" the voice said. God is calling us
out of Babylon, out of the world's system of thought and
practice. We must be in this world, but not of it (John 17:15).

Building the Tabernacle in the Wilderness

The people of God in Moses' generation had become a
nation of craftsmen. At Mt. Sinai they received God's plan for
the Tabernacle in the wilderness, God's earthly dwelling place
in their generation. But what good is a plan and skill to build if
the craftsmen do not have materials? There in the wilderness,
these anointed skillful craftsmen had exactly the materials
needed for God's dwelling place. Upon their exit from Egypt
their former masters loaded them with riches. What a miracle!
They built their Tabernacle in the wilderness with the
combination of their craftsmanship, God's plan and the recap-
tured wealth of creation. The wealth of Egypt came from God
at the act of creation; it was created to give pleasure to Him.
These ancient craftsmen of Israel restored that wealth to its
rightful place in the kingdom of God.

At the time of Solomon the craftsmen of Israel had experienced several generations of tradition and inherited excellence. God gave them the plan for the Temple. God raised up a
warrior king in David to secure the borders of Israel so the
riches of creation could freely flow into the hands of craftsmen. Like the Tabernacle, the craftsmanship of God's people

built the Temple as the plan of God, reclaiming the riches of creation from the heathen nations.

This is the pattern of worship that pleases God—daily craftsmanship of such a high order that we are actually building lives on this earth fit to be His habitation.

- We have our skills (craftsmanship),
- His plan (the Bible) and
- We are recapturing the riches of creation (information, education, resources, technologies, materials, art forms) and
- With these creations we build our lives.
- God resides in us just as He did in the Tabernacle and the Temple, shining with His *Shekinah* from the Throne Room of our hearts.

As He shines in us each day we become lights in the darkness. Collectively, believers shine as a luminous city set on a hill which cannot be hidden, glowing in the dark as the One who is called "The Light of the World" gleams in hearts and hands where Jesus lives and rules. We have built Him a Tabernacle in our wilderness.

The church should be a productive center of activity. We should be using our skills to build the habitation of God by His Spirit, reclaiming the waste places where Satan has stolen or polluted the resources of creation. God will indwell the work of our hands if it is done unto Him and not unto men. Call to mind the promises found in the models of worship and apply them to daily craftsmanship. When we work as unto the Lord:

- The Throne of God is established,
- God rules in our lives;
- The River of Life flows from His Throne and
- Wherever the waters go, there is healing and fruition.

In the same way, we believers in Jesus incarnate Him into the world through the craftsmanship of our daily living.

Incarnation Is the Key

What is meant by the Church "incarnating" Jesus? Just as Israel was chosen among all nations to bring the Messiah into the world, and just as Mary was chosen among all women to bear God's Son, we have been chosen to bear Jesus into our world. Neither Israel nor Mary created Jesus. God is eternally existent as Father, Son, and Holy Spirit. This nation and this woman served only to incarnate Him into this world, to put Him into flesh by the power of the Holy Spirit. This is the exact mission of the Church. To incarnate Jesus into our world is not to create Him but to bring His love, His power, His truth, and His character into flesh, our flesh, our very lives!

Worship cannot stop with public ceremonies or even with private audiences with the King. If we are to bring Jesus to our world, it must go on to affect our daily living with the passion and reason of True Worship. As we love God with heart, soul, mind and strength, He flows through us, empowering us to love others, from our neighbor to our nation and beyond. What an awesome privilege. *"Whatsoever craft"* becomes a blessing to God and man. Babylon is depleted and out of the excellence of Zion, God shines.

Creativity

The creation of man was a special event, separate from the stream of creative acts when God called things into existence. God crafted man out of the clay and personally breathed into him His own life, imparting the eternal to time-locked man. A bit of heaven was squeezed into an earthly frame, and a spark, a creative spark, jumped like lightning from the mind and heart of God to the mind and heart of man.

Creativity is another aspect of the character of God resident within the heart of man. I believe creativity is the exclusive province of man and God. Angels are messengers carrying information, warriors fighting battles and guardians standing watch, but it is not recorded that they have ever originated anything. God and man originate things thus creativity is something only we share. Satan, a fallen angel, is clever but does not originate things. (When he is described in Ezekiel 28:11-19, he is described more as an musical instrument than as a musician.) He will corrupt the things that man and God create but he will never come up with anything new. Possibly this ability to create is what Satan lusts after most.

Of course, man's creativity pales besides that of God, but its source is God's character. We are made in His image: He is the creator; we are creative. Creativity, then, is one of the joys of life that Satan has pounced on and smashed into a burden and a bother. Jesus has come to reawaken the creativity within us so the Holy Spirit can flow through it to the healing of the nations.

The creativity of mankind is also eternal. Why? Because the Christian's creativity flows as part of his worship. We worship God because His character is revealed to us. It is the river that cannot be crossed, totally without limitation. Just so, there is no limit to the creative expression of man through all the arts in the praise and worship of God's limitless character. We will spend eternity discovering new things about God and expressing them in word, in song, and in graphic display. Our creativity is an eternal link with God.

What is the difference between creativity and craftsmanship? The difference between these complimentary concepts can be expressed in terms of the craftsman and the originating artist. Every artist needs to be a craftsman whether he is an artist who brings new works into existence or an interpretive artist who brings existing works to life. But every craftsman is not an originating artist. The difference is with the process of origination. The artist tries to do something original and do it very well. The craftsman is primarily concerned with the quality of the piece. The interpretive artist tries to do an existing work in an original manner. The world needs many more craftsmen and interpreters than originating artists. One original creation can supply many craftsmen with satisfying work to do. A playwright originates a play and creates work for a whole company of craftsmen, the producer, director, stage manager, actors, technicians and so forth. A composer creates an original piece supplying the editor, publisher, conductor and performer with work to do. The artist is not superior to the craftsman and craftsmen certainly need to be creative. These are two complimentary sides to the creative nature of God implanted in the human spirit; God is both creator and craftsman. The world and the kingdom of God need both.

Creation in the Garden

For biblical support of this view we turn to the beginning. Man, this special product of God's personal craftsmanship, was alone in the garden and that was not good. One needs someone to share with if he is be creative. God caused a deep sleep to overtake Adam. God tore his side, took from the wound a rib and healed the wound. From the rib He fashioned the woman and breathed into her the breath of life, making her His final and ultimate creation. He hid her, awakened Adam and brought Eve to him. Adam rejoiced in his wife, as all right-thinking husbands have done since and called her Eve, "the mother of all living." God granted to her special creative gifts. We think of some of them as mothering instincts, but really they amount to a creative spark given only to women who must participate in the creation of, of all things, people. God always gives a special touch for a special task.

Male and female created He them and He pronounced that they were good, even very good. The fall of man is so obvious to us it is difficult for us to imagine the goodness of man. But before the fall, man was good, very good. God said so. That meant that the inventory of things God put into man contained no mistakes, nothing which God did not intend to be there. A partial list would read:

- the arts (all expressive activity),
- industry (the ability to work together),
- family (marriage and child rearing),

- love (between husband and wife),
- leadership (the selection of some to guide others),
- curiosity (the desire to know and discover),
- gamesmanship (the fun and games of life), and
- craftsmanship (the need to make things).

It was all good, very good, for it came from God who had a plan for it all.

We are beginning to recognize that our creative abilities have an important role to play in the drama of end-time events. Like a good dramatist, God knows that things that are to be significant in the final act must be introduced in the opening act. Creativity and craftsmanship are not in man by accident; they are for a purpose—God's purpose! He expressed the plan in the commands given to Adam and Eve.

- *"Be fruitful and multiply."*—be productive; be creative.
- *"Subdue the earth."*—Conquer creation; unlock its potential; discover its mysteries.
- *"Have dominion."*—care for the animals, the environment, the earth; rule creation wisely and lovingly.

Creation was to be man's school, his work place, and his vacation/vocation paradise. This garden of Eden was for man's delight.

But sin was lying in wait beneath the green-speckled shadows of Eden. Satan, as a serpent, beguiled Eve, corrupting her God-given desire for knowledge into a violation of God's clear instructions. Doubt was his beguiling song. Eve had no knowledge of evil, only good. She and Adam knew the Tree of Life—love, relationship, truth, joy, discovery, creativity. But Satan took her to the Tree of Knowledge, knowledge of good *and evil.* If knowledge was good, went the song of the temptor, the knowledge of good *and evil,* must be good; exquisite to the taste, pleasant to the eyes, desirable to make one wise. "You shall not die," he said, "God just wants to hold you back. He doesn't want you to be like him." She believed the lie and tasted of the forbidden. The knowledge of evil overwhelmed her as, for the first time, she was separated from God.

She hurried to Adam. Would she be separated from him, too? Yes. For a moment, Adam was suspended between a sinless God and a sinful humanity, a position from which another Adam, the seed of the woman, would someday bruise the serpent's head. This first Adam, powerless to remove the separating sin, forsook his God and joined his wife in rebellion.

New themes were added to the repertoire of man's expression: suffering, separation, defeat, treachery, betrayal, and death. Craftsmanship became toil. Man would now create only by the sweat of his brow. Just as Babylon captured Jerusalem, Satan captured the creativity of man. He has used that divinely given creative passion of man to light the path to hell. Man's creativity has become Satan's opportunity to beguile the children of Adam and Eve to worship at his footstool.

Recovering the Gift of Creativity

The arts are concerned with truth and beauty. Some have confused the arts with entertainment. Entertainment may be artfully done and art may be entertaining but these are two different forces in the world. The concern of the entertainment world is the amusement of a mass audience. The literal meaning of "amuse" is to be without (the prefix "a") thought or inspiration ("muse"). This means that entertainment is always seeking the common appeal of as many customers as possible; ticket sales, subscriptions, copy sales, etc. Art has a much different goal. Instead of dulling thought, art seeks to stimulate thought; if you will, to "muse" not "amuse." The art worlds of music, painting, sculpture, literature, dance, theatre, television, and film all have their own small audiences quite separate from the entertainment wings of these same pursuits. Sometimes one is called "serious" art and the other, "commercial" art. The artist wants to confront his patron with his view of truth and beauty to persuade him of the validity of

252 / Stephen R. Phifer

the artist's vision. "Serious" artists sometimes venture into the entertainment world to make a living, bringing with them their views of truth and infusing entertainment with those views.

"Truth has stumbled in the streets." Prior to the twentieth century, it was generally considered that truth was absolute, true for all men at all times. During the nineteenth century the scientific and art worlds came to the conclusion that there is no absolute truth. As we enter the twenty-first century, the worlds of art, science, education and entertainment have all become united in this belief in the one absolute of relativism: "There is no absolute truth."

Modern man may believe this intellectually but something in his heart will not buy it. Just because man believes he is not a spiritual being, does not mean his spirit goes away somewhere. It is still there, needing what it needs and sending man into confusing attempts to feed the spirit: New Age philosophy, scientology, reincarnation, the occult, etc. Even art and education have become religions for some who think that food for the soul will nourish the spirit. Some even worship the physical body as if fitness or fatness can cure a leanness of heart, a starving spirit.

"In Adam's fall we sinned all." Isaiah records the plight of fallen man, his creative gifts taken captive by the enemy, in his 59th chapter. As you read through these verses, bear in mind the terrible state of the creative world today;

- the perversity in the arts,
- the wickedness of the entertainment world,
- the darkness of the educational community, and
- the tragic spiritual barrenness of the scientific community.

THE FALL OF TRUTH
Isaiah 59

SIN SEPARATES FROM GOD.

But your iniquities have separated you from your God; your sins have hidden his face from you, so that he will not hear. (2)

IMMENSE GUILT PLAGUES THE SOUL.

For your hands are stained with blood, your fingers with guilt. Your lips have spoken lies, and your tongue mutters wicked things. (3)

JUSTICE, FAIRNESS, RIGHTEOUSNESS, AND PEACE ARE UNKNOWN.

No one calls for justice; no one pleads his case with integrity. They rely on empty arguments and speak lies; they conceive trouble and give birth to evil. (4)

The way of peace they do not know; there is no justice in their paths. They have turned them into crooked roads; no one who walks in them will know peace. (8)

So justice is far from us, and righteousness does not reach us. We look for light, but all is darkness; for brightness, but we walk in deep shadows. So justice is driven back, and righteousness stands at a distance; **truth has stumbled in the streets,** *honesty cannot enter. (9,14)*

DESTRUCTION IS THEIR WAY, DARKNESS AND SADNESS, THEIR LOT.

Their feet rush into sin; they are swift to shed innocent blood. Their thoughts are evil thoughts; ruin and destruction mark their ways. (7)

Like the blind we grope along the wall, feeling our way like men without eyes. At midday we stumble as if it were twilight; among the strong, we are like the dead. (10)

We all growl like bears; we moan mournfully like doves. We look for justice, but find none; for deliverance, but it is far away. (11)

THEIR WORKS FAIL TO SATISFY THEIR OWN HEARTS.

They hatch the eggs of vipers and spin a spider's web. Whoever eats their eggs will die, and when one is broken, an adder is hatched. (5)

Their cobwebs are useless for clothing; they cannot cover themselves with what they make. Their deeds are evil deeds, and acts of violence are in their hands. (6)

THEIR TRANSGRESSIONS MULTIPLY.

For our offenses are many in your sight, and our sins testify against us. Our offenses are ever with us, and we acknowledge our iniquities: rebellion and treachery against the LORD, turning our backs on our God, fomenting oppression and revolt, uttering lies our hearts have conceived. (12,13)

TRUTH, ETERNAL, ABSOLUTE TRUTH IS THE CASUALTY, MAKING THE INNOCENT THE HUNTED PREY.

truth has stumbled in the streets, (14)

Truth is nowhere to be found, ("so truth fails" NKJ) and whoever shuns evil becomes a prey. (15a)

All of these fallen systems have succumbed to evil because the creative heart of man has fallen to sin and Satan's kingdom. From these verses we see the Fall of Truth, and with it, the fall of man's ability to express truth and beauty through the arts.

"Truth has fallen in the streets." So complete has been Satan's capture of the creative heart of man that the very things intended to refresh the heart such as music, literature, drama, dance, and graphic display have been used instead to preach hell's half-truths and crush the heart of man. Man's creative passion has been severed from godly reason. *"So truth fails."*

The Rescue of Truth and Creativity of Man

Truth is also God's concern, His very essence, in fact. A moment ago we stopped midway in verse 15. As we continue, we see that the failure of truth was something God could not tolerate.

> *The LORD looked and was displeased that there was no justice (15b). He saw that there was no one, he was appalled that there was no one to intervene; so his own arm worked salvation for him, and his own righteousness sustained him. He put on righteousness as his breastplate, and the helmet of salvation on his head; he put on the garments of vengeance and wrapped himself in zeal as in a cloak.* (Isaiah 59:15b,16,17)

When the failure of truth was beyond the ability of man to redeem, God sent Jesus, His own arm, clothed in righteousness, salvation and judgment to restore what had fallen into Satan's hands. Jesus came as *"Truth"* to restore truth to man. "For since by man came death, by man came also the resurrection of the dead. For as in Adam all die, even so in Christ shall all be made alive" (I Corinthians 15: 21,22). Jesus came to restore all that had died. This must include the creativity God put into the heart of man in the Garden of Eden.

The Second Adam and the Second Eve

There, in a garden unlike Eden, one brimming with death's residue instead of life's promise, lay another Adam. His body also slept but this was the deep sleep of death. His side was also torn but this wound, from the jagged edge of man's sin, would never close. By the blood of this Adam's wounds, God fashioned a bride. The Holy Spirit awakened this second Adam on the first day of the week. Fifty days later, that same Spirit breathed the breath of God into the Bride and she, the Church, the Second Eve, was presented to the Second Adam, fully prepared by the Spirit to be the "mother of all living" in Christ. The Second Adam took a bridegroom's deep joy in His bride, the Second Eve—*the Church!*

Through the Church, the Lord wants to reveal His character to the world and touch a hurting humanity. This is another sense in which, the Church incarnates Jesus to the world. The Bible remains just a book to those who never open it until someone starts to live it before them. Jesus is the embodiment of truth and beauty. The artist who is a Christian is gifted in talent and temperament to express truth and beauty, therefore, the joy of the Christian artist is to incarnate Jesus through the works of his craft. This does not mean that every painting must have representation of Jesus in it, that every story written or dramatized must be a Bible story, or that every song (except perhaps in the context of a worship service—*psalms, hymns, and spiritual songs*) has to be a "Christian" song. Artists need to address all areas of life with eternal truth.

The Lord is restoring within the Church all that was taken captive, all that fell:

- the heart and all its contents (the arts),
- the mind and all its potential (industry, education, science),
- the body and all its senses (sexual love within marriage, pleasure, athletics), and
- the spirit in all its power (worship, prayer, the Word).

Calvary restores it all and the Holy Spirit empowers it all—*joy in the Holy Ghost!*

As we read in Isaiah's prophecy, we see the Bride, the Second Eve, in all her resplendent and fruitful glory. For two reasons, I believe the time of the fulfillment of these verses is the church age: Jesus proclaimed His earthly ministry from these passages, (Isaiah 61, Luke 4) and, the age described is not one of universal peace, as the Millennial Reign will be.

THE RESTORATION OF TRUTH AND CREATIVITY
Isaiah 60, 61

PEOPLE (INCLUDING GENTILES) ARE TOLD TO ARISE AND SHINE.

"Arise, shine, for your light has come, and the glory of the LORD rises upon you. See, darkness covers the earth and thick darkness is over the peoples, but the LORD rises upon you and his glory appears over you. Nations will come to your light, and kings to the brightness of your dawn. (60:1-3)

SONS AND DAUGHTERS SHALL RETURN TO THE LORD.

"Lift up your eyes and look about you: All assemble and come to you; your sons come from afar, and your daughters are carried on the arm. (4)

THE HOUSE OF THE LORD WILL SHINE WITH HIS GLORY.

I will adorn my glorious Temple. (7) I will glorify the house of my glory. (AV)

"The glory of Lebanon will come to you, the pine, the fir and the cypress together, to adorn the place of my sanctuary; and I will glorify the place of my feet. (13) I will make the place of my feet glorious.(v. 13 AV)

THE EXCELLENCE OF GOD WILL SHINE IN HIS PEOPLE.

"Although you have been forsaken and hated, with no one traveling through, I will make you the everlasting pride and the joy of all gen-erations. (15) Instead of bronze I will bring you gold, and silver in place of iron. Instead of wood I will bring you bronze, and iron in place of stones. I will make peace your governor and righteousness your ruler. (17)

THERE WILL BE SUPERNATURAL SUSTENANCE.

The sun will no more be your light by day, nor will the brightness of the moon shine on you, for the LORD will be your everlasting light, and your God will be your glory. (19) Then will all your people be righteous and they will possess the land forever. They are the shoot I have plant-ed, the work of my hands, for the display of my splendor. (21)

THE PEOPLE WILL EXPERIENCE THE MESSIAH'S MINISTRY.

The Spirit of the Sovereign LORD is on me, because the LORD has anointed me to preach good news to the poor. He has sent me to bind up the brokenhearted, to proclaim freedom for the captives and release from darkness for the prisoners, to proclaim the year of the Lord's favor and

the day of vengeance of our God, to comfort all who mourn, and provide for those who grieve in Zion—to bestow on them a crown of beauty instead of ashes, the oil of gladness instead of mourning, and a garment of praise instead of a spirit of despair. They will be called oaks of righteousness, a planting of the LORD for the display of his splendor.(61:1-3)
THEY WILL REBUILD THE THINGS SATAN HAS DESTROYED.
They will rebuild the ancient ruins and restore the places long devastated; they will renew the ruined cities that have been devastated for generations. (4)
THEY ARE KNOWN AS PRIESTS AND SERVANTS.
And you will be called priests of the Lord, you will be named ministers of our God. You will feed on the wealth of nations, and in their riches you will boast. (6)
THEIR WORK WILL BE DIRECTED PERSONALLY BY THE LORD.
. . . and I will direct their work in truth. (v. 8 KJV)
THE LORD AND HIS PEOPLE ARE LIKE BRIDEGROOM AND BRIDE.
I delight greatly in the LORD; my soul rejoices in my God. For he has clothed me with garments of salvation and arrayed me in a robe of righteousness, as a bridegroom adorns his head like a priest, and as a bride adorns herself with her jewels. (10)
THIS WILL HAPPEN AS SURE AS PLANTING AND HARVEST.
For as the soil makes the sprout come up and a garden causes seeds to grow, so the Sovereign LORD will make righteousness and praise spring up before all nations. (11)

Man's heart is a garden. At the moment of creation, God sowed good seed into that garden. When that heart kneels at the cross, it is reborn and the good seed rejuvenated. As the Holy Spirit moves upon that heart, stripping away the binding vestiges of sin, the good seed springs forth as righteousness and praise before all nations. This includes the creativity of man. Joy is restored! Reason, the truth of God, rescues passion, the truth of man.

Christian Creativity—
God's people do original work.

Is There A Revival of the Arts?

Let us ask the question in other ways. Does God love the artist? If creativity is a gift from God, then it is special to Him. If creativity is a link between God and man and if God has plans to use that creativity in His work, then it must be important to Him. What happens to the singer, instrumentalist, painter, writer, actor, director, dancer, or artist of any discipline, when he is restored by the Lord?

Under proper pastoral guidance, he will infuse his work with the truth and beauty of Jesus. If artists love the Lord, and their abilities come from God's heart, surely He has plans for them in His work. What would then be the result of thousands of artists coming to know Jesus? Thousands of spiritually reborn artists would start creating works of art that reflect the glory of God and the truth about the human condition. Some have sought to think of a revival of the arts as an abstraction, disconnected from real life or real people. What we are seeing is a revival among artists. Because they come to know the Lord and center their lives on Him, there is a revival of the arts. In the same way, there should be a revival in banking as bankers find Jesus, a revival in education as educators come to the Lord, a revival in government as leaders become committed to Jesus on and on we could go.

The Lord has much that He wants to say to the Church and to the world. through the ministry of each believer. He has gifted many men and women with creativity. He has infused them with truth and showered them with light. These creative craftsmen are waiting in the Church for someone to recognize this and to employ them in harvest. If these people are anointed to sing, play, direct, act, and so forth, God's power will flow through them as they obey Him in their anointing. They bring more than the power of the truth and beauty of Jesus—they also bring His joy.

We are not all artists, but each of us has that creative spark in some area. Just as our craftsmanship is a key to a joyful life, so our creativity awaits deep within our hearts for opportunity to emerge from the shadows where life has driven it. As we center our lives on God himself, and as our passion is focused by the reasoning of the Word of God, our creativity and craftsmanship can flood our daily living with our inheritance—the Joy of Jesus, the Creator.

Thou art worthy, O Lord, to receive glory and honour and power: for thou hast created all things, and for thy pleasure they are and were created.
(Revelation 4:11 KJV)

—

Chapter Eleven

KEEPING THE JOY
Worship as Confrontation with Spiritual Opposition

Elisha's Servant

It's hard sometimes to make the connections. A heathen leper had been healed by dipping in the Jordan the way Elisha told him to. A Shunamite woman, the one who made the room for Elisha, had her dead son brought back to life when the prophet stretched out on him. A lost ax head had dutifully floated to the surface when Elisha needed it. Gehazi, the servant who had, until recently, been chief among the servants was now a leper because Elisha had sent Naaman's leprosy on him. But what did all that have to do with an enemy army that had them surrounded? It will take more than floating axe heads or dips into Jordan to get out of this!

"Our army is bigger than theirs." Elisha said, when his servant expressed his fears.

That's really good to know, thought the newly appointed chief servant, but when will it get here? Seeing what had happened to Gehazi, he had decided to keep a tight reign on his tongue. But when you work for a prophet of the Most High God, the One who knows all, it doesn't really help to keep your mouth shut. It is almost like He can read your thoughts.

The prophet sighed and patiently prayed to God to open the servant's eyes.

Those eyes were searching the horizon in the waning daylight, looking for some promising cloud of dust that could only mean that Elisha's army was about to rescue them. So focused was he on the horizon, he did not really notice that the air seemed to clear before him, as if a curtain had been pulled aside. Another army, indeed, much larger than the heathen horde, was standing before him, behind the enemy. Quickly he looked toward the flank. How large was this army? He could not find a flank. He would remember later the amused look on Elisha's face as he had passed through his astounded servant's field of vision as he spun around passed his original position. This army had the enemy surrounded!

The servant looked around at Elisha. The prophet was profoundly amused. Quickly, the servant of the prophet, looked back at the army. There was something he had to figure out. He had observed something . . . different about this army. He thought he saw what he saw, but he needed to look again. He stared intently at the soldiers, the chariots, the horses. Their flesh seemed to . . . glow. It looked like they were made of . . . fire. That couldn't be, of course.

Suddenly the obvious thought exploded in his brain. He looked at the heathen army. There was no alarm. Sentries and watch fires revealed no panic. The heathen army did not know they were surrounded! Then, like a cloud passing in front of the face of the moon, the whole scene before him of impending battle began to dim. Soon all he could see was the enemy and the vacant horizon. But that horizon did not disappoint him nor did the enemy army frighten him any longer.

"Our army is bigger than theirs," he said to himself.

Elisha smiled at him and turned to gaze out over the heads of the enemy.

Spiritual Warfare

"Fight the good fight of faith." "Wage a good warfare." Paul's militant exhortations to believers in his day still ring true for us today. Some shy away from military images in worship music, seeing no reason to sing "Onward Christian Soldiers" in this enlightened age. Well, the devil is not yet in chains and he is nowhere near the pit. *The Christian life is spiritual warfare.* This being the case, worship must have a role in the conflict.

We have come a long way and learned much about establishing the Lord's kingdom through our worship. We have learned about our righteousness before God and our peace with God. We have even learned about craftsmanship and creativity, the keys to our joy in the Holy Spirit. But, if we do not know how to resist the devil so that he must flee, all this knowledge will not bring us joy.

No matter how passionate and excellent we are with thanksgiving, exaltation, adoration, and communion, Satan will still come against us. No matter how reasonable we are or how faithful to the deep pools of peace we know as public worship, between services the enemy will attack us. Regardless of our skill as craftsmen or our cleverness as creators, our adversary will still oppose us. We cannot be joyful; we cannot know God's peace; and we cannot enter fully into the righteousness of Jesus if we are defeated. In this chapter we learn how to resist the devil through our praise and worship.

The Church Is God's Spokesman in the World.

We have discussed our identity in Jesus as priests, now it is time to see ourselves as prophets, also. Prophets are those who speak forth the Word of God as well as those who foretell future events. Paul told the Ephesians that God has called out the Church for just this type of proclamation. In Chapter 3 Paul speaks of the Church as a mystery hidden from the prophets but now revealed to apostles. He describes the Church as a coming together of Jews and Gentiles as "fellow-heirs, and of the same body, and partakers of his promise in Christ by the gospel" (Ephesians 3:6 KJV). In this passage he reveals one of the intentions God had in creating the Church.

To the intent that now the manifold wisdom of God might be made known by the church to the principalities and powers in heavenly places, according to the eternal purpose

*which He accomplished in Christ Jesus our Lord, in whom
we have boldness and access with confidence through faith in
Him.* (Ephe-sians 3:10-12 NKJ)

God intends to speak to mankind through the Church.

- We have the gospel story of Jesus to tell.
- We understand we must admonish and teach one
  another, echoing the timeless truths we have learned.
- We see the importance of speaking to God in praise,
  worship, prayer and singing to Him with our sacrifices
  of praise.

*But, have we realized that from the beginning God has intended
that we speak to the powers and principalities arrayed against the
kingdom of God?* This purpose of the Church is a major theme
of Scripture. Through our speaking, as well as our obedience
to God, we resist the enemy; and when we resist the devil, he
must flee. "Submit yourselves therefore to God. Resist the
devil, and he will flee from you" (James 4:7 KJV).

What do we speak? This Ephesians passage gives us much
to say. We are "to make known the manifold wisdom of God."
In other words, we resist the devil with the declaration of
praise, when we proclaim the multifaceted wisdom of God.
"The manifold wisdom of God" is the theme of our praise and
worship as we declare who God is and what He has done;
"God is great! His mercy endures forever! God is wise! He is
the Loving Creator of all things. Worthy is the Lamb! Holy is
the Lord!" Satan will flee before this! He cannot co-exist with
our praise.

There Is a Battle in the Heavenlies and One on Earth.

There is a battle in the heavenlies. "For we wrestle not
against flesh and blood, but against powers, against the rulers
of the darkness of this world, against spiritual wickedness in

high places" (Ephesians 6:12). Satan's kingdom is "above" the earth, not so much in its direction as in its nature; it is a spiritual kingdom. Though we encounter people as we fight the good fight every day, we must learn to see the spiritual "above" the human. Many times Satan's forces are there, influencing the attitudes and actions of those who are against us.

But this is not the whole story. There are other sources of evil in our lives. John provides the other side of the picture for us. There is also a battle on earth. "For everything in the world— the cravings of sinful man, the lust of his eyes and the boasting of what he has and does—comes not from the Father but from the world" (I John 2:16). The lust of the flesh and of the eye and the pride of life are such powerful forces of evil, there is little need for the enemy to dispatch his forces to tend them. A Christian struggling with the flesh, with envy, or with pride may seek victory by resisting the devil when there are no demons involved at all—just the wickedness of his own human heart. We always want God to deliver us from the evil of spiritual wickedness arrayed against us (and He does!) but in these cases the victory comes through discipline, not deliverance. Discipline is just as much a work of grace as deliverance and probably of greater long-term benefit. But, "over" every conflict of soul, taking advantage of every weakness, lust, and prideful thought, there is a wicked spir-itual kingdom "over" the earth—a battle in the heavenlies.

The basic issue of the conflict is worship: Who will rule? Who will serve? Satan lusted after the worship that belongs only to God and he was thrown down from heaven. Slithering there in Eden, with envy greener than any leaf in the garden, he watched as God crafted man and woman and then fellowshiped with them. This was the relationship, expressed by Adam and Eve in worship, that Satan had to break up. If God wanted mankind to worship Him, then Satan must capture man's heart and bend him toward his throne. He uses man's innate desire for relationship with God against both man and God. He has a plan:

- **Step One**—have man worship idols;
- **Step Two**—have man worship Satan.

The idols change from age to age and culture to culture. The image doesn't matter. They can range from wooden images of animals, to grotesque humanoid figures, abstract institutions (government, education), documents (the Constitution), organizations, sports teams, entertainment personalities or even man himself. These are all idols—Step One. Satan is content as long as we do not worship Jesus as the only begot-ten Son of God. When the final victory is won, the result will be True Worship by all remaining mankind as well as heaven's hosts. Every knee shall bow and every tongue will confess that Jesus Christ is Lord. Thus, the conflict of the ages began over worship, and worship will be its conclusion. In between the beginning and ending, worship is also the warfare we wage and our victory in it.

Waging the Warfare

The weapons of this warfare are not the fleshly or soulish weapons of man. We cannot resist the devil in our strength. The weapons we need are spiritual, full of God's power, and able to pull down the strongholds of the enemy.

> *The weapons we fight with are not the weapons of the world. On the contrary, they have divine power to demolish strongholds. We demolish arguments and every pretension that sets itself up against the knowledge of God, and we take captive every thought to make it obedient to Christ.* (II Corinthians 10:4-5)

We do not go into battle defenseless or without offensive power. God has provided us with what we need to wage a good warfare. Let's visit the arsenal of the Army of God! Here are *some* of the weapons we use in our warfare:

THE WEAPONS OF OUR WARFARE

The Name of Jesus (Eph. 1:21)
The Word of God (sword of the
the Spirit (Eph. 6:17)
Praise (Ps. 149:6; Eph. 3:9-12)
Tithing (Mal. 3:8-12)
Fasting (Is. 58:1-14)
Spiritual language (Rom. 8:26-27)

The blood of Jesus (Rev. 12:11)
The word of our testimony (Rev.
12:11)
Spirit-walk (also called, holy life,
obedience, faithfulness) (Matt.
24:45-47)
Spiritual armor (Eph. 6:10-17)

Prayer (including worship) is more than a weapon . . .
IT IS THE BATTLE ITSELF!

Ancient Warfare

To understand the biblical illustrations of Spiritual Warfare we must think of war as it was fought in the Bible era. In ancient times, before it became the province of machines, warfare pitted soldier against soldier with few weapons that did not depend upon the arms and legs of the warrior or his animal. Ancient armies waged three basic types of warfare.

- First was the raid. A small force would move quickly into enemy territory, do as much damage as possible, and retreat to safe ground.
- Second was the assault. A large force would attack an enemy position head-on in an attempt to capture new ground and destroy the enemy force.
- Third was the siege. An army would surround an enemy stronghold, cutting it off from supplies, communication, and reinforcements until it had to surrender.

All three of these types of warfare are mentioned in Scripture. They correspond to the three types of warfare the Christian must wage against the spiritual wickedness:

- personal worship,

- public worship, and
- daily craftsmanship.

The Raid Private prayer is like a personal raid on the enemy. You and all the heavenly raiders you can summon strike
off behind enemy lines in a sequence something like this:

- First, you enter His gates with thanksgiving and dwell
  in His courts with your praise.
- Next, you come into the holy place of prayer in the
  light of the Holy Spirit, placing all your personal petitions before Him.
- Then you enter the Holy of Holies by the blood of the
  Lamb and worship the Lord there, communing spirit-
  deep with Him. There you hear the Spirit's call to
  battle, His "muster" call, summoning you to battle over
  a specific issue. The effectual, fervent prayer of the one
  righteous man, Jesus Christ, begins to well up in your
  spirit and you allow the Spirit to pray for you the
  manifold wisdom of God. (James 5:16; Romans 8:26,27)
  Your own effectual, fervent prayer resists the enemy.

You have entered Satan's territory (the heavenlies) and
you are resisting him, disrupting his communications with
perfected praise and petition. Strongholds begin to crumble as
hell's forces are weakened. *The kingdom of God is advanced!*

The Assault Public worship is like a pitched battle, an assault by a huge army on a strongly defended enemy position.
When a body of believers gathers for worship in their city,
they are actually assaulting the powers and principalities
"over" that city.

- The Lord leads the Church into battle.
- The holy-royal priesthood gathers, forming a mighty
  army.
- We enter His gates with thanksgiving and dwell in His
  courts with praise.
- We make offerings of our money to the Lord.

- We celebrate the Lord's presence with special music.
- We dwell in the holy place of the Word and of prayer in the light of the Holy Spirit.
- We honor the boldly proclaimed Word of God.
- We enter the Holy of Holies by the blood of the Lamb, and in the name of Jesus, and we worship within the realm of the splendor of His holiness. There we hear the Spirit's muster call, summoning all the divisions of the army to prepare for an assault. Corporately we intercede in the power of the Spirit.

The forces of darkness retreat before the forces of light. *The kingdom of God is advanced!*

The Siege Daily, joyful craftsmanship is like a siege. The army of God fans out to each soldier's appointed position along the line of siege. Some are teachers, others students; some are salesmen, others purchasers; some are managers, others the managed; each one a soldier on the line of siege. Heretofore we may have thought that though we feel like a mighty army on Sunday, on Monday when we go out into the world we are really an outnumbered force. *Actually, we have got the devil surrounded!* As we joyfully live our lives of craftsmanship unto the King we lay siege to Babylon.

- We honor God's gifts in our heart, our talents and skills as we submit these abilities to the work of the kingdom of God as expressed in our place of service— God's plan for our life.
- We are Christ-like in our attitudes toward work and co-workers, and we are led of the Spirit in our choices and decisions.
- By the Spirit's power, we are joyful in spirit, even in times of stress—the joy of the Lord is our strength.
- We resist the constant influence of Babylon all around us, holding fast to our Jerusalem citizenship for we live as godly people, not according to the world's rules.

We minister to God by ministering to man and the dark kingdom's hold on those around us is weakened by our joyful, relentless obedience. *The kingdom of God is advanced!*

Yes, we are priests, but we are also prophets of the eternal Word who proclaim the manifold wisdom of God through our praise. Yes, we are worshipers, but we are also warriors raiding the enemy's territory with our private prayer, assaulting his strongholds with our public worship, and laying siege to his capital city with our daily craftsmanship. Hell has no defense for a passionate, praying, praising, obeying, reasoning church! Behold the powerful ministry of the believer whose life is centered on God himself!

Let me use an old football story as an example. It was Jr. High football and we had a championship team. I was big and slow so they made me a tackle. (A "lineman" is one of the big slow guys who "block" or clear the way for sleek, fast "backs" who carry the ball.) We had a little running back named Sam who scored many touchdowns running through my spot in the line. One of our most successful plays was a cross-block, a play that depends on deception. My job was to convince the player in front of me that I was about to knock him over. (There is much edifying communication among the players on the field just before the football is snapped.) Then when the center gives the ball to the quarterback, I would leap to my right and block a different player than the one I had been "communi-cating" with. I always enjoyed this legal, moral deception. Sam would scamper through the hole in our line and score a touchdown. I will never forget how it felt to run along trailing the play while the crowd went wild for Sam scoring the six points. The people were cheering for Sam, but the other linemen and I knew that *we* were the ones who had cleared the way for Sam. In football terms, we had "opened the hole in the line of scrimmage."

Many years later, I was still bigger and slower and I became a worship leader. I was on the staff of a great, growing church. People were gloriously saved every week, whole families, old and young, of all races—it was great. I would hear the people cheering the Pastor much as the football crowd had our little fullback, Sam. But I knew that we worshipers had helped open the hole in the opposition for the pastor to run through with his message and altar call. We are all a part of the victory God is winning today. Our job as worshipers is illustrated in my football story. We must do the warfare before the preacher takes the pulpit.

PSALM 149—A Song of Spiritual Warfare*

*Praise ye the Lord. Sing unto the Lord a new song,
and his praise in the congregation of saints.
Let Israel rejoice in Him that made him:
let the children of Zion be joyful in their King.
Let them praise His name in the dance:
Let them sing praises unto Him with the timbrel and harp.
For the Lord taketh pleasure in His people:
He will beautify the meek with salvation.
Let the saints be joyful in glory: let them sing aloud
    upon their beds.*
**LET THE HIGH PRAISES OF GOD BE IN THEIR MOUTH,
AND A TWO-EDGED SWORD IN THEIR HAND;**
*To execute vengeance upon the heathen, and
    punishments upon the people;
To bind their kings with chains, and their nobles
    with fetters of iron;
To execute upon them the judgment written:
This honour have all His saints. Praise ye the Lord.*
*KJV

CONCLUSION

"Let us hear the conclusion of the whole matter," said King Solomon at the end of his great work on the meaning of life, "fear God and keep His commandments: for this is the whole duty of man" (Ecclesiastes 12:13). The word translated "fear" means, in a moral sense, to reverence God—in other words, to worship God. The word "duty" is not in the original language but was added for clarification in both the New International and King James Versions. It should be printed in italics. When it is removed, we hear King Solomon making a much broader statement than one concerning just the duty of man. The world-weary king is telling us that to worship and obey God is the whole of man, his passion and purpose, his duty and reason, his joy and strength, and his eternal calling. This, of course, is the same conclusion we have reached in this study.

Seeing these things—these models of worship, these principles and directives, these keys to joyful living—what do we do now? How should we think and feel about them? What effect should these things have on our lives? We should think, speak, and experience a revolution of peace and joy in the presence of the Lord.

A Revolution of Self-worth—*Righteousness.* It is time for a revolution in the hearts of believers in their understanding of who they are in God. With no cause for boasting, and with hearts filled with profound humility we must realize that we are Holy-Royal Priests unto the King of kings and Lord of lords! With this revelation comes a new appreciation for the value of our private worship before the Lord. As a priest unto the King, we are to minister to Him above all others. He has called us to spend time with Him. He has summoned us as one would a friend to come into His Office-Place, His Throne Room, beyond the veil into the very Holy of Holies, to be with Him, to drink in His glory and to exchange our weakness for His strength. "Draw near to God," James, the Lord's brother, says, "and He will draw near to you"(James 4:8).

We are also anointed, creative craftsmen unto the King, skillful servants of the Most High God! Our creative gifts are from His hand for His glory and our joy. Satan's business is to kill, steal, and destroy them. But the Holy Spirit has quickened our gifts in us to new life and power and now He guides us in their use each day to the glory of the Lord and to our immense joy. Fruitful branches in the True Vine are we!

We are also mighty warriors—in the public worship service, on our knees in our homes, and in our work-places. The sound of our personal praise can shake the armies of the enemy arrayed against us. The power of our intercession can put the wicked hosts to flight for thousands of warrior angels stand ready to attend our petition and praise at the command of Jesus their captain. Holy-Royal priests, anointed-joyful craftsmen, mighty warriors—such is the revolution of self-worth brought about by worship that pleases God.

A Revolution in Public Worship—*Peace.* The Church needs a revolution in understanding of public worship and all the related disciplines involved. "Having church" is not just a sequence of unrelated events or a cultural exercise for the enjoyment of man. "Having church" is a kingdom of priests gathering to minister to the Lord. True Worship is ascending the hill of the Lord, Mt. Zion, to meet with heaven's citizens, sing heaven's songs, and see heaven's King.

When we worship we invite the King to reign upon the Throne of our praise, to inhabit our praise, and to manifest His presence among us. As we minister to the Lord, we provide Him an Office-Place, at the expense of our pride, from which to do the work of His kingdom.

Worship that pleases God is the experience of entering into the River of Life, which flows from the Throne of God, first ankle deep with our thanksgiving, then knee deep with our exaltation, waist deep with our adoration, and finally waters for swimming as we commune with Him and are changed.

A Revolution of Our Daily Living—*Joy.* Worship is not something we lay aside when we leave home to face the day. The presence of the Lord is not just a once-a-week promise. Each of us can take the "whatsoever" we do and make it praise unto the King. If we view our life's skills as craftsmanship unto the King and creativity as an eternal connection of our heart with God's heart, the joy of Jesus can follow us through every day. Our daily lives can be filled with the joy of being chosen by God (our anointing) to do ordinary things with extraordinary power (also our anointing). We can take joy in our work just as God did, knowing our creativity is a lifeline through which He can flow to lift our work above the ordinary to the excellent and make it shine with His glory. Like a tall healthy tree we will bring forth fruit in season. Our season will be perpetual; our leaf will not wither; and whatever we do shall prosper. We will know the joy of productivity not just profit.

The Lesson of the Oak Tree—
The Joy of Productivity

My family and I were out on a beautiful North Carolina mountain one fine fall day. Magnificent oaks covered the mountain and had produced a bumper crop of acorns. I couldn't help filling the pockets of my jacket with acorns and rolling them in each hand as we toured the park. We decided to hike down a steep grade to some waterfalls. As we topped the crest of the ridge, I could see the expanse of the mountainside before me, the tall oaks and the ground covered with their acorns.

At that moment, the Lord spoke clearly to my heart. "Son, do you see how little concern the oak trees have for the acorns they have produced? I have made them joyful in just producing their fruit. They leave to higher powers the destiny of what they produce." I knew that some of the acorns would feed the squirrels, others would rot underground to feed worms, and a few would end up in my pockets. But I also knew that each of them had the potential to become a mighty oak.

In that moment God started setting me free to enjoy my work. I was discouraged about my songs. I felt I was laboring in obscurity and I always would. I had confused a profit motive with a ministry motive, judging my success as a musician by the standards of men—publication, recording, recognition. I had almost stopped writing songs because I could not properly promote what I had already written. Each new song became a burden added to my back.

But the word from the Lord changed all that. I decided to be like the oak tree. I would take joy in producing songs, arrangements, writing projects and all the other fruit God has anointed me to produce and leave to Him which acorns would become oak trees, if any at all.

That fall day was the beginning of a new phase of productivity for me. This book is one of the acorns from the tree of my life. It takes its place among the worship services, the choir and orchestra anthems, and the seasonal productions. They are all just acorns—mine to produce and enjoy and His to use as He pleases.

The Joy of Change and Constancy

This many-faceted joy in the Lord is encouraging:

- the joy of craftsmanship,
- the joy of creativity,
- the joy of victory, and
- the joy of the oak tree.
- The joy of daily living includes both the joy of *change and constancy.*

Change is joyful to those who have a vision of what God wants to do. *If we believe prayer changes things, we must either learn to get excited about change or stop praying.* Constancy is also joyful. When changes frighten us, we can take joy in that which will never change:

- the character of God,
- the Word of God,
- the faithfulness of God.

Have no doubt that the things that can be shaken will be shaken so that those which cannot be shaken can remain. The things that remain are the things of the kingdom:

- righteousness,
- peace, and
- joy in the Holy Spirit.

His kingdom endures.

"Go Through the Gates!"

God burned a special passage from Isaiah into my heart. For months I had been absorbing Chapters 58 through 61, letting the plight of those whose creativity has been captured by the enemy sink deep into me and finding a vision of the creative haven God intends for the Church to be.

One day I felt I should go on and read Chapter 62. There I saw verse 10, and in it I felt a sense of urgency in the heart of God. I marked that verse in a Bible I said I would make no marks in. It has become a life-verse for me.

Isaiah 62:10, NKJ

Go through, go through the Gates!
Prepare the way for the people;
Build up, build up the highway!
Take out the stones,
Lift up a banner for the peoples!

Go through the Gates! What we have learned demands action. You and I must go through the gates every workday and every Lord's Day! Jesus opened these gates by His life's blood; all He asks is that we go through them. There is nothing on which to wait. No further word from God is required. God and the world He wants to reach await our passionate and reasoned obedience.

Prepare the way for the peoples. We have learned, though God's plan is revealed in Scripture, that we must prepare "the way" for the people. Not our way, like King David's new cart, but His way. It is time for all of us—Pentecostals, "main line" believers, Evangelicals and Fundamentalists—to cast off traditions of men if they do not conform to "the way." It is time for us to travel "the way" ourselves, to release control of our public worship to the leadership of the Holy Spirit through His anointed worship leaders.

Come alive in church! Worship God with all your might, with all your heart, soul, mind and strength. There is no subsequent event for which to save your passion. In so doing, you prepare a way for the unsaved and spiritually dead to get to God. He inhabits *your* praise!

Build up the highway! There are dangerous potholes in the highway we offer to the Lord each week. We must build them up! *Use* the truths presented in this study, those you find in other books and especially those God burns on your heart from the Scripture. Take these reasonable things and *implement them!* Potholes of ignorance must be filled with reason and with biblical truth.

Take out the stones. There are hindering boulders of man's tradition, culture and our own personal preferences that need to be blasted out of the way by the dynamite of biblical truth. It takes courage; it takes humility; it takes unity but it can be done. Entire congregations can hear about True Worship and obey the Lord. Through teaching and example, leaders can *"take out the stones."*

Lift up a banner for the peoples. Above all, lift up Jesus, our banner! Lift Him up on songs, on shouts, and on standards of obedient living. He is *"The Lord Our Banner, Our Victory."* Let us center our lives on Him. Let us rally to Him as warriors to a battle flag flying high above the smoke and dust of man's efforts. He is mustering us for battle for souls are in the balance. He is their only hope and He flows through our lives. They need a King, and He has promised to reign upon our praise. He will take it as His office where He will meet their needs.

This is worship that pleases God—True Worship; Worship in Spirit and Truth; worship with passion and with reason. This is what it means to love God with heart, soul, mind, and strength; and this is the ministry of every believer!

By Him therefore let us offer the sacrifice of praise to God continually, that is the fruit of our lips giving thanks to His name. But to do good and to communicate forget not: for with such sacrifices God is well pleased.

(Hebrews 13:15,16)

Let Us . . .

**Praise Him, worship him, obey Him,
and share Him with others
as we center our lives on Him.
In so doing we extend His Kingdom
and experience His righteousness,
peace, and joy.**

This is worship that pleases God!

In the light of the moment when we each stand before Him, is there anything that matters more than this?

APPENDIX ONE

A Biblical Defense of the Tabernacle of David

W hat is the relevance of the Tent on Mt. Zion? This is one of the most important questions of our day. Traditional theology gives little place or importance to the Tent on Mt. Zion. Most commentaries will mention that the word "tent" refers to the house of David—his royal line. Other references will be interpreted as having millennial significance but no meaning for today.

Obviously, I give the Tabernacle of David much more relevance and a much broader interpretation than traditional theologians. Let me call my biblical witnesses. David's Tabernacle, or Tent, might remain an obscure oddity of Scripture if not for the following passages.

Old Testament Witness: Asaph's Interpretation of History. Asaph, King David's chief musician, gives us what surely must be David's own understanding of what was happening when he put the Ark in the Tent on Mt. Zion and not back in Moses' Tabernacle.

> *Then he rejected the tents of Joseph, he did not choose the tribe of Ephraim; but he chose the tribe of Judah, Mount Zion, which he loved. He built his sanctuary like the heights, like the earth that he established forever. He chose David his servant and took him from the sheep pens; from tending the sheep he brought him to be the shepherd of his people Jacob, of Israel his inheri-tance. And David shepherded them with integrity of heart; with skillful hands he led them.* (Psalm 78:67-72)

Old Testament Witness: Isaiah. While Solomon's Temple still stood, Isaiah saw this:

> *In mercy the throne will be established: and One will sit on it in truth, in the Tabernacle of David, judging and seek-*

ing justice, and hastening righteousness." (Isaiah. 16:5 NKJ)

Old Testament Witness: Amos. When worship had become ritual at Solomon's Temple, Amos saw this:

> On that day I will raise up the Tabernacle of David which has fallen down, and repair its damages; and I will raise up its ruins, and I will rebuild it as in the days of old: That they may possess the remnant of Edom, and of all the Gentiles, who are called by my name, says the Lord who does this thing. (Amos. 9:11,12 NKJ)

New Testament Witness: James. At the Council in Jerusalem, James brought peace to the conflict with these words:

> "Simon has declared how God at the first visited the Gentiles, to take out of them a people for his name. And with this the words of the prophets agree; just as it is written, 'After this I will return, and will rebuild the Tabernacle of David, which has fallen down. I will rebuild its ruins, and I will set it up, so that the rest of mankind may seek the Lord, Even all the Gentiles, who are called by my name, says the Lord, who does all these things.'
>
> "Known to God from eternity are all his works. Therefore I judge that we should not trouble those from among the Gentiles who are turning to God, but to write to them to abstain from idols, from sexual immorality, from things strangled, and from blood "
>
> Then it pleased the apostles and elders with the whole church. (Acts 15:14-20 NKJ)

New Testament Witness: The Writer to the Hebrews. The writer to the Hebrews compares Old Testament worship with New Testament worship by comparing Mt. Sinai with Mt. Zion. David's Tabernacle was the first structure of worship to be built on Mt. Zion.

You have not come to a mountain that can be touched and that is burning with fire; to darkness, gloom and storm; to a trumpet blast or to such a voice speaking words that those who heard it begged that no further word be spoken to them, because they could not bear what was commanded: "If even an animal touches the mountain, it must be . . . stoned." The sight was so terrifying that Moses said, "I am trembling with fear."

But you have come to Mount Zion, to the heavenly Jerusalem, the city of the living to the church of the firstborn, whose names are written in heaven. You have come to God, the judge of all men, to the spirits of righteous men made perfect, to Jesus the mediator of a new covenant, and to the sprinkled blood that speaks a better word than the blood of Abel. (Hebrews 12:18-24)

This stream of biblical witness (Psalm 78:67-72; Isaiah 16:5; Amos 9:10,11, Acts 15:17-22 and Hebrews 12:18-24) elevates the Tabernacle of David above the level of obscure historical fact. The Lord has some important things to teach about His Church through this model.

If so, why has so little been taught in Evangelical circles about the Tabernacle of David? As previously stated, there are godly scholars who believe that biblical references to the Tabernacle of David refer only to the house and lineage of David. The "Tent of David" refers only to the re-established rule of King David's greater Son, King Jesus. They attach no significance to the Tent on Mt. Zion, no relationship between that tent and the one referred to by the prophets, and no relevance of that dwelling place of God to New Testament worship. I certainly agree that the passages regarding the "Tent" of David refer to his house and his kingdom rule. But one of the most important facets of David's rule was the restoration of the Ark. It is historical fact, not personal interpretation that he put the Ark in a tent on Mt. Zion. Indeed, the establishment of Mt. Zion as the dwelling and ruling place of God is at the heart of the rule of King David. The meaning of

282 / Stephen R. Phifer

the Tent is the subject of interpretation. It is better to let Scripture interpret Scripture than to interpret solely on the basis of what scholars of previous generations have said. A century ago, most Evangelical scholars would not have accepted the gifts of the Spirit as sound doctrine because it was not the agreed upon view. But the gifts were in the Book and they became a part of accepted Pentecostal / charismatic / Evangelical theo-logy in this century. We must keep updating our theology to match the Bible. God is still speaking through His Word, still unfolding His heart to us in the pages of Scripture. We must be careful to judge our traditions by the Word of God using sound interpretive principles such as letting Scripture inter-pret Scripture, keeping passages in context, etc. It is precisely the context of Acts 15 that keeps the relevance of David's Tabernacle squarely centered in the New Testament age, not the millennial age to come. The assumption that Isaiah and Amos referred only to the house of David and not the Tent on Mt. Zion is one that scholars bring to the passage. To the best of my research (*Strong's Exhaustive Concordance of the Bible*) the original words do indeed mean house and line of David, but they also mean a literal tent or booth. We are left to decide what the words might mean in the passages. If there had been no historical record of a Tent on Mt. Zion that was the center of worship for more that a generation, then all the passages could mean would be the house of David. But the Tent was there and it signaled the beginning of a new order, sound, and look for worship. There is nothing in the text that denies the possibility of a double reference to both the house of David *and* the Tent on Mt. Zion.

On the point of what is and what is not strictly biblical, it is interesting to note that "Tabernacle of David" is a biblical term (Isaiah 16:5, Amos 9:10,11, Acts 15;) but "Moses' Tabernacle" and "Solomon's Temple" are terms not found in the Bible. Clearly, Moses had a Tabernacle, Solomon had a Temple, and David had a Tent on Mt. Zion. All of these dwelling places were inhabited by the Lord *but the only one that included Gentiles was the Tabernacle of David!* This is the passage used as proof to the believers in Acts 15 that God was indeed including the Gentiles in the New Testament church. The Tent on Mt. Zion was God's way of predicting through David's actions that "All the ends of the earth will remember and turn to the LORD, and all the families of the nations will bow down before him, for dominion belongs to the LORD and he rules over the nations" (Psalm 22:27,28).

Biblical References to the Tent on Mt. Zion

Scripture	Meaning
Psalm 78:67-72	Asaph teaches history of David's acts. God abandoned Moses' Tabernacle and chose David and Zion
Isaiah 16:5	The Messiah will sit and judge from the Tabernacle of David.
Amos 9:11,12	The Lord will rebuild the tabernacle of David so that all mankind can seek the Lord.
Acts 15:17-22	James settles the dispute over the salvation of the Gentiles by quoting Amos 9. The establishment of the N.T. Church is the rebuilding of David's Tabernacle.
Hebrews 12:19-24	The writer says that that New Testament believers have come to Zion not Sinai to worship. The first place called Zion was the Tent on the hill in Jerusalem.

I believe the Lord is emphasizing this truth as we turn from the twentieth to the twenty-first century just as He did the truth about the fullness of the Spirit in the early 1900's. For years many believed that the Tabernacle of David was a reference to the restored Israel in the millennial reign. Is this millennial or current truth? Yes and yes. It is both!

The throne of David *does* refer to Israel restored in the millennial reign, but Jesus told Pilate that He rules a kingdom "not of this world." Just as surely as Jesus will reign upon this earth for a thousand years of peace, Jesus also reigns over a spiritual kingdom during the Church Age. Since God is always the same, His rule is the same from age to age. The wonderful prophecies of the millennial kingdom are foreshadowed in the rule of Jesus in the Church. The Acts 15 conference proves this. The question settled by the quotation of Amos about David's Tabernacle and the Gentiles had nothing to do with the millennial kingdom but it had everything to do with the Church. James and the disciples acted upon the truth then. They did not wait for the Millennium. I believe the restored Tabernacle of David is a prophetic picture of the New Testament Church.

It is important for us to study the Tabernacle of David, the rule of King David, the times of David, and the early part of Solomon's reign. During this era, the heart of God was revealed in many of the religious and political systems. Of course, all observations must be reinforced by New Testament truths before we build our ministry systems upon them. I find the Tabernacle of David a rich source of inspiration and instruction in the ministry of worship and the arts.

APPENDIX TWO

Principles of Worship Leading: Let the River Flow

W e must take all that we have learned about worship: the attitudes of the heart, the relationship we have with God, the concepts of the priority of worship, the principles and directives, and the confidence in our anointing to worship and apply these things to the actual planning and execution of the worship service. We will look at worship leading with two lenses: a wide view that looks at the whole service from beginning to end and a narrow view that looks at the congregational praise and worship time.

The Entire Service of Worship

It is essential that the worship planner keep the whole service in mind. If one is a musician, he will naturally focus his attention on the music segment of the service. If one is a pastor, his primary concern will probably be the sermon time. Both the chief musician and the pastor are worship leaders. Each must follow the other's leadership: the pastor worshiping God with all his might and the musician intently following every word the pastor speaks. In this way both deflect attention away from themselves and back to the leader in the pulpit whether he is leading in praise and worship music or preaching the Word.

When a chief musician first learns about the destinations of worship services (the Throne Room, the Holy of Holies, and the Lord's Office-Place) it is natural for him to want to take the people *all the way* into those places while the praise and worship music is being offered to the Lord. This is not necessary. We need to pass through the veil at *some point* during the service, but not always during the praise and worship music. Again, I am indebted to my friend Larry Hartley for an illustration from his ministry.

His worship leading was doing well. The people were following him, and in every service they were moving through the outer courts and having powerful times in the Holy of Holies. Larry's pastor began to withdraw from his normally unrestrained worship. After a few weeks, Larry was greatly concerned. (A good chief musician wants to please God *and* his pastor!) As men of God and pastoral team members *must* do, they talked it out.

Larry's pastor's wisdom does much to ease any strain between the forces of "spirit" and the forces of "truth." "Why do you have to take them all the way into the Holy of Holies every time you lead worship? Why can't we stop for a while in the Holy Place? That is a good place to be, the place of prayer and the Word in the light of the Holy Spirit."

Larry told me this and then went further with the truth. "It's OK, Steve, to stop in the Holy Place for a while. The veil is torn. We can see the Ark from there! All is well in the Holy Place!" I, too, had been struggling with the strain of feeling that I was supposed to bring the congregation *all the way* to the goal in praise and worship time. I can remember how this revelation relaxed that drive in me. God is interested in the *whole service* not just the music time or the preaching time.

With all that we have learned, we can now chart the worship service from beginning to end. We will look at only the spirit and truth elements in a service 90 minutes in length. Of course the amazing thing about a worship service is that it is essentially a *spiritual event* and can never be nailed down as neatly as this chart. This chart only serves to illustrate the flow from praise to worship, from spirit activity to truth activity. Different biblical models are charted by this illustration.

APPLICATION OF WORSHIP MODELS TO THE WORSHIP SERVICE

PRAISE/WORSHIP/PRAYER/OFFERINGS | READING/PREACHING WORD/RESPONSE

45 Minutes	45 Minutes
Spirit	Truth
Praise	Worship
Gates, Outer Courts	Holy Place, Holy Of Holies
Thanksgiving, Exaltation	Adoration, Communion
Ankle Deep, Knee Deep	Waist Deep, Waters for Swimming
Establishing His Throne with Praise	Abiding Near Throne
Ascending the Hill of the Lord	Standing in Holy Place
Ministering Unto the Lord	Visiting His Office
Presenting Our Bodies to Him	Renewing The Mind
Preparing a Way for The Lord	The Glory Revealed

God's Holy Spirit can do thousands of different things all at once in the same room. One worshiper may have a Throne Room visit beholding God's majesty and submitting to His sovereignty while the next person may be exchanging his weakness for the Lord's strength in the Holy of Holies and another may be visiting the Lord's Office-Place just to be held for a while in the arms of the Lord.

It may be that the Holy Spirit desires to take the whole congregation into one of these manifestations of the Lord's presence all at once during the music time. It would be wonderful for an entire sermon to be a visit to the Holy of Holies. Remember these models are merely illustrations. They are clay in the hands of the Holy Spirit to be molded by Him to reveal Jesus to us. Our role as worship leaders is to be sensitive to the Holy Spirit's wishes when we plan and execute the service.

Congregational Praise and Worship Music

Terminology is important. Will we have a *"song service"* or a *"praise and worship"* time? Will the leader be a *"song leader"* or a *"worship leader?"* What is the difference? *A song leader* leading *a song service* is this: a person leading other people singing songs, and instrumentalists accompanying them.

A *worship leader* leading a praise and worship time is so much more: people praising and worshiping God with and without songs; instrumentalists praising and worshiping God with the sounds of music; people praising and worshiping from their hearts while the instrumentalists play (which may be what *Selah* meant); gifts of the Spirit in scriptural operation; "Psalms and hymns and spiritual songs" flowing; the Lord indwelling the praise of His people and finding our praise worthy to be His Throne; the Lord using our worship as His Office-place; the River of Life flowing from His Throne to our restoration and healing; Heaven and earth coming together at Mt. Zion in the unity of praise and worship to the Lamb on the Throne; the call of God going forth to those He has anointed to specific areas of service; the church moving forward in unison in the will of God; the testimony of the church that Jesus is alive validated by the manifestation of His presence; and unbelievers falling down and worshiping God with us, saying that God is in us *"of a truth."*

Given a choice of these two things, a song service or a praise and worship time, we would certainly desire the latter. This is exactly the choice we have. It takes leadership to transform a song service into a worship service. God is always the same. God is not on a circuit whereby He only visits us once in a while. He wants to Tabernacle with us *every time we gather to worship!* The River of Life is always flowing from His Throne. If there are inconsistencies they must be ours, inconsistencies in the way we lead worship. We need to closely examine the leadership of the praise and worship time within the service.

Basic Questions About Worship Leading
Who Is a Worship Leader?

A worship leader is a man or woman who is called of God to lead in worship. If we want the power of God to flow in our worship, the leader must be a person *GOD* has selected.

The anointing is as essential to this ministry as it is to any other ministry. Those whom God calls, He enables. Without this enablement the worship time will be mired in imitation and fleshly effort. Many congregations are waiting, week after week, for song leaders to become worship leaders or yield the position to a worship leader. Anyone who is so prideful of the "song leader" position that he will not share leadership with other anointed leaders is probably not called of God. Leaders who are anointed of the Lord hold their positions among men with a light grip. They have no trouble making way for others who are anointed. However, those who have been placed in a leadership position by the hand of man must hold tightly to it with their own strength.

Musical skill and understanding are essential. Music must be handled properly or it will inhibit the flow of God's Spirit. A skillful musical mind can release the powers of music to support the expression of God's people. On the other hand, unskillful handling of music can spoil the sacrifice of praise of the whole church, the Holy-Royal Priesthood.

The worship leader must be broken before the Lord and remain broken. Through Isaiah, the Lord makes it clear that He visits His presence upon those who are humble before Him.

> *For thus saith the high and lofty One that inhabiteth eternity, whose name is Holy; I dwell in the high and holy place, with him also that is of a contrite and humble spirit, to revive the spirit of the humble, and to revive the heart of the contrite ones.* (Isaiah 57:15 KJV)

> *Thus saith the Lord, the heaven is my throne, and the earth my footstool: where is the house that ye build unto me? and where is the place of my rest? For all these things hath mine hand made, all those things have been, saith the Lord: but to this man will I look,("This one will I esteem", NIV) even to him that is poor and of a contrite spirit, and trembleth at my word.* (Isaiah 66:1,2 KJV)

Music and music ministry can be done in a prideful manner, lifting the musician up with pride in performance and position. Worship leading is the exact opposite. Pride is incompatible with God's presence. *When the performance musician succeeds, all eyes are on him and the applause of men floods his heart. When the worship musician or worship leader succeeds, he disappears, for all eyes are on Jesus and all applause goes to the Lord.* Because they are soulish and physical in their origin, music, thanksgiving, and even praise can be humanly generated. But the manifest presence of the Lord is a heavenly visitation given to those who have a poor and contrite spirit and who tremble at the Word of the Lord. It cannot be generated by man; it is a gift of God. Of all musicians, the worship musician must be humble The difference between church musicians who are performance-oriented and those who are worship-oriented is obvious. Performers are proud and worshipers are humble.

Human nature teems with pride for everyone, musicians included. In your experience, if humble church musicians have been few in number, call to mind the action of culture and personal preference we discussed in Chapter One. Pride is a cornerstone of the music education system that trains most musicians. But when a musician decides to minister to the Lord, when he desires for God's presence to be visited upon his music, he finds he must repent of pride and forsake it. God simply will not be enthroned upon prideful music. In the same way, a worship leader must be humble to lead a congregation before the Throne of God. He cannot take people someplace he has not been. He and his music must take the background and allow the Holy Spirit's work to take the foreground. Most musicians dislike performing background music. We want to be listened to when we make music. But worship music (while it is certainly not "elevator music") must be music in submission to God, deflecting the attention back to Him. The humility this requires from musicians is always a supernatural work of the Holy Spirit. A worship leader performs his or her ministry *together* with the congregation, the pastor, the choir, the orchestra, and the worship singers in humility and obedience. Worship leading is in every way a service to the congregation and not something of leadership *over* the church. God may call anyone who is qualified to serve in this way.

A Worship Leader is someone who is:

—*called of God* to lead in worship,
—*musically skillful* and/or understanding,
—*spiritually broken* before the Lord.

What Is Worship?

The relationship between praise and worship has to be held clearly in the mind of the one who plans and leads a worship time. Praise (thanksgiving and exaltation) should precede worship (adoration and communion). This praise-worship sequence is the reasonable order of worship referred to in Romans 12:1. This is not to say that a sovereign God cannot short-circuit this order and visit us with His manifest presence in times when we have not praised Him. We all may have experienced such astounding times of visitation. *But, the goal of the worship leader is not the occasional sovereign move of God, but the pattern God's Spirit has given us in Scripture.* God has also sovereignly chosen to move in the logical, praise-worship sequence. If we are to lead worship, we must understand and submit to this.

Praise is an action of soul and body, a time of thanking the Lord for what He has done and exalting His name, His character, and His deeds. Here are the gates to His presence and the outer courts of His dwelling place. This is wading ankle deep and knee deep into the River of Life. It is ascending the hill of the Lord where the Tabernacle of David is found. This is the presentation of our bodies to Him. By these things we establish His throne as we minister to the Lord with our

Living Sacrifice of Praise. Through praise we prepare ourselves for the revelation of His glory.

**Worship is a response of the spirit, a time of expressing
our adoration and devotion to God, giving Him an exclusive
place in our hearts.** Communion is abandoning ourselves to
His presence, contemplating His glory, dwelling inside the
veil, and drinking in His righteousness. It is the solemn
sovereignty of His Throne Room, the holiness of the Holy of
Holies, the deep waters of the River of life, the tenderness of
His Office-Place, the renewing of the mind, and the glory
revealed. True worship transports the worshiper out of time
and into eternity. There is a timeless quality to these spiritual
destinations.

The worship leader must be careful not to stop with praise.
Our goal is to enter His presence with praise so that we may
respond to Him in worship. Of course it is always proper to
thank and praise the Lord. We begin these expressions in the
outer court and bring them with us into the inner court.

These differences can be seen in the music itself. The
music of thanksgiving and exaltation can be either upward in
direction, thanking and praising God, or it can be outward in
direction, speaking to others about God, encouraging them to
praise. The music of worship is almost exclusively upward in
direction, speaking directly to God. The pronouns in the text
signal the direction of the song. A song of mine illustrates.

From Psalm 29:1,2 comes a song of praise:

> *Give unto the Lord, O ye mighty.*
> *Give unto the Lord, glory and strength.*
> *Give unto the Lord the glory due His name;*
> *Worship the Lord in the beauty of holiness.**

From the Revelation comes a second part, still in praise:

> *Give Him blessing; Give Him honor;*
> *Give Him glory; Give Him power!*
> *Give unto the Lord the Glory due His name;*
> *Worship the Lord in the beauty of holiness.**

To use this song in a worship time, after we have praised the Lord, I would adapt the lyric:

We give You blessing; We give You honor;
We give You glory; We give You power!
We give unto You, Lord, the glory due Your name:
*We worship You, Lord, in the beauty of holiness.**
**"Give Unto the Lord"* ©Copyright 1986 by Gospel Publishing House

By adjusting the pronouns we personalize our expression, sending it upward to the Lord. The worship leader must be sensitive to the direction of the songs. I keep this in mind by imagining the heads of the people turning upward when we sing to God and from side to side as we sing to one another. If I look at a series of songs I have planned and see the people getting sore necks from all the direction changes, I have to re-think that sequence. When we see an entire congregation actually looking upward for substantial periods of time as the music carries their individual sacrifices up to the Lord, do we really want to give them a song that brings their attention back to earth to sing to one another *about* God? How much better it is to sing *to Him!* **God knows the end from the beginning and so must the worship leader—praise leads to worship! It is the revealed pathway to the presence of God.**

There is also a manifestation of *"spirit and truth"* in the character of praise and worship music. Paul told the Corinthians that he was determined to sing *"with the spirit and . . . with the understanding also."* (I Corinthians 14:15b) Some praise and worship songs are very much *"truth"* exercises having many verses and developing complex messages of theology or exhortation. These are songs we sing with understanding. Other songs have only a word or a phrase repeated again and again as in "Hallelujah," "We exalt Thee," "Worthy is the Lamb," and "I Love You, Lord." Some musicians and theologians have decried the lack of content in such songs. But as we sing these vital words again and again our spirits soar. We are singing *"with the spirit."* Of course, we have all heard worthless little songs that say nothing and give no important expressions of praise and worship. These have nothing to recommend them. Paul's testimony gives us biblical permission to enjoy songs of spirit and truth, those presenting great truths as well as those whose simplicity lets our spirits minister to the Lord.

Understanding Praise and Worship

Praise is an action of soul and body, a time of thanking the Lord for what He has done and exalting His name, His character, and His deeds.

Worship is a response of the spirit, a time of expressing our adoration and devotion to God, giving Him an exclusive place in our hearts.

How Does One Lead in Worship?

The first rule of worship leading is this: a worship leader must himself worship God without reservation. He must give himself to praise and worship, hungering above all things for the manifestation of the presence of the Lord. There have been times I thought my heart would pound its way out of my chest as the awe of His majesty broke upon me. With rule number one in mind, this is the step-by-step procedure I recommend.

The worship leader must do these things: *Prepare his heart* to approach the Lord with the people of God. *Prepare the leadership* for positive change. *Prepare the people* for a systematic way of approaching God. *Prepare a sequence of songs* that will take us on that journey and *communicate the plan* to all the singers, instrumentalists, and technicians who must know where we are going and the musical route chosen. *Execute the plan* as he is led of the Spirit and as he praises and worships God with all his might, whether the people follow him or not.

Rule Number One:
The Worship Leader must worship God with all his heart, soul, mind, and strength

---

Prepare the heart. In preparing the heart to lead worship, a vision for worship is essential. My prayer is that by now your vision for worship has expanded beyond a "song service." We must have a vision of His majesty. The critical phrase from Psalm 29 is *"the glory due unto His name."* This is the biblical standard given to the worship leader. Until a leader has the vision of the majesty and glory of the Lord Jesus, he cannot be an effective worship leader. Throughout the Bible a transforming vision of God is the turning point in the lives of the leaders of God's people from Abraham to Moses to David to Isaiah to Peter, James, John and to Paul. One of the greatest evidences of the resurrection of Jesus is the refusal of the witnesses who saw Him after His death to retreat from their vision of a risen Lord. A vision of Jesus our Sovereign is the goal of every praise and worship time.

Prepare the leaders. The Lord must awaken a hunger and thirst for this vision of Jesus the King within the pastor, the board, the worship leader, the music department and the people. The pastor is the key personality. The church cannot go deeper into the presence of the Lord than the pastor will go. If he watches his watch during the praise and worship time, or talks to the person next to him, or studies his notes or is merely passive while the people are offering their sacrifices of praise, the church will never surmount the pastor's personal obstruction.

To illustrate: a worship leader moved to a new church, one that was more involved in praise and worship than his previous church. At his former church, the revelation of God came through preaching not worship; worship was seen as an altar-time experience. The first time this man led worship in his new church he was amazed that so many of the people were worshiping God with all their might. After a few minutes the worship leader's old instincts told him it was time to stop before this thing got out of hand. He stole a glance at the pastor to see if he was checking his watch. What he saw explained everything. The pastor had no thought of the time. His hands were spread out toward heaven and his head was thrown back with his eyes closed. A broad smile graced lips lost in the praise of His Redeemer. The worship leader then knew why the church was worshiping—the pastor was worshiping! And so it will always be.

Wouldn't it be wonderful if all pastors and guest speakers worshiped with all their might like King David. However some do not even come into the service until after the corporate praise and worship time, send-ing the message that it is really not that important, only a warm-up for the main event. Such non-verbal messages are hindrances to the revelation of Jesus through corporate worship.

On the other hand, the worship leader must not go beyond the pastor's vision for worship. Conflicts result when musicians are exposed to the kinds of biblical truths we have explored in this study but the pastor is not. When this is the case, the worship leader must be very careful. Usually the flow of theological instruction goes from pastor to staff member and not the other way. Hopefully, two spiritual leaders can sit down and discuss Scripture and arrive at a mutual plan.

The three questions posed in Chapter One (Will I worship to please myself? others? or God?) will simplify the process. The heart of a True Worshiper is a patient heart submitting to the pastor's vision. God is never pleased if His truth is used to divide a church or to cause turmoil. The worship leader must never allow a "worship party" to form. God is not in political processes. A "party spirit" is something God hates.

How can a worship leader proceed if his pastor does not share his vision for worship? First, he must realize that worship is not his property. It is God's. Second, he must realize no one knows better than God how to work in the pastor's life. Remember that the true-hearted worship leader never touches the Lord's anointed. Next, the worship leader must pray as he has never prayed before. It may be the Lord is doing something in his life that cannot happen in his current location. We must remember that God is not as wrapped up in our present situations as we tend to be. He loves us more than He does our ministries. If He has birthed a ministry in our hearts, He will find a place for us to fulfill it. If He has called us to be a worship leader, He will find us a place where we can lead worship.

Prepare the people. Together, the pastor, the board, and the worship leader must obey the command of Isaiah 40: "Make straight in the desert a highway for our God." There may be valleys of insufficiencies that must be built up: insufficient vision for what True Worship should be, insufficient understanding of how to go about worship, insufficient time (importance) given to worship, or, insufficient musical skills to release worship. There may be hindering mountains that have to come down: mountains of religious tradition, mountains of attitudes based upon cultural factors, mountains of musical or spiritual pride, mountains of false spirituality (fads, false teachings) or, mountains of insensitivity to the Holy Spirit on the part of those leading various parts of the service. Crooked places in the church procedures may need to be made straight: worship practices that are non-biblical; worship practices that are simply not anointed of God (yielding no supernatural results),or, worship practices that emphasize things neither spirit nor truth. The people may have grown used to rough places that need to be made smooth: careless service planning careless praise and worship planning, careless musicianship, careless treatment of the congregation by failing to provide words for songs, or, careless purchase and maintenance of instruments, materials, and facilities.

These types of hindrances can reach so deep into the life of the congregation that only a united effort by the pastor, the board, the worship leader, and the church musicians can root them out. Yet, this is exactly what is needed if the worship service is ever to be the highway of the Lord.

Prepare the sequence of songs. The pastor and the worship leader must find God's will for each service. God's agenda for each service includes the songs (to be found by the worship leader) and the message (to be found by the pastor). *Prayerful sensitivity during the week is the key.* Just as the pastor must start thinking about the message before Saturday night, the worship leader should have the worship music close to his heart all week. In fact, the music of praise and worship needs to be a part of the worship leader's daily life. Songs of praise, prayer, and worship should abide in his mind and dwell in his heart. He is constantly stocking his storehouse of new songs. Learning new hymns and choruses is his passion, making them a part of his private devotions long before they are given to the congregation. As early in the week as possible, if the pastor senses a certain theme or emphasis, he needs to point the worship leader that way.

The song sequence should be worked out by midweek, at least. This means the leader has time to do some important things: prepare his heart to lead this set of songs through prayer and meditation; prepare materials needed to execute the plan; prepare the singers and instrumentalists and teach any new songs, and, refine the plan in consultation with the pastor. By preparing through the week the praise and worship plan becomes the prayerful product of the worship leader's heart. It must establish and maintain a flow of worship and every element should be connected so that it flows together effortlessly.

Two biblical illustrations of excellent preparation come to mind: the seamless robe of Jesus and Solomon's Temple. The robe the soldiers gambled for was valuable because it was woven in one piece. If the Lord is to wear the robe of praise we prepare for Him, our motivations must be woven of one material: His glory, not ours. We are not showcasing our talents; we are honoring Him. We are not pumping up the people; we are praising the Lord. We are not performing for men's applause; we are humbling ourselves before men, seeking God's presence. The Temple of Solomon was so well planned the workmen did not need to use the hammer or the iron tool to make the blocks of stone fit together. That is the way a praise and worship plan should be. For me, there have been times when things went wrong. Perhaps chords were mismatched among the keyboards or a transition was muffed. (Any number of things can go wrong!) The thought in my mind was "Oh, I just heard a hammer!" "Wow, I had to use an iron tool to get between those two songs! Forgive, me, Lord, I'll plan it better next time!"

What makes praise and worship flow? Connections. Thoughts flow together when the last line of one song connects to the first line of the next. Thanksgiving flows into praise which flows into worship. Moods flow together also: joy gives way to majestic wonder which leads to reverent awe. Musically, the praise and worship will flow when songs are grouped together by their musical elements: key, tempo, and style.

The music of congregational praise and worship differs in this respect from the music of performance, even when that performance is ministered unto the Lord. Performance musicians are trained to surprise the listener with all sorts of musical devices: sudden modulations, sudden stops, rubato, fermatas, contrasts in style and tempo, and so forth. The purpose of these things is to keep the audience's attention riveted to the performer. The goal of the worship musician is to point the listener's attention to Jesus, not to himself. Therefore these elements must be used in ways that support the praise and worship, not detract from it. Music that is constantly jumping back and forth in tempo, or style, or constantly starting and stopping, or attempts to defy the natural flow of music from key to key will not flow as a corporate worship experience because it is constantly calling attention to itself. When minister-

ing *to* the congregation, we can let our creativity and craftsmanship soar, but when ministering *with* the congregation, we
must use our musical skill to facilitate the flow of the music.
The skillful musician must be careful not to leave the congregation behind on his personal ascent of Mt. Zion.

A praise and worship experience will flow if it has a destination. Many times the pastor knows what should happen in
the service and gives the worship leader a theme: missions, the
Lord's Supper, Prayer, and so on. Often, however, the worship
leader must depend on the Lord for direction. God always
knows what He wants to do in a service. Through the Holy
Spirit we can be guided to the right ideas and find the songs to
carry them. Through our musical understanding and our sensitivity to the Holy Spirit we can craft these songs and
thoughts into a plan that God can use.

I will outline my process. Planning worship is such an
interplay of songs, truths and the personality of the worship
leader that I hesitate to generalize as if all worship leaders
plan the way I do, or that they should. I think of the models as
basic guidance from the Holy Spirit. When I begin to plan the
worship I will sometimes sense a desire to crown Jesus King
among us, so I put together a set of songs that take us to the
Throne Room. At other times I will sense that we should really
celebrate the Lord's presence so I put together a musical ascent
of Mt. Zion to worship at David's Tabernacle. At still other
times, I will sense the Lord's desire to dwell with His people
in the healing fullness of His holiness, and I will let thoughts
of the Holy of Holies guide my selection of music. I think of
what I am planning as the Living Sacrifice of Praise for the
Holy-Royal Priesthood. On and on we can go through all the
models. They serve this dual function: to help us understand
worship and to guide our thinking as we plan worship.

Many times the Lord impresses me first with how He
wants the praise and worship time to end and I work toward
that specific goal. At other times a certain chorus or hymn will
be the definite starting point and I start connecting last lines to
first lines, keys to keys, and styles to styles until I joyfully

discover, song by song, where the Holy Spirit wants to take us. However God leads the worship leader, the worship plan is not something that is just thrown together at the last minute. The worship leader seeks and prepares it as a pastor would a Word from the Lord! It is a product of the worship leader's devotional life, his sensitivity to the Holy Spirit, and his musicianship.

Communicate the plan. A simple sheet of paper for each service should be provided to each singer, player, and technician who will help in the service. The number of things the leader can communicate with a one page outline of the service is amazing: keys, modulations, introductions, interludes, differing orchestrations on hymn stanzas, solos, anticipated transitions and repeats, anything that can be thought out ahead of time.

Execute the plan. Leading in worship only begins with the plan. During the time of praise and worship in the service, the worship leader has to exercise sensitive leadership as the plan unfolds. It is at this point that he must walk a tightrope: he must worship God with all his might, but still be thinking ahead in the plan; he must give himself completely to the praise and worship of his God, but still gauge how the people are responding to the plan he is giving them; and, he must take charge of the musical aspects of the sequence (tempo, transitions, etc.) but *never feel like he is making something happen*. (Leading worship is a process of *letting* something happen, not *making* something happen.)

STEPS TO WORSHIP LEADING

Prepare the heart
Prepare the leaders
Prepare the people
Prepare the songs(old and new)
Communicate the plan
Execute the plan

These things need to be in place for this to come about: the plan must be available to all who need it, and signals must be used and the words must be provided. Use **simple signals** during the service. There are some things that cannot be planned ahead of time. The worship leader needs a set of signals. Again, let me share the ones I use as these are the only ones I can vouch for. Make eye contact with the pianist just before the next modulation in the plan. Because all the musicians have the plan, they are all looking for my signal as to the moment when we will do the modulation. The pianist makes sure the organist and the rhythm section know that the time is coming—and it happens! All from a written plan and a glance! I walk around quite a bit as I lead worship, so it is easy for me to give the signal without the congregation noticing. (I have had to work with the piano in all possible locations, behind me and to either side, but I have never had to abandon "the look" as a signal for the next modulation.)

A signal for a transition is needed. I put my right hand in the air and all the musicians know I am about to conduct something. I conduct all transitions, getting the tempo changes I want or creating pauses between songs. (I do not conduct all during praise and worship. Once a tempo is set, there is no need to beat it out. In this way, when I *need* to conduct something, my gestures have meaning.)

A "last time" or coda signal is needed so the musicians can know when the last time through a song is upon them, especially if there is a special ending. I use my right fist in the air. *All of the signals only work if players are watching.* With their utmost attention given to the worship leader, such signals can be discreet. The whole congregation should not be distracted by them.

People cannot be expected to sing songs if they do not know the words. As an act of invitation and courtesy, provide the words. The old ways of singing from memory do not serve the growing church of today. When there aren't a lot of new people coming to the church each week, there is little need to provide words for the home folk. When new people are coming to houses of worship, some were not raised in church. They may not even know the words to "Amazing Grace!". In an effort to reach out to them and make them feel welcome, we must provide words on all the songs we sing, new or old. Pastor Gifford (of the Wichita church) said this of memorized singing, "It makes the visitors feel like they are on the outside looking in, as if we were saying to them, `See all the neat songs we know! If you stay here long enough, you can learn our songs, too, and then you can join us.'" This is not the message the worship leader wants to send. On the other hand, if we provide the words to all our songs, we are saying, "We're glad you are here. We love to sing unto the Lord. Many of our songs may be new to you but we want you to join us and sing!" This is the message of the effective worship leader.

The songs themselves have changed today; there are more of them and they are more complex than those of yesterday. To do justice to the songs we select requires visual help. Today's songs have much more content and much less repetition; words are needed. God always has music for each stage of growth through which He takes the church. New songs soar on the winds of revival. They are the life of the praise and worship of the church.

A balance of old and new songs is best as we learn to value all anointed songs. Those who by nature love the new songs must learn to appreciate the old songs. Those who love the old songs must learn to respect the new songs. New songs are a command of Scripture but Scripture also says for one generation to declare God's works to the next. Previous generations have left us their songs! Older songs still have much to say and their use can be enhanced by projecting of words as well. Old and new, songs that exalt the Lord, edify the body and flow decently and in order are works of the Holy Spirit and should be esteemed as such.

Rule Number Two:

Be prepared and be flexible. Have a plan and know how to modify it as the Holy Spirit Leads.

Let the Music Flow

Music is designed by the Lord to flow. There are certain ways it will flow and other ways it simply will not. To illustrate let me recall an incident from the second or third grade. A taxidermist visited our class with a small, stuffed animal, a raccoon I think, on a wooden stand. The teacher carefully walked down each aisle to let each one of us touch the stiff beast. When it was my turn, I stroked it from the back toward the head. The fur did not grow that way so all I did was disturb the work of the craftsman, making the smooth hairs stand up in awkward clumps along the path of my hand. The teacher corrected me, "Steve, the hair didn't grow that way. Stroke it the way it grows!" I suppose it embarrassed me enough that I have never forgotten that moment, but in latter years I remember it with a musical application. Sometimes worship leaders do not understand the way music flows, and they try to make it flow backwards. Their praise and worship times end up being a series of awkward clumps, like that raccoon's fur after I finished with it. To avoid this, let's look at the way music is designed to flow.

The flow of tonality involves the relationship between keys. The worship leader cannot just simply put down songs without reference to their keys because music does not jump around from any key to any key. The major keys are related to each other by the interval of a fifth. The key of C is the fifth of the key of F, so it is quite natural to flow from C to F between songs. When planning a worship series and I am in one key searching for the next song, I search two lists, the one for the key I am in, and the one for the key up one fourth (called the subdominant). Adjacent keys (up 1/2 step, up 1 step) are also easy to move up to by playing the five (the dominant) of the new key. The important thing to remember is that keys flow upward, not downward. One can easily do a song once in Eb and then in F, but to do it the other way around is awkward and does not flow. Based on these observations I use three modula-tions: up 1/2 step, up one step, and up one fourth. These three modulations simplify things for our musicians; they know the modulation chord is always the five of the new key.

Minor keys are more challenging. Once a minor tonality is established it is best to stay in that mode for a while. When it is time to leave, the options are to go directly to the parallel major (F minor to F major) or to go to the relative major (G minor to Bb major).

MOST COMMON KEY CHANGES

Major Keys: up perfect fourth   Minor Keys: up 1/2 step
    up 1/2 step   up whole step
    up whole step   to parallel major
                                    to relative major

Tempos flow together also. Once a tempo is established, it is best to stay with it until you are ready to go to another tempo for another *set* of songs. It is distracting to change tempos on every song. Here is a common plan: fast tempo (several songs) / medium tempo (one or two songs) / slow tempo (several songs). Song sequences should not always start fast, move to medium tempo, and finish with slow songs. The models should free us from such rigid thinking. For instance, if we want to scale Mt. Zion to worship at David's Tabernacle, we may begin our ascent with slower songs, build to the medium tempo songs, then the fast songs, and finish with songs in a majestic tempo. There are many ways songs can flow together in various tempos.

Styles and meters need to flow together too. As with tempos, songs should be grouped together according to style. Not all songs in the same tempo are in the same style. A medium tempo song can have a triplet feel or a 16th note pulse or an 8th note pulse. It can be distracting to try to "swing" one song and then do the next with straight 8th notes even though the two are in the same tempo. The same guidelines apply to meters. Music that is constantly switching from 4/4 to 3/4 to 9/8 to 6/8 and so forth, will not flow. Use one meter until it has served its purpose then go to another.

Flowing Elements of Music
Tonality
Tempo
Meter
Rhythmic Style

The worship leader must master the art of transition. *Leading the singers, instrumentalists, and worshipers through the transitions between songs and sections of praise and worship is the most critical skill the worship leader must develop.* Our songs might be well thought out, the keys may be right, and everyone prepared to the best of his ability, but that does not guarantee a smooth flow. The worship leader must negotiate the end of every song and the beginning of the next in a natural, easy way that does not attract attention away from the worship. Grouping the songs together by thoughts, keys, tempos, meters, and styles should make it easy to go directly between those songs without stopping. When a change is necessary it should be well thought out in a sequence of changes with never more than two at one time. For example, suppose we had just led four up-tempo songs in F. They were all in the same meter and style so we simply went from one to another without stopping. The next song is slower, much slower, for we are moving from praise to worship, from singing about God to singing to God, and we are moving to Bb. To abruptly slow everything down and change tonality, the direction (remember the pronouns) and songs all at once will shut down the momentum the praise songs gave us. A transition is needed. Here's what I would do:

STEPS IN A TRANSITION—
A Sequence of Changes

1. I raise my right hand to signal that I am about to conduct a tempo change;

2. Conducting the new tempo, I repeat the last line of the final up-tempo chorus at a slower tempo; perhaps repeat it again;

3. I make eye contact with the pianist to signal that this is the last repeat—the modulation is next;

4. When I hear the 7th of F, I imagine the first note of the next song in Bb and start into it.

Analysis of Change Sequence

Let's examine this common transition. I took control of the tempo when I put my hand in the air and started conducting. (If I had been conducting all along, this would have no meaning.) When I repeated the last line of the fast song at a slower tempo, I did two important things: I emphasized the truth of that song, and I signaled the end of a section and an oncoming change. People, from platform musicians to those in the pew appreciate knowing that a change is coming. Changes are pleasant when we are ready for them. Here are transitions I use most:

1 . Repeated last lines or half choruses in the old tempo, (signals an ending or transition)

2. Repeated last lines in the new tempo (if slower),

3. Spoken prayer, praise or applause unto the Lord,

4. *"Selah"* times when the orchestra plays while the people praise and worship the Lord,

5. Instrumental interludes, introductions, or endings; and,

6. Vocal cues for the words we are about to sing.

There is a common transition I rarely use—talking! Why should we stop people from worshiping to talk to them? They are going to hear a sermon in a few minutes. What they need to do now is sing unto the Lord. Never preach at the people. And, especially, never, *ever* chide them when they are not entering in the way you want them to. Why? Because it does not work. It is not your place and you only discourage those who *are* entering in. A worship leader should never give the impression he is expecting the people to perform up to his standards.

King David is my model. He danced before the Ark with all his might with little thought for who was dancing with him. When the congregation looks at the worship leader they should see a worshiper who is ministering to the Lord, not someone trying to get a response out of them. One more "never"—never teach about worship when it is time to worship. Worship leaders who talk too much are their own worst enemies. A *few* words of exhortation at the beginning of the praise and worship time is my limit. Those extremely rare occasions when God prompts me to exhort during praise and worship have a great impact because God is in it and it does not happen every week.

Effective Transitions

- Repeated last lines or half choruses in the old tempo,
- Repeated last lines in new tempo (if slower),
- Spoken prayer, praise, or applause unto the Lord,
- "Selah" (instruments playing, people worshiping)
- Instrumental interludes, introductions, or endings,
- Vocal cues, (giving part of song to sing next)

Rule Number Three:

Let the worship flow—
(the music, the message, the mood).
Master the transition.

What Is Worship Leading?

Worship leading is not making something happen, that would be more like cheer-leading. It is letting something happen, in your own heart first and in the service next. It is *not* a musical *tour de force*. However, it *is* a musical offering selected from our repertoire of the church to be the Living Sacrifice of Praise of the Holy-Royal Priesthood as the ancient Hebrew worshiper would select a spotless lamb from his flock.

The Three Rules of Worship Leading:
#1. Worship God
#2. Be prepared and be flexible.
#3. Let the worship flow.

Worship leading comes from the overflow of the worship leader's life. A passage from Isaiah contains a wonderful promise to the worship leader.

> *Therefore the Lord, the Lord of hosts, will send lean-ness among his fat ones; and under his glory He will kindle a burning like a burning of a fire. So the light of Israel will be for a fire, and His Holy One for a flame. It will burn and devour his thorns and his briars in one day.* (Isaiah 10:16,17)

The context of these verses is the wasting of Israel to prepare for the restoration of Israel. The nation had to go through the purging of fire to be at a place where God's glory could shine. So it is with the worship leader. He or she must pay the price in the secret place if God's presence will be visited upon him or her in the public place. Under a *"canopy of His glory"* (NIV) God will burn away that which does not please Him in our lives. We must not take the covering of His glory (His blessing upon our worship leading) to mean He is finished with us. It *does* mean that while He is using and blessing us, He is still at work under that canopy of glory, making us more like Him.

The worship leader must *"tremble"* (Isaiah 66:2) at the Word of God. Song leaders can immerse themselves in music only but a worship leader must also immerse himself in the Word of God. As we, under a canopy of His glory, seek to build up our personal valleys, bring down our individual mountains, straighten out our well-worn crooked places, and smooth out our rough, careless ways, He is revealed in all His glory as we lead the people of God in ministry to the Lord. And remember, *"All flesh will see it together"*! The revelation of His glory will bring the righteousness, peace and joy of His reign.

Worship Leading is not *making* something happen. It is *letting* something happen, in your heart first and then in the service.

Ten Tips for Worship Leaders

Advice gleaned from more than 30 years of worship leading

1. Make your own worship song book. Some people use computers, some notebooks, but an effective worship leader keeps a copy of at least the titles and keys of the songs the church has used in worship. This is an invaluable tool. It should be organized by keys, function, subject, etc. and it should be easy to update. Source books and page numbers should be noted so that music can be quickly found.

2. Devise your own technique for teaching new songs to the church. Here is mine:

> Step One: Teach the singers and players first. (Sight-reading is not a pleasant experience in front of the whole church.)
>
> Step Two: Sandwich the song between two familiar songs. (Be sure to provide words for congregation.)
>
> Step Three: Use the song again soon. (Learning must be re-enforced.)

Other new song introduction techniques include using a new song to open the service or letting the singers do it first as a special. Don't try to teach too many songs in one service.

3. Use leadsheets. Provide the leadsheets to all improvising musicians and to all singers. It is essential that everybody sings and plays the same version of the songs the worship leader has selected. I consider the published version of the song to be the definitive version. Local "improvements" on the harmony or melody should rarely be used. Respect the songwriters. There has to be a standard, some way to settle on how a song should be played. I strongly suggest using the published version. This is objective and does not favor any local personality. If orchestra is being used, the rhythm chart becomes definitive. You should not expect to change orchestrations to match the chords that local keyboardists want to play. When orchestrations are being played, everyone is in subjection to the score.

4. Use the songs in their published keys. Leadsheets are the life line of a worship ministry but asking musicians to transpose is not generally well received. Songs should be pitched for the congregation, not for the comfort of the worship leader or musicians. Publishers usually place the song in an average range, not too high and not too low. If you place a song too far away from its published key you will make the congregation uncomfortable. That is never helpful when you want them to sing.

There are altos and basses who lead worship. Songs are usually published for the 2nd tenor/2nd soprano range. This means that these worship leaders must lower some songs slightly in order to sing them. To do that without losing the congregation, lower the song 1 half-step or at most 1 whole step. Transpositions down a minor 3rd will take many songs out of the average voice range. If half-step-down modulations get into difficult keys, (C down to B, F to E, etc.) a whole step must be used. Congregations can handle things down a little, but not more than a 3rd. If the song is still too high for the worship leader he or she must learn to depend on the higher voices in the worship team for a phrase or two. It is much better for the worship leader to be uncomfortable for a few notes than to place the song out of reach of the people he or she is trying to lead in worship.

5. Learn how to warm-up your worship team. It is so important to help your leaders focus on the business at hand. Adequate pre-service time should be allotted to learn or touch up any new music and to teach any transitions, introductions, endings, etc. After all that is done, find a private place and pray together. Review the goals of the service and the music you have planned. Help them settle in mentally and spiritually so they can help you execute the plan God has given you. The last few minutes before the service should not be spent in a frantic search for leadsheets or powerpoint or in last minute rehearsal. These moments should be reserved for spiritual preparation.

6. Stay within your time allotment. You have met with the pastor so you know his goals. You have prepared your music to fill the time allotted. Be sensitive to the Holy Spirit. If He leads past the time given to worship no one should question it. But if the worship leader artificially carries on beyond the time given, most people will know that, too. The worship leader has broken a trust. Those who know how to use wisely the time given them will be asked to lead again. Those who abuse their time will most likely not be asked again.

7. Lead worship, not just songs. When a congregation becomes dependent on songs, the people cannot give thanks, proclaim praise, express worship, or even pray unless they are singing. Many times the worship leader has done much to create this situation. If he or she hurries from song to song, showing more concern for each transition than for the worship that is taking place, then he or she is leading songs not worship. We must be careful to let people express themselves, and we must never hurry them. There is an element of waiting on God in worship leading. This is why transitions that involve the spoken praise, worship, and prayers of the congregation are effective. These transitions, allow praise and worship to happen between the songs.

Take special note of songs that give commands—"Praise the Lord", "Exalt the Lord our God," "Give Him glory", etc. Many times these songs will be followed by a time when the order of worship is to obey the command of the song. The Worship Leader must allow time for this.

I learned this when a friend was leading worship. He led in a great song that invited me to spend time loving the Lord. I was ready to do this when suddenly we were starting another song. I couldn't fulfill the command of the last song. It frustrated me. I cried in my spirit, "Let me worship my God!" I have never forgotten that moment. It has changed my worship leading. There is much more waiting now, more sensitivity to the moment. Really, the next moment is more important than the next song.

8. Listen to the people. The pastor and the congregation have entrusted us with planning and leading their sacrifices of praise. They should have a say in the matter. Not everyone who has a complaint is a critical spirit or a tradition-bound saint. God will use people to instruct you as a worship leader. He will even use those with critical spirits and those who are tradition-bound because they are sometimes right. I wish it were not so, but it is. The fact is we need people who are watching because we can't see ourselves lead worship. We are so focused on what we are doing that we are blind to things

314 / Stephen R. Phifer

that others see. God will help us sort out the truth from the
negativism and learn from it.

9. Do not polarize the people. The role of the worship
leader is to unite the people. But sometimes worship leaders
unconsciously polarize the people they are trying to unify.
They do this by constantly referring to the songs: old, new,
high church, low church, Pentecostal, charismatic, Baptist,
black gospel, southern gospel, hymns, choruses, Scripture
songs, traditional, contemporary. Really, these worship leaders are emphasizing the differences between the people who
like or dislike those songs. They are building the walls between those people higher and stronger. They are causing the
worship to be all about the songs. On the other hand, if we
insist that the songs be all about the worship (thanksgiving,
praise, humility, adoration, worship, prayer, testimony) then
we can tear down the walls and unify the people.

10. Don't talk too much. There really isn't much to say to
the people, if what we want to do is lead them in worship.
Let's get to the business at hand—worshiping God! Sometimes
things need to be said. How can we judge what is proper and
what isn't? Here are some good questions:

Is what I have to say about me or about God?
Does what I have to say bring attention to me or to the
  Lord?
Am I tempted to complain about how the people are or are
  not worshiping?
Am I seeking to vent frustration or anger?
Am I treading water, trying to figure out what to do next?
Do I have a word of exhortation or encouragement?
Am I emphasizing the songs or the truths of worship?
("Let's all sing Stuart Hamblin's great old song, *How Great
Thou Art;* " "My mother used to sing this to me . . .;" or, "God
is great and powerful. He is worthy of our praise today . . . ")

If you have planned well, your songs do most of the talking. All the worship leader needs to do is encourage the wor-

shipers by keeping the focus of the proceedings on God himself.

TEN TIPS TO WORSHIP LEADERS

1. Make your own worship song book.
2. Devise your own technique for teaching new songs to the church.
3. Use leadsheets.
4. Use the songs in their published keys
5. Learn how to warm-up your worship team.
6. Stay within your time allotment.
7. Lead worship, not just songs.
8. Listen to the people.
9. Do not polarize the people.
10. Don't talk too much.